The Shawnees and Their Neighbors, 1795–1870

The Shawnees and Their Neighbors, 1795–1870

STEPHEN WARREN

University of Illinois Press
URBANA AND CHICAGO

First Illinois paperback, 2009
© 2005 by the Board of Trustees
of the University of Illinois
All rights reserved

∞ This book is printed on acid-free paper.

The Library of Congress cataloged the cloth edition as follows:
Warren, Stephen, 1970–
The Shawnees and their neighbors, 1795–1870 / Stephen Warren.
p. cm.
Includes bibliographical references and index.
ISBN-13: 978-0-252-02995-0 (ISBN-13/cloth : alk. paper)
ISBN-10: 0-252-02995-X (ISBN-10/cloth : alk. paper)
1. Shawnee Indians—Ethnic identity.
2. Shawnee Indians—Politics and government.
3. Shawnee Indians—Missions.
4. United States. Office of Indian Affairs. Shawnee Agency—History.
5. Black Bob Indian Reservation (Kan.)—History.
6. United States—Race relations.
7. United States—Social policy.
8. United States—Politics and government.
I. Title.
E99.S35W37 2005
974.004'97317—dc22 2005006500
PAPERBACK ISBN 978-0-252-07645-9

Contents

Acknowledgments

The process of completing a book has a tendency to blur the lines between the personal and the professional. Therefore, I could not possibly fail to mention friends and family who have stepped in and kept me and this project moving forward. First, I would like to thank Dick Murphy and Bob Harrmann. Before they died both men taught me a great deal about the joy of living even as heart disease and cancer carried them from this world. Their courage and resilience lit a path that I can only hope to follow. Joe Hatton, Bill Trimmer, and Matt Berg reminded me that hiking, fishing, and hanging out in dimly lit pizzerias can be far more interesting than professional responsibilities. My brother, Michael Warren, and my friend, historian Thomas Appleton, Jr., copyedited the manuscript. I am grateful to them for creating a space for me and my work in their busy lives.

R. David Edmunds inspired me to further study American Indian history and to pursue a dissertation on the Shawnees. A charismatic teacher, Dr. Edmunds supervised an undergraduate honors thesis on the Shawnee Indians that, in hindsight, became the genesis for *The Shawnees and Their Neighbors.* Dr. Edmunds has been an invaluable mentor, and I want to thank him for his encouragement and good humor over the years.

Peter Iverson, Susan Gray, Albert Hurtado, and Kenneth Morrison at Arizona State University helped me to make the painful transition from undergraduate to graduate studies. They have all been enduring mentors. Peter Iverson's ongoing good counsel at the annual meetings of the American Society for Ethnohistory has been an immense help.

As a Ph.D. student at Indiana University, I was blessed to learn ethnohistorical methods from some of the best practitioners in the field. In anthropology, Professors Raymond J. DeMallie and Loretta Fowler showed me how to incorporate Shawnee social organization into this historical study of change and continuity in Shawnee leadership. I am also grateful to Professors Steven Stowe, Wendy Gamber, and Lawrence J. Friedman for helping me to become a better writer, critic, and scholar. The department of history at Indiana University was also blessed with a large number of remarkable graduate students who have become both good friends and good critics. They include Alan Shackelford, Scott Stephan, Patrick Ettinger, John Dichtl, Tom Lappas, Frances Flavin, Lynn Pohl, and Paul Schadewald. Doug Winiarksi and Christina Burke, from religious studies and anthropology respectively, have also been a great help.

Rebecca Kugel and the anonymous reviewers of the University of Illinois Press have made essential contributions to this book. Dr. Kugel's insights into Shawnee history, and Indian–white relations more generally, deepened my understanding of the evidence. I want to thank them for helping me evaluate this manuscript from a distance.

Randolph Noe and I devoted countless hours to Shawnee history as we traveled to and from Oklahoma. We shared fry bread and good fellowship with the Shawnees during their annual War Dance. Randy's book, *The Shawnee Indians: An Annotated Bibliography,* proved to be an invaluable resource as my research revealed gaps in the primary source record. Before his death in May 2003, Randy actively shared his knowledge with academics as well as Shawnee tribal members. He has been sorely missed by us all.

As this study points out, the Shawnees in the first half of the nineteenth century were dispersed over a wide geographic area. Consequently, this project would not have been possible without the financial support of numerous organizations. I am grateful to the American Philosophical Society for granting me the Phillips Fund Grant for North American Research, the Kansas State Historical Society for the Alfred M. Landon Historical Research Grant, and the University Graduate School at Indiana University for both the Doctoral Student Grant-in-Aid of Research and the Wiseman Fellowship. I have traveled to Ohio, Missouri, Kansas, Illinois, and Washington, D.C., to research Shawnee history. This project would have been much more limited in scope were it not for the generous support of these organizations.

A research grant from Eastern Kentucky University funded travel to and from Oklahoma and laid the foundation for my current relationships with the Absentee Shawnee, Shawnee, and Eastern Shawnee tribes. In summer 2001, Ken Blanchard, then lieutenant governor of the Absentee Shawnee Tribe, was kindhearted enough to sit down with me during my initial visit to the tribal headquarters. Since then I have become indebted to innumerable members of the Absentee Shawnee Tribe, including Ken and Serena Daugherty, George and Sue Blanchard, Elroy Alford, Jennifer Makaseah, Helen Ramirez, Scott Miller, Karen Kaniatobe, and Pauline Wahpepah. I would also like to thank Rebecca Hawkins, Greg Pitcher, and Linda Cox with the Shawnee Tribe and Chief Charles Enyart, Glenna Wallace, and Lamont Laird with the Eastern Shawnee Tribe. Their collective assistance has transformed my perspective on American Indian history.

Researching and writing a book can be a solitary endeavor. But at the end of each day I have been fortunate to share in this journey with my partner, Kristy Nabhan-Warren. Kristy is a wonderful scholar and writer in her own right. Her intelligence and work ethic have set standards (mostly unobtainable) that I have pursued over the years. Her dedication and commitment has inspired my own small successes. And now, with the arrival of our son, Cormac Nabhan-Warren, our shared passion for teaching and research has been put into perspective once again. Thanks, Cormac!

The Shawnees and Their Neighbors,
1795–1870

Introduction

The Shawnee elder told me that I "was just guessing." Her perspective on my work came crashing down on me in Shawnee, Oklahoma, at the Absentee Shawnee tribal headquarters. Mrs. Helen Ramirez, a Shawnee elder and member of the Cultural Advisory Council, had this to say about my project and, by extension, any scholarly treatment of her people from the colonial period through the nineteenth century. She elaborated on her indictment of the scholarship by making clear the connection between language and power. Mrs. Ramirez calmly explained that "most of us didn't speak English until the 1930s. Heck, I don't even speak it that great now." As a child, she continued, Quaker missionaries had washed her mouth out with soap when she spoke Shawnee. Now in her seventies, she and others like her work tirelessly to reclaim the Shawnee language on the same grounds that those missionaries had once used to eradicate its use. Mrs. Ramirez described, in a matter-of-fact way, how those who have translated Shawnee culture and history over time have held the literal and metaphorical bar of soap. Available source material derives from individuals who diligently worked to take away what it meant to be Shawnee. How then, she asked, did I intend to write a *Shawnee* history?[1]

When I meekly replied that I had committed more than ten years of research to the recovery of every Shawnee voice that I could find in the sources, she elaborated on the intersection between language and power among the Shawnees and their Indian neighbors. To her mind, those Shawnees who spoke English did not understand the vast majority of those Shawnees who did not. English speakers remained a tiny percentage of the overall population until the twentieth century. Educated at boarding schools far removed from their communities, these Shawnees often grew apart from tribal members who had stayed behind. I realized that if I hoped to recover a comprehensive picture of Shawnee life, I had better rethink the sources I used and the methods I employed to explain them.

I have been haunted by Mrs. Ramirez's words since this meeting. Her sentiments have been echoed by various members of the three federally recognized Shawnee tribes. Historians such as myself typically examine source material written by missionaries and bureaucrats committed to the cultural assimilation of Indian people. Most of us also inquire into sources left behind by a tiny fraction of Shawnee intermediaries, who often promoted assimilation with the paternalistic determination of the most committed American missionary. The basic sources of Shawnee history, scattered across archives in Pennsylvania, Ohio, Indiana, Missouri, Kansas, and a host of other states, were created by men and women who actively promoted the destruction of the Shawnee people through warfare, or the death of their culture through assimilation. Mrs. Ramirez repudiated much of the available scholarship because of the inescapable moral problems raised by the sources on which they are based.

As a historian, I have come to regard meeting with the Shawnee people as essential to my archival research. Invariably, someone such as Mrs. Ramirez offers fresh insights into the politics of history and the challenges faced by contemporary historical interpreters of their people. Field work among the Shawnees has provided dramatic evidence of the radically different epistemologies that have shaped contrasting Shawnee and academic discourses about history. The Shawnees possess their "own particular sense of the past." And, as anthropologist Peter Nabokov writes, "Indian pasts . . . are often personal and ever present."[2]

The undeniable immediacy of the past and the Shawnees' sense of connection and belonging with their ancestors inform their criticism of academic histories. In an April 1968 interview, an Absentee Shawnee named Clifton Blanchard put it this way: "I look at [the] past to see [the] future." He went on to describe how his grandfather, a famous Shawnee chief named Big Jim, "told the government that he had been pushed enough so if they would give him and his people the worst land in Oklahoma, then no white man would want it anymore." To no one's surprise, the government agreed with Big Jim's request and gave the Shawnees "sand hills" and "red dirt." Nevertheless, Blanchard recounted how his 160-acre allotment had been cut down to one-half of an acre when, in 1965, the state of Oklahoma flooded the land and created Thunderbird Lake. He then linked his unwillingness to share information about Shawnee history and ritual with the tribe's long struggle against forced removals and land loss. Far more than a simple narrative of his life, Blanchard conveyed a great deal about a common inheritance of betrayal promoted by imbalances in power between colonizers and the colonized. Notwithstanding these differences, he left behind an epic tale about an ongoing history perpetrated on the Shawnee people by Americans and their forebears. Anthropologist Julie Cruikshank explains that oral histories offer more than a "record" of the past. In her view, oral traditions reveal how "the past is culturally constituted and discussed." Blanchard's story of kinship and survival amid colonizers was virtually interchangeable with that of his grandfather, Big Jim, and his famous great-great grandfather, Tecumseh. He had connected time.[3]

Tribal members are as interested in the authors of their history, and the context in which they wrote, as they are in the interpretations they provide. An acute understanding of the intersecting strands of history and memory, and the impact these understandings have had on their contemporary circumstances, inform their criticisms of the sources—from manuscript materials to the informants scholars have consulted. "Official" historical knowledge contained in treaties and academic publications has had a direct bearing on everything from economic-development initiatives to the settlement of cases stemming from the Native American Graves Protection and Repatriation Act (NAGPRA). More often than not, academic histories, and the sources on which they have been constructed, have been used by the courts and the Bureau of Indian Affairs to undermine the Shawnees' struggle for self-determination. Hard experiences have shaped the Shawnees' critique of historical methods and their interpreters. They understand that interpreters of Shawnee history have been so influenced by the context in which they lived and wrote that they have created—sometimes intentionally, sometimes inadvertently—harmful myths about the tribe.

The Shawnees' well-placed wariness toward their interpreters has a long history. During the War of 1812, William Henry Harrison, then territorial governor of Indiana, left behind a voluminous record of his violent struggle with Tecumseh, the "Moses" of Shawnee history. In November 1811, Harrison crushed a major site of pan-Indian resistance, Prophetstown, on the Tippecanoe River. After a series of conflicts, Harrison met Tecumseh in battle on October 1813 at the Battle of the Thames, where Tecumseh was killed. Pan-Indian resistance in the Old Northwest effectively died with Tecumseh. Through spies and personal exchanges with the most famous of all Shawnee warriors, source material created by Harrison and his henchmen has shaped our understanding of Indian–white relations in the Old Northwest. Subsequently remembered as "Old Tippecanoe," Harrison parlayed his battlefield experiences into a successful bid for the presidency of the United States in 1840.[4]

Several generations later, a descendant of Tecumseh named Thomas Wildcat Alford wrote a tribal history entitled *Civilization and the Story of the Absentee Shawnees.* Along with a handful of other young Shawnees, Alford was educated at Hampton Institute. Upon graduation in 1882, Alford returned home and promoted the Dawes General Allotment Act among his people. Alford's role as an educator and allotment advocate brought him into frequent conflict with a sizable number of tribal members who opposed such policies. As an old man, Alford combined his own traditional knowledge with available written sources to create *Civilization.*[5]

Fieldwork with members of the three federally recognized Shawnee tribes invariably leads to important discussions of this long line of interpreters and their individual and collective impact. A sense of history pervades the language, culture, and daily conversation of the Shawnees with whom I have spoken. Tribal histories are featured prominently on everything from tribal Web sites to the reverse side of their breakfast menus at one of their tribally owned restaurants. But their knowledge of history transcends print media—the genre preferred by academic historians.

"History" is also personal and familial, and it is conveyed at a range of rituals throughout the year, such as the Shawnee War Dance. In August 2002, near Little Axe, Oklahoma, I was privileged to attend an Absentee Shawnee War Dance. Designed to honor male warriors, living and dead, the dance also reintegrates male warriors into their community after battle. Since the mid-nineteenth century, the War Dance has become associated with honoring Shawnee men who have served in the U.S. military. Before the men entered the camp circle, I could hear them singing in the woods just beyond where I sat with my host family, one of perhaps twenty other families that had formed a circle around the tribal dance ground and ceremonial arbor. A tribal official explained that I heard the dancers praying along with the ritual leader of the dance, who had just opened the sacred pack, full of items from the time when the world began. Only the warriors know what the sacred pack contains. Its viewers understand that each object has a meaningful history—a lesson—that is unique to the Shawnee people.

After they viewed the sacred bundle and prayed over its contents, the men rode into camp on horseback. They circled the camp four times, ritually purifying themselves from the world and the battles they had endured. Once purified, young and old veterans of American wars began dancing, a process that stretched from mid-morning until deep into the night. As they danced, individual warriors recounted their military exploits in the Shawnee language. Yet as each individual described his experience, it was clear that his power derived from sharing his exploits in a group context. As they listened to their accomplishments, younger Shawnees were taught that "there is meaning in every step" of the ritual dances.[6]

Toward noon, the dancers took a break. They had danced for several hours, and their hunger and thirst must have been overwhelming, for the temperature reached beyond ninety degrees and they had been fasting since the previous evening. As the men sat down outside the ceremonial arbor, Shawnee women began carrying enormous watermelons to the dancers. After the dancers devoured the meat of the watermelons, women brought in traditional foods prepared on the cooking fires established by each of the familial camps. Then we all began to eat, and a new round of dancing began after an hour or so of visiting and conversation.

Performing the War Dance continues to shape the Shawnees' understanding of themselves. Observers and participants learn much about Shawnee gender roles and the complementary, but separate, functions of men and women. The Shawnees take great pride in both the preparation and conduct of the War Dance as well as the other ceremonials that mark the tribe's movement from one season to the next. The War Dance also provides tribal members with a sense of "deep time," of the rituals that have linked all Shawnees together for centuries.[7]

History is also conveyed through language. To the northeast, in Craig County, Oklahoma, tribal elders in the Shawnee Tribe teach younger Shawnees the tribal language as it was intended to be learned: through informal, oral communication. Two of the three Shawnee tribes run language classes for tribal members that involve intensive collaboration. In everything from language acquisition to tribal rituals, Shawnees learn who they are from networks of relatives. While academic histories grace the bookshelves of the tribal library, they remain peripheral. Most, if not all, Shawnees continue to learn about their history through the annual rituals and tribal gatherings that unite them as a people.

Explorations of silences, mythmaking, and misinterpretation are essential to this case study of the Shawnee people. To this end, a portion of this book is devoted to an examination of the producers of knowledge about the Shawnee Indians, the sources they have created for popular consumption, and the methods they have used in the production of that knowledge. This study of Shawnee history operates from the assumption that the nexus of myth and history produced by these Shawnee interpreters is essential to understanding their unique history. Based on a range of sources, including oral history, tribal histories written by Shawnees, and the historians' traditional documents, including government correspondence, what follows is my best attempt at understanding Shawnee history from a distance. As yet another interpreter, I am keenly aware of how time, geography, and culture have separated me from the people I struggle to understand.

Yet in my attempt to understand Shawnee history and culture from a distance, I began to notice patterns in the mythmaking and silences revealed by the sources. At peculiar times and places, rank-and-file Shawnees rose above the clamor of assimilation-minded people inside and outside the tribe. The interests of the majority of the tribe became clear when Shawnee nationalism was at its weakest. As a small clique of tribal members marched toward nationhood, a process that culminated in 1852 with the adoption of a tribal constitution, the range and diversity of Shawnee perspectives receded. In contrast, when Shawnees resided in multiethnic villages led by hereditary chiefs, as happened in Ohio and Missouri between the American Revolution and the War of 1812, a clearer picture of Shawnee life emerged from the sources. Put another way, the Indian Removal Act of 1830 and the consolidation of all Shawnees on a united, tribal reservation diminished the range and diversity of Shawnee voices and drove the vast majority into a protracted silence that has nearly destroyed the Shawnees' language and culture. Mrs. Ramirez reminded me, as yet another interpreter of Shawnee history, to be aware of both the limitations of historical methods and the invariable silences and misinterpretations that grow out of this complex matrix of language, power, and nationalism.

The Shawnees and Their Neighbors begins in 1795 in Ohio and Missouri at a time when Shawnee political organization was diffuse, multiethnic, and village-centered. I conclude the study in 1870, when the Shawnees were removed from Kansas to Oklahoma. By that time, the Shawnees' village-centered world had been replaced by an institutionalized national government that drew its leaders from the ranks of economically successful, mixed-blood leaders. Shawnee leaders interested in accommodation helped transform their people from members of culturally related villages to a politically unified nation. In the process, these individuals limited the diversity of actors and the varied Shawnee responses to colonizers that had characterized Shawnee history from the beginning of contact with colonizers.

In this way, this book devotes significant attention to the internal dynamics of the various Shawnee communities that came together as a nation in modern-day Kansas. Between the sixteenth century and the late nineteenth century, the Shawnees occupied more than two hundred villages stretching from Maryland to Mexico. Waves of colonizers ripped the Shawnees from their traditional homelands in the Ohio River Valley. As a result, Shawnee culture became largely divorced from sacred places and tribal members learned how to recreate their identity as part of a transient culture. The various branches of the Shawnee Tribe formed a wide range of alliances and geographically specific survival strategies. Consequently, the imposition of what historian Donald Fixico calls "a single Indian voice" would be a fiction at best. This case study of the Shawnee people from the 1795 Treaty of Greenville, which established American dominance in the Old Northwest, to their removal to Indian Territory in the early 1870s does not offer a monolithic assessment of Shawnee identity. Rather, *The Shawnees and Their Neighbors* explores the range and diversity of Shawnee identities in this crucial period of their history.[8]

Most historians of the Shawnees and their neighbors have focused the majority of their attention on small numbers of militant resisters such as Tecumseh and his compatriots farther west. In contrast, I argue that multiple approaches to American expansion characterized this period in Shawnee and Algonquian history. For example, a majority of the roughly 3,000 Shawnees voluntarily emigrated beyond the Mississippi River between 1783 and 1815. The Western Shawnees avoided the drastic cultural changes demanded by government officials and missionaries, including the reformation of traditional gender roles, by ceding control over their Ohio homelands. In contrast, more than 1,000 Shawnees chose to remain in Ohio. Leaders such as Black Hoof of Wapakoneta, Ohio, and Tecumseh at Prophetstown, Indiana, illustrate the wide disagreements between those who stayed behind. Black Hoof led the vast majority of Eastern Shawnees in an attempt to accommodate the Americans and retain tribal homelands. Meanwhile, Tecumseh and his brother Tenskwatawa led a small minority of Shawnees in a militant, pan-Indian resistance movement. The collapse of that effort after the War of 1812 allowed Black Hoof and some Missouri Shawnee leaders to consolidate their power over the emerging Shawnee nation. Together, these groups initiated a new era of centralized authority and cooperation with the United States.

To accomplish these sweeping reforms, mixed-blood Shawnees, along with government officials and their missionary allies, attempted to diminish substantive alliances between Shawnees and their Indian neighbors. Prior to the Indian Removal Act of 1830, colonial and multitribal alliances linked the Shawnees and other Central Algonquian-, Muskhogean-, and Iroquoian-speaking tribes, including the Kickapoos, Creeks, and Cherokees. British, French, and Spanish colonizers heavily influenced these alliances and shaped their responses to subsequent American expansion. Indeed, loyalty to an older, village-based political order helped many Shawnees resist the changes being imposed on them. By this time, the Shawnee nation, backed by a tribal constitution, had already been formed. But the vast majority of the Shawnees continued to resist political consolidation and ultimately succeeded in destroying the Shawnee nation by the time of removal in 1870.

Americans loathed multiethnic alliances, and following Tecumseh's defeat, they set about dismantling these villages and creating unified tribal governments in their place. By embracing constitutional democracy as a universal ideal, early republican reformers rejected cultural pluralism and ignored the obvious cultural and political differences between Indians and Americans. In Machiavellian terms, tribal governments modeled after the United States contributed to the dispossession of tribal lands. First articulated by the Washington administration and then refined by Thomas Jefferson, U.S. policies were designed to create pliable leaders and uniform political hierarchies within tribes. Democratically elected government chiefs lent an air of legitimacy to U.S. designs. These new, culturally homogeneous tribal governments eased the way for treaty-makers but widened the divide between tribal leaders and tribal members. For Shawnees accustomed to village-based autonomy, such governments were anathema.[9]

Andrew Jackson shared both Washington's and Jefferson's disdain for multiethnic alliances. But for Jackson, the southeastern tribes had been far too successful in building national governments. Tribes with constitutions modeled after the United States had become an impediment to the sovereignty of newly created states. As a result, Jackson and his successors became committed to the removal of these tribes and to the ultimate destruction of their national ambitions. He and his successors desired centralized tribal governments that were subordinate to both the authority of the federal government and the states in which they were located. U.S. officials and the tribal leaders whose interests they had advanced thus found themselves at cross-purposes. Meanwhile, Shawnees who believed in village-based autonomy felt betrayed by both the Americans and those Shawnees recognized as national leaders. Openly opposed to national tribal governments, the vast majority of Shawnees preferred the multiethnic models of alliance and authority they had known prior to removal.

The Shawnees and Their Neighbors thus explores the Shawnees' understanding of themselves as both a cultural group and a tribe immediately before and after the establishment of U.S. dominance throughout the central United States. Anthropologists, including Erminie Wheeler-Voegelin and Charles Callender, have argued that the Shawnees and other Central Algonquians began as politically coherent tribes, united around hereditary chiefs and supporting leaders. Historical evidence offers a different narrative, one in which "being Shawnee" depended less on political allegiance and more on language, gender, and the ritual practices that affirmed these cultural beliefs.[10] This book thus challenges the long-accepted paradigm that Central Algonquians derive from politically unified tribes by analyzing the crucial role that individuals, alliances, and colonizers played in shaping modern tribal governments. A messier, more complicated history of migration and conflict emerges in this study of the Shawnee people in the nineteenth century.

After removal, the Shawnees and their neighbors began identifying themselves as members of nations rather than the more ethnically diverse villages that preceded them. The object of this book is to understand how and why this shift in the political consciousness of the Shawnees took place. The answer to these questions is important not only for historiographical reasons but also because of the Shawnees' unique position as architects of pan-Indian resistance. Perhaps no other tribe had such a wide geographic range of settlements and contacts with other tribes. As a tribe with cultural practices common to both Algonquians and Muskogeans, the Shawnees are recognized as the keystone of resistance to white expansion east of the Mississippi between 1754 and 1815. Consequently, it is essential to make sense of the ways in which the Shawnees, a people of hybrid cultures and varied historical experiences, came together as a "tribe" and "nation" between 1795 and 1870.

The Shawnees and Their Neighbors is also designed to restore the historical reputation of an important set of Shawnee leaders who rose to power amid Tecumseh's efforts to foment pan-Indian resistance to U.S. expansion. Interested in consolidating their power as leaders of a new Shawnee nation, these men spoke of a future of reform rather than a tradition of resistance based on somewhat nostalgic, precontact conceptions of Indian power. The experience of Tecumseh's survivors raises important questions about the historiography of the American Indian experience and challenges the historian's obsession with militant resisters who fought Americans to the bitter end. Ultimately, I hope to recover this important period in Shawnee history in order to make a case for the importance of American Indian history after military defeat.

Tecumseh's historical popularity as the archetype of Shawnee identity can be seen in the numerous biographies dedicated to the man. In contrast, one searches in vain for recent titles on any one of the many Indian leaders who favored accommodation with Americans. These leaders, including Black Hoof of the Shawnees, Captain Anderson of the Delawares, Crane of the Wyandots, and Keokuk of the Sacs, remain obscure despite the fact that they managed to keep the majority of their kinsmen in the Ohio country and the Upper Mississippi Valley at peace.[11] The only major counterpoint to the myriad biographies of Tecumseh and other militants in the Midwest is Harvey Carter's *The Life and Times of Little Turtle,* which concerns a prominent Miami leader who fought and died on behalf of the American cause in the War of 1812.[12] Several important articles exist on Indian partisans of the

Americans, but little is known of their later resistance to removal and the role their children played in defining Algonquian life in Indian Territory. The story of the survivors of the middle ground and their equally heroic efforts to save a way of life has been lost to us. This history of the Shawnees immediately before and after the War of 1812 shows that the individuals seriously committed to the work of maintaining the cultural and economic viability of their communities did much to create a world of possibilities during a time most historians characterize as an era of diminishing opportunities and closing doors.[13]

In most U.S. history classes, the "end of the trail" for the Algonquian tribes occurs shortly after their military defeat and forced removal from the eastern half of the United States. Sculptor James Earle Fraser understood that for most Americans, military conflict makes American Indians interesting and central to the grand narrative of U.S. history. Those early historians who created an intimate connection between American Indian and frontier history are partly to blame for this phenomenon. Since Francis Parkman set out to prove his manhood in *The Oregon Trail* in the 1840s, attempting to test himself in a time and place he thought might soon vanish, writers have sought to discover the period in which Euro-Americans and Indians contested for land, game, and cultural primacy as more or less equal adversaries. This definition of the frontier—as a distinct economic and geographic realm in which Indians and whites coexist, yet remain independent of each other—has severely limited the importance and relevance of American Indian history to larger, postnational, and postcolonial narratives of American history.[14]

The widespread obsession with Indian people before they became "dependent" on Euro-Americans ignores the fact that economic, military, linguistic, and cultural borderland crossings remain a perennial aspect of human existence. The divorce of American Indian history from the frontier of Parkman and Frederick Jackson Turner is of fundamental importance if we are to include marginalized groups like American Indians—from the past to the present—in larger narratives.[15]

The Turner paradigm, which describes the process by which the Indian frontier is subsumed by more settled, agricultural communities, limits the presence of American Indians in narratives about the postremoval era to this day. As a predecessor of Turner, Parkman viewed these disappearing personal and national moments of contact between Indians and whites as the foundation of American exceptionalism, the basis for the national identity of the upstart American nation. Like Parkman and Turner, George Bancroft argued that in the United States "humanity is steadily advancing, that the advance of liberty and justice is certain." These evolutionary theories of American history have left a distinct imprint on the field of American Indian history. Historian Frederick Hoxie explains that "modern historians . . . while rejecting the racism of Parkman, still fall back on the view that American history is essentially a story of civilization overcoming primitivism."[16]

Constant attention on militants such as Tecumseh adds to the perception that American Indians were stubborn resisters to change. His opponents within the Shawnee tribe, including the noted chief Black Hoof of Wapakoneta, Ohio, and Captain Lewis of Lewistown, are poorly understood figures from this crucial period. Many historians dismiss them because of their cooperative stance toward Americans, describing militant resistance and "tradition" as the twin pillars of Indian survival, and viewing peaceful cooperation as an inevitable yet destructive reality perpetrated by largely corrupt leaders. Such oversimplifications inhibit more complex—and useful—perspectives on belief and behavior in American Indian life.

Black Hoof and his successors lost the battle against removal but survived the bloodshed and helped to shape Shawnee life before and after Tecumseh's death. It is true that the reforms they advocated required cooperation with missionaries, government officials, and their white neighbors. But in transforming their villages, the Shawnees innovated in ways that did not wash away long-held understandings of leadership, gender, and ritual life. Cultural transformations cut in several different directions, toward a future among an overwhelming number of Americans, and a past based on the principles of local autonomy and the separate but complementary roles of women and men. Shawnee leaders used assistance from missionaries and the federal government to procure material support, enhance their own political prestige, and test the American promise of cultural pluralism in the nineteenth century. That they often failed says more about the cultural chauvinism of the United States than the ability of American Indians to move from "savagery to civilization."[17]

1. Tribal Identity in a Time of Multiethnic Confederacies, 1795–1813

In December 1823, General Lewis Cass, then territorial governor of Michigan, hired his personal secretary, Charles C. Trowbridge, to record what remained of Indian languages and customs throughout the Old Northwest. As part of his assignment the following July, Trowbridge interviewed Tenskwatawa, the Shawnee Prophet, hoping to record what remained of Shawnee culture and history before his tribe was forcibly removed from the Old Northwest.[1] Tenskwatawa, age fifty, did not speak English and relied on a translator to convey Shawnee history and culture to the strange twenty-four-year-old American. In turn, Trowbridge probably hired an Ottawa speaker to translate from Shawnee to English.[2] Tenskwatawa traveled to Detroit, a short distance from his place of exile among the British at Fort Malden, Ontario. The Prophet and approximately twenty-five of his supporters, most of whom were close relatives, had lived as refugees at Malden since the War of 1812. By the time of their interview, Lewis Cass had already approached Tenskwatawa about assisting the Americans in persuading the Ohio Shawnees to leave Ohio and resettle beyond the Mississippi. Tenskwatawa may have hoped that his long years of exile might come to an end by cooperating with Trowbridge and facilitating Shawnee removal from the Great Lakes.[3]

In the spring of 1825, Trowbridge and Cass traveled on horseback to Wapakoneta, Ohio. The first of many encounters between government officials and the Shawnee people about removal had begun. Cass and Trowbridge invited Tenskwatawa and a delegation of Shawnees and Senecas from Lewistown, Ohio, to Wapakoneta, the central village of the Shawnee people, located on the Auglaize River in northwestern Ohio. Some members of their delegation seemed to favor a new life in the West. But their hosts at Wapakoneta most certainly did not, and their village chief, Black Hoof, led the Shawnee resistance to American plans for them. Black Hoof had devoted the last thirty years of his life to creating a lasting peace with the Americans, and in the process he had grown to despise former militants such as Tenskwatawa. In fact, he had worked hard to counteract the influence of Tenskwatawa and Tecumseh among his kinsmen. He particularly resented the Shawnee Prophet's new incarnation as a removal advocate. Black Hoof, who was then in his eighties, granted the interview in this context of betrayal and loss.[4]

Trowbridge thus managed to gather two contrasting visions of a people besieged by American settlers and their federal and state representatives who had become increasingly committed to the elimination of Indian people—and the land they occupied—in the midwestern United States. Both Black Hoof and Tenskwatawa struggled against American plans for them, albeit in radically different ways. The contest for power between militants such as Tenskwatawa and accommodationists such as Black Hoof was ultimately decided by their extensive ties with relatively unknown local leaders both inside and outside the Shawnee tribe. Trowbridge's interviews—and the tumultuous history of Black Hoof and Tenskwatawa's power struggle—illustrate the relative weakness of tribal governments during an era in which multiethnic villages dotted the midwestern landscape.

As an active participant in this process of Native American land loss and extinction, Trowbridge assembled a list of questions. Ranging from Shawnee knowledge of giant mammoths to "family government," his questions were intended for a dying people. The bizarre range of questions, and his equally puzzling fascination with extinct Ice Age creatures, must have puzzled the two Shawnee leaders. Nevertheless, both Tenskwatawa and Black Hoof managed to weave important stories about their people into the interviews—stories of survival and persistence amid an unpredictable series of changing circumstances. Both men described a people who had endured long migrations across the Americas, achieved close partnerships with a wide array of other tribes, and worked to bring together the variant groups encompassed by the Shawnee name.[5] As two of the most renowned leaders of the Shawnee tribe, Black Hoof and Tenskwatawa recognized the important role their competing memories would play in Shawnee history.

Both the Shawnees and Americans acknowledged Wapakoneta as the most important Shawnee village in the Old Northwest since 1795, when the Americans and their former enemies signed a peace treaty designating boundaries between Indian and non-Indian land in the Ohio country. Black Hoof solidified his authority as the spokesperson for the Shawnee people following the Treaty of Greenville through his hereditary role as peace chief and his outspoken support for the United States in the War of 1812. Yet despite Black Hoof's cooperative stance toward the United States, knowledge of the English language, and esteemed position among the Shawnee people, the aged chief's interview is much shorter than the interview with Tenskwatawa. It could be that Trowbridge, like most Americans then and now, was far more interested in militant resisters and their memories of the past than in advocates of adaptation and cultural continuity such as Black Hoof.[6]

It is easy to imagine Trowbridge blushing at the Prophet's sometimes bawdy description of the creation of men and women and their first attempts at sexual intercourse. Yet behind the overt sexuality involved in their oral histories, it is clear that both Shawnee leaders paid specific attention to politics and to the unique characteristics of the Shawnee divisions. Both men characterized Shawnee society as a world in which loyalty to kin and village determined belief and behavior. Tenskwatawa explained that the Shawnees "do not pretend" to believe that the divisions were "made for the purpose of government." Rather, the divisions "were originally single families, the heads of which bore the names by which their descendants were afterwards distinguished."[7] Accordingly, Black Hoof and Tenskwatawa described the Shawnees as a group of semiautonomous villages rather than a single, distinct tribal group from the beginning of time. And in more than fifty years of incessant warfare with Europeans, the Shawnee divisions had become even more independent and decentralized.

Leaders of the Shawnee divisions entered into partnerships with widely divergent groups of Native Americans and colonizers, from New Jersey and Pennsylvania to Kansas and Texas, between the early eighteenth century and the 1820s. While the Kispokothas built alliances with Southeastern tribes, including the Creeks and Cherokees, the Maykujays established ties with Algonquian-speaking peoples, including the Miamis and Delawares. All Shawnees shared diverse attachments to peoples from different regions and cultural groups, a unique by-product of the Fur Trade Wars (c. 1640–1700) and other violent conflicts with colonizers and the Indian communities allied with them. Trowbridge's interviews reflect these long-range alliances and offer ambiguous perspectives on what it meant to be Shawnee from the perspective of two rivals within the tribe. Both Black Hoof and Tenskwatawa had cultivated alliances with a confusing array of Indian tribes and colonizers in their lifelong rivalry as competitors for Shawnee leadership. Tenskwatawa and Black Hoof managed to convey that the Shawnee people were united more often by language and culture than by politics and leaders.

Tenskwatawa, a member of the Kispokotha division, began his account with the creation of a single man and woman, and their subsequent move to the island "which rests upon the back of a great turtle that carries it as a load." Upon their arrival on "the first earth they saw," the original man, *Kwee koo laa,* instructed his children to travel "in a northern direction from them and at a great distance." After a long journey northward, Shawnee elders asked their young men to hunt. The young men were told that if they killed any game, they must remember to "bring it all home." Nevertheless, the young men did not fulfill their elders' wishes, leaving behind the backbone of an enormous elk—one so large that they could not carry it all back to their camp. Upon their return, the old men noticed the backbone's peculiar absence, and sent the young men out once again to retrieve it. After one failed attempt to collect all of the elk's bones, the young men returned to the kill site and found "an Indian whose body was red and could give no account of himself." The Shawnees incorporated him into the tribe, placing him in charge of warfare and initiating the "Piccaway family" (or Piqua division) of the Shawnee people.[8]

A short time later, "a man unknown to them all" burst in amid deadlocked negotiations for the appointment of a medicine man. On the next day, the man rose in front of the council and "told the members that he was of the Mekoche [Maykujay] family or tribe of Shawanoa's" and that he alone would be in charge of the tribe's medicine. The members of the council tested his abilities and eventually forced him to concede to the superior power of the Chalagawtha division. The Maykujay thus became the "counsellor for the whole nation" rather than the division providing the tribe's most powerful leaders.[9]

Black Hoof, a member of the Maykujay division, recalled a similar chain of events—from encounters with strangers to their incorporation as full members of the tribe—in the early days of the Shawnee people. Yet for him, the Shawnees were far more decentralized than the Prophet's account suggests. Black Hoof recalled that the Shawnees "had previously constituted a separate band or tribe" but that their name had since been adopted by members of the "confederated tribes" (the Shawnee divisions) because "the Shawnees were the most numerous." Significantly, Black Hoof claimed that the Thawegila division (one of several divisions that had voluntarily removed west of the Mississippi River during the 1770s) was now extinct. Using Trowbridge's fascination with tribal lore for personal gain, Black Hoof essentially claimed that his division, the Maykujay, was solely responsible for the election of tribal chiefs such as himself. The significance of this claim could not have been lost on Trowbridge. Black Hoof ensured that his division, and the Shawnees at Wapakoneta, would play a decisive role in tribal politics for years to come. Political motives aside, it remains true that divisional identities associated with specific villages were very important to Black Hoof, who believed that the members of different Shawnee divisions could be "easily distinguished as members of the[ir] respective parent stocks."[10] For both men, the tribe known as the Shawnees was in fact a constellation of independent groups that had negotiated the formation of an organized tribe.

These oral histories help provide a cultural context for the historical record on the Shawnees at the dawn of the nineteenth century. Between 1795 and 1825, when Trowbridge set out to record Indian histories of the Old Northwest, the Shawnees struggled to preserve their lands from American encroachment. As cross-cultural experts, Black Hoof, Tenskwatawa, and his brother Tecumseh cultivated long-standing alliances and animosities among their villages and their neighbors. Leaders of Shawnee villages, whose power was based on the tribal divisions, often advanced radically different views on how to respond to American power. But several different divisions, and sometimes large numbers of people from other tribes related through marriage and trade, lived within each village. The Shawnees settled the question of who should lead by selecting chiefs from the numerically superior division in each village. In this way, the Maykujay's numerical superiority at Wapakoneta prefigured Black Hoof's dominance. However, such leadership formulas sometimes broke down in practice. Village leaders struggled to bring together competing opinions about the appropriate response to American colonizers and their cultural agents—missionaries and political ambassadors such as Trowbridge—within these tidy understandings of kinship and power. Leaders thus became mediators of political and military objectives among unstable populations of kin.

Black Hoof and his Shawnee rivals for power, Tecumseh and Tenskwatawa, struggled to maintain the support of their people between the Treaty of Greenville and the conclusion of the War of 1812. All three men were unable to stop the erosion of Shawnee lands—and people—in the Old Northwest. Indeed, a majority of the Shawnees lived west of the Mississippi. Soon after the War of 1812, an estimated 1,400 Shawnees lived in Missouri, compared with eight hundred Shawnees remaining in Ohio at that time.[11] Evidence suggests that Tecumseh and Tenskwatawa's mother, Methoataske, left her children behind and traveled to what is now southeastern Missouri in 1779. Having lost their father in war and their mother to migration, the Shawnee brothers were raised by an older sister and her husband.[12] Methoataske and a majority of her Shawnee relatives chose to remove themselves voluntarily from their lands in the Old Northwest rather than adapt to the vagaries of American power in the Ohio River Valley. Harassment from neighboring Americans, who numbered 231,000 in Ohio by the time of its statehood in

1803, forced most Shawnee families to search for territory less overrun with settlers in what is now Missouri and Arkansas.[13] Methoataske's reasons for leaving her children behind remain a mystery. But in an ironic twist of fate, her children would ultimately lead the few remaining militants in a final conflict for control of the Old Northwest.

In Missouri, Ohio, and Indiana, Shawnees shared a weakened sense of tribal loyalty and a heightened sense of the need for multitribal alliances. Shawnees everywhere made up for their small numbers by allying themselves with other tribes and colonizers. The most famous multitribal alliance the Shawnees participated in was located at Prophetstown, near present-day Lafayette, Indiana. There Tenskwatawa and his brother Tecumseh spearheaded a militant Indian counterpoint to American expansion.

Yet even before Tecumseh and Tenskwatawa founded Prophetstown, American officials worked hard to disperse the vast numbers of tribes represented at villages scattered throughout the Old Northwest and to minimize the threat they posed to white settlements. Henry Knox, as secretary of war under George Washington, became the architect of the United States' Indian policy in the years after the Battle of Fallen Timbers and the subsequent Treaty of Greenville. American officials focused their energies on the geographic and political consolidation of tribes onto "small reservations around their villages and there to promote their civilization." Concomitantly, Knox desired "an orderly westward advance" through the peaceful transfer of lands from the Great Lakes tribes to the United States. After the election of 1800, Thomas Jefferson continued Knox's strategy and established trading houses throughout the Old Northwest designed to promote indebtedness. In a private letter to William Henry Harrison, then territorial governor of Indiana, Jefferson observed that when "debts get beyond what the individuals can pay, they become willing to lop them off by a cession of lands."[14]

Harrison was responsible for implementing this policy of land loss and civilization in Indiana and Ohio. He soon discovered just how difficult it was to achieve land cessions given the tremendous diversity of the Old Northwest. Conflicting land claims, shifting alliances, and uncertain leadership meant that negotiations were long, tedious, and contested. American officials attempted to deal with this problem by reinventing American Indian societies. Between the Treaty of Greenville and the removal treaties of the early 1830s, Harrison and others like him steadily reduced the number of treaty signers and consolidated authority around a handful of tribal leaders willing to negotiate.

Alliances with members of other tribes were not simply designed to disorient American officials hungry for Indian lands. Rather, multiethnic alliances helped to stem the loss of kinsmen through warfare, disease, and out-migration. Such partnerships were not new. In fact, historians have focused increasing attention on the Ohio Valley tribes and the difficulty of defining American Indians along tribal lines in the region.[15] Throughout the eighteenth century, it is easier to describe the divided loyalties in the Old Northwest than the equally important tribal identities anchoring them to the region. Village leaders operated independently from other Shawnee villages as well, except in matters of grave importance to the tribe as a whole. For the Shawnees, kinship ties reached beyond the tribe, attaching diverse groups through an array of cultural, political, and economic motives.[16]

After 1795, the vast majority of American Indians who did not have access to leadership positions struggled against centralizing forces inside and outside their villages. Tenskwatawa and Tecumseh argued that all Indians from east of the Mississippi, regardless of their linguistic and cultural differences, should come together as a pan-Indian force. Similarly, the United States attempted to consolidate the autonomous and multiethnic, yet interdependent, villages that had defined the Great Lakes region for more than a century. In this way, Harrison, Cass, Trowbridge, Black Hoof, and Tenskwatawa shared a single-minded obsession with coercive, and centralized, authority. All five men believed that a handful of leaders, united around a single ideology, could speak and act for thousands of others. But a careful reading of the sources reveals a series of diverse cultural worlds in which local interests, rather than national ideologies, determined the outcome of important events.

Elaborate kinship relations between tribes were the foundation for both peaceful and militant alliances before the removal era. The Shawnees typically referred to the Wyandots as "elder brothers," the Delawares as "grandfathers," and the Miamis and Ottawas as "younger brothers." While violence sometimes erupted between the Shawnees and their "younger brothers," the Miamis and Ottawas, Tenskwatawa claimed that his people "had never fought against the Wyandots, Delawares, and Creeks." Similarly, Black Hoof recognized the long-standing ties between the Shawnees and their neighbors in 1817, when he reminded the Shawnee subagent, John Johnston, that negotiations for what would become a massive land cession, bringing most of northern Ohio and eastern Michigan under American control, would not be possible unless a number of related tribes agreed to the treaty. According to Black Hoof, "the Wyandots will feel reluctant [if] the Delawares and Miamis" were not invited to attend negotiations at the Maumee River that September. Evidence of this multiethnic political spirit can be found within most villages of the Old Northwest as well. For example, a number of Delaware, Seneca, Nanticoke, and Conoy Indians lived with the Shawnees at Wapakoneta until their removal in 1832. Leaders such as Black Hoof defined themselves as both Shawnees and as members of extended, multitribal kin networks.[17]

Leaders of pan-Indian revitalization movements, from the Ottawa leader Pontiac in the aftermath of the Seven Years' War to Tecumseh in the War of 1812, helped to create a climate of fear between Indians and whites. In addition, Spanish and French traders and their creole children, many of whom were tied to Indian communities through marriage, continued to trade with the Indians in the western Great Lakes.[18] American settlers in the Old Northwest lived under the shadow of competing empires. They felt threatened by the once-powerful alliances that had existed between the Native people remaining in the Old Northwest, even though a clear majority of the tribes favored peaceful relations with the United States. Anywhere confederacies took shape, Americans worried. Government officials viewed the polyglot villages west of the Mississippi as seedbeds for revolution. The western expatriates' long association with the Spanish and French only worsened the fear of a general Indian conspiracy. In February 1803, Secretary of War Henry Dearborn was convinced that "certain persons among Indian nations . . . were agents from the french or spanish [*sic*] government" who were trying to "engage the several tribes" in a general war against the United States.[19]

Rumors of a coordinated Indian attack "from the Floridas to the Lakes" intensified after the Louisiana Purchase nearly doubled the size of the United States. Writing in 1805 to General James Wilkinson, the governor of the Louisiana Territory, Major James Bruff warned of ubiquitous anti-American resistance. According to Bruff, "not an Indian has visited this post [St. Louis] or neighbouring town since last fall." Residents of St. Louis, confused over their neighbors' absence, and accustomed to daily interaction with a host of Algonquian, Caddoan, and Siouan speakers, suddenly felt as if they knew next to nothing about the people and the lands surrounding them. Anglo-American mistrust was made worse by the fact that the military men protecting them from Indian attack were "mostly half bloded [*sic*] and effect to believe there is no danger from Indians." The perceived threat from the Louisiana Territory forced Governor Wilkinson to spend much of his time "worrying about the effect of British and Spanish influence on the Western Indians." Like Wilkinson, settlers between Missouri and Ohio looked across the landscape of human settlements and saw explosive volatility in the variety of languages and ethnicities surrounding them.[20]

Nevertheless, the multiethnic texture of Native American life in the Old Northwest continued to flourish before the War of 1812, despite American attempts to terminate such associations. Black Hoof and the Shawnees at Wapakoneta concentrated on transforming their village economy from a mixed hunting-agricultural subsistence cycle to an economic plan better suited for the more settled world of the Great Lakes region. Members of the Maykujay and Chalagawtha divisions dominated Wapakoneta in spite of frequent out-migration. With the help of the federal government and Quaker missionaries, Black Hoof intended to concentrate on livestock raising, intensive agriculture, and the leasing of tribally controlled lands. The Wapakoneta Shawnees linked this transition with their ability to remain in Ohio, behind the American frontier. American depredations on their livestock and on the remaining game on their lands increased after the Treaty of Greenville. The Wapakoneta Shawnees and their Delaware and Wyandot allies in Ohio lobbied for a clear division between Indian and white territory and sought legal title to their lands in order to counter illegal squatters and other forms of American encirclement.[21]

Those who stayed behind hoped to participate in new economic ventures designed to increase their relevance to the new order brought by American settlers. For example, in a joint effort with the Delawares, the Shawnees sought ownership of a salt spring on the Wabash River. Perhaps their preoccupation with a rivalry between themselves and another pro-American leader, Little Turtle of the Miamis, enabled them to ignore the existing claims of the Wabash tribes to the territory. The Shawnees and Delawares recognized that the spring, described by Harrison as "perhaps the very best in the whole extent of the country," would bring a large amount of money to their villages. They intended to sell salt from the spring to neighboring whites. Harrison rejected the Shawnee claim, explaining that because "every tribe in the country would expect to partake in the benefits of the lease," it would be easier simply to "extinguish the title to the spring and a small tract around it." Governor Harrison further justified his decision by explaining that granting the Shawnees and Delawares control over the salt spring would place white settlers at a tremendous disadvantage by forcing them to pay high prices to the tribes for this precious resource. Secretary of War Dearborn agreed with Harrison and instructed him "to ascertain the smallest sum for which the Nations will convey the salt spring." American officials preferred to increase annuity payments rather than to lend support for the entrepreneurial endeavors of the Native people remaining in the Old Northwest.[22] Jefferson directed Dearborn and Harrison to delay the economic independence of the Shawnee people until after these land cessions had occurred.

The Wapakoneta Shawnees pressed on in spite of these setbacks and recruited sympathetic missionaries to assist them. In fall 1804, two representatives of the Baltimore Yearly Meeting of Friends, George Ellicott and Gerard Hopkins, traveled west to Wapakoneta. The two were impressed with what the Shawnees had accomplished, noting that the tribe possessed some "40 head of cattle & make butter and cheese." These missionary forays bore fruit three years later in June 1807, when Black Hoof, Black Beard, and the people of Wapakoneta welcomed the Quaker missionary William Kirk. The Shawnees hoped that Kirk's mission would improve their existing agricultural output. Within a year of his arrival, the Wapakoneta Shawnees had more than five hundred acres of corn, beans, squash, and other crops under production. In addition, Kirk assisted in numerous building projects, including the construction of a sawmill, gristmill, split-rail fences, and log cabins.[23]

Kirk received support from a number of important but lower-ranking leaders of the Wapakoneta Shawnees. A man named Black Beard, the second chief at Wapakoneta before his death in 1809, recognized that the wanton slaughter of game animals by neighboring whites would make the economic transition both more difficult and imperative to the tribe's survival in the years ahead. Like Black Hoof, Black Beard was a Maykujay Shawnee who had fought against the Americans during the Revolutionary War. But Black Beard had become an old man in his years as a warrior, and he abandoned militant resistance soon after the Battle of Fallen Timbers in 1794. In fact, on a diplomatic mission to Washington, D.C., in 1806, Black Beard spoke of his desire to persuade his people to transform their way of life.[24] In a speech to Thomas Jefferson, he observed that the white people's "Great God" provided "plenty of tame animals that you might kill them at your doors when you pleased." He then asked the president to grant his people time in making the transition from hunting to raising domesticated animals.[25]

Black Beard asked Americans to be patient with the Shawnees during their transition to intensive agriculture and stock raising because village chiefs lacked the authority to do more than merely appeal to their kinsmen. Treaties changed this time-honored pattern by granting a select group of village chiefs significant control over tribal resources. The Wapakoneta Shawnees, composed primarily of the Maykujay division, benefited from government treaties and the policy of establishing a core group of tribal chiefs. Wapakoneta chiefs attempted to establish themselves as the legitimate leaders of the tribe so that those opposing acculturation would not be entitled to a significant amount of the tribal annuity. In this way, Black Beard married the Jefferson administration's policy of centralized authority to the political aspirations of the Wapakoneta Shawnees. The Shawnee diplomat told Jefferson that his division (the Maykujay) "was the first born and all our youngest brothers came and listened to me." Since that time, a "great disturbance" had taken place that destroyed the unity between the Shawnee divisions. Nevertheless,

Black Beard predicted that someday the Shawnees would "live in one place and never move . . . and that everyone will look on us [the Maykujay and Chalagawtha divisions] as formerly." The Missouri Shawnees and the small number of Tecumseh's supporters in Ohio, composed primarily of the Kispokotha, Thawegila, and Piqua, greatly resented the Wapakoneta Shawnees' quest for tribal authority and American favoritism. The consequences were severe for Shawnees outside of the Wapkoneta community. For example, the Wapakoneta chiefs had been the recipients of the Shawnee annuity payments since the 1795 Treaty of Greenville.[26]

With Jefferson's support, tribal leaders from western New York to Indiana Territory increased their authority over their people.[27] Accordingly, Jefferson underwrote Black Beard's assessment of the need to centralize tribal power and convert to intensive agriculture. Jefferson and Harrison believed that increasing the Shawnees' dependency on annuity payments would create an entrenched elite capable of forcing the divergent bands into cooperation. Jefferson encouraged the Wapakoneta Shawnees to do all they could to diminish the power of their opponents within the tribe. In exchange, Jefferson assured Black Beard that if the United States "can be of any service in bringing you all together into one place, we will willingly assist you." The president hoped that annuity payments would force other tribes to acknowledge the necessity of geographic and political centralization.[28]

American officials made the breakup of multiethnic Indian villages a central goal of their efforts in the Old Northwest. William Wells, the Indian agent at Fort Wayne, began manipulating Native dependency on annuity payments. In a letter to Secretary of War Dearborn, Wells argued that "each nation should be collected together and some regular sistam [*sic*] of government established among them." To this end, Wells used treaty annuities in cash and supplies to entice villagers to choose their tribal identity and to declare the territory in their possession. American officials crafted these policies in response to the numerous revitalization movements of the colonial and revolutionary era and to the widespread, multiethnic opposition to American expansion such movements engendered.[29]

American policies enhanced the authority of tribal leaders who cooperated with American officials after the Treaty of Greenville and inspired their opponents to coordinate their efforts with other, similarly aggrieved leaders. Tenskwatawa and his brother Tecumseh became vocal critics of the American civilization strategy and those who accepted the new political and economic order in the Old Northwest.

Power Struggles: The Diversity within Revitalization Movements

Tecumseh and his brother Lalawethika, later known as Tenskwatawa, grew up amid Indian–white warfare that pushed the Shawnees from their lands and debilitated Indian tribes across the Old Northwest. Between the early 1770s and 1794, the Ohio River Valley was the site of continuous warfare between the Shawnees and the Americans. The "Long Knives" (as Shawnees called the Americans) had forced the Shawnees and their neighbors from their villages and hunting grounds in what is now West Virginia, Kentucky, and all but the northwest corner of Ohio by 1803. Settlers consistently thwarted British and American plans for a restrictive, rationally organized line of settlements in the trans-Appalachian West. Unlike the majority of their relatives who had fled the violence and were now living west of the Mississippi, Lalawethika and Tecumseh stayed behind with fewer than one hundred members of their immediate family, the few remaining members of the Kispokotha division in the Old Northwest. Lalawethika's life devolved to the point where he became "a perfect vagabond" who "would not hunt and became a great drunkard." He represented an extreme example of the ill effects of land loss, violence, materialism, and the erosion of family ties that had come with American domination in the Old Northwest.[30]

In a strange twist of fate, during an ugly drinking binge Lalawethika observed some itinerant ministers preach in western Ohio. The religious fervor espoused by these men at the height of the Second Great Awakening deeply affected Lalawethika during his drinking years. Then, during the winter of 1805, when he was approximately thirty-five years old, Lalawethika experienced a vision along the White River in Indiana Territory in which he reached a crossroads. The Master of Life forced him to choose either a "right hand road" free from evil or a "left hand *way*" full of "*bad wicked* people who would not *be good*." The "good spirit" told Lalawethika to use his medicine against an array of evils, including alcoholism, Indian–white marriages, hide hunting, dependence on trade, and spousal abuse. Particularly vivid for Lalawethika was the punishment reserved for alcoholics. In his vision of an alcoholics' purgatory, drunkards were forced to consume an endless supply of melted lead. Upon their refusal to drink more, attendants stepped in to urge them, "saying come, drink, sure you used to love liquor—now you must drink it." A recovering alcoholic since his vision, Lalawethika began a new life under a new name, Tenskwatawa, or "the Open Door" (or, more commonly, "the Prophet"). The Shawnee Prophet saw American culture and the alcohol trade

Ten-sqúat-a-way, The Open Door, Known as the Prophet, Brother of Tecumseh. By George Catlin. Smithsonian American Art Museum, Gift of Mrs. Joseph Harrison, Jr.

as the primary cause of despair among the Indian tribes. Like other leaders of revitalization movements before him, Tenskwatawa merged the larger political goal of preventing further land cessions with these strict moral codes.[31] Tenskwatawa believed that his own suffering and redemption should act as a template for all other American Indians.

Tenskwatawa directed his newfound moral superiority at Shawnees allied with the United States.[32] Yet neither those Shawnees allied with the Prophet nor their opponents at Wapakoneta were traditionalists. Both groups called for innovations to the decaying political, economic, and cultural order. Chief among these reforms was the centralization of authority. These competing ideologues struggled with each other to determine the path of change in Shawnee society, not whether the Shawnees should return to traditional practices. Average Shawnees, like most of their Indian neighbors, resisted both extremes and were frustrated by the simpleminded dichotomy between war and peace proposed by the Prophet, Black Hoof, and Harrison between 1795 and 1813.

Those Shawnees remaining in Ohio fiercely resisted the Shawnee brothers' dream of uniting the Great Lakes tribes around a reform-minded, political vision of Indian power. Approximately eight hundred Shawnees, most of whom were Maykujays and Chalagawthas, remained east of the Mississippi by the War of 1812. Black Hoof's people worked hard to demonstrate their loyalty to the United States by distancing themselves from their militant relatives. Some of their American neighbors embraced the Wapakoneta Shawnees and believed that they were "watchful safeguard[s] to our habitations." Unlike Tecumseh and the Shawnee Prophet, Black Hoof consistently emphasized the common bonds between Indians and Americans. Black Hoof believed that the Shawnees were "one man with the whites" and that because "treaties have always considered us as Americans . . . we look upon ourselves to be such now." Both the Shawnees and the Americans were "dropped on the same island," Black Hoof argued, and because of the common creation of Indians and Americans, both "ought to be bound in the ties of friendship."[33]

Allies of the Wapakoneta Shawnees, including the Miamis, Delawares, and Wyandots, feared the Prophet and the very real threat of violence posed by his supporters. Among the Miamis, Jean-Baptiste Richardville, a métis chief who had grown wealthy through the fur trade, joined Little Turtle in rejecting the ambitions of the militants. Both men used their wealth and their influence with American officials to retain the loyalty of their people. Similarly, Tecumseh and Tenskwatawa persuaded a mere forty Shawnee warriors to join them between 1805 and 1811. By contrast, tribes to the north and west of the Ohio-Indiana border, namely the Kickapoos, Potawatomis, Winnebagos, and Ottawas, supported the resistance movement. The Kickapoos, Potawatomis, and Winnebagos in Illinois and Wisconsin, and their Chippewa and Ottawa counterparts in Michigan, were just beginning to experience a surge in American settlement. In the Illinois country alone, over thirteen thousand Americans relocated between 1800 and 1814.[34] Many tribespeople in Illinois,

Wisconsin, and Michigan believed that armed resistance might turn back American settlers. In contrast, emigrant Indian villages in southern Missouri were more concerned with resisting Osage attacks and maintaining the fur trade than with joining their kinsmen in the East.

Tecumseh and Tenskwatawa placed few requirements on their supporters. They chose to emphasize the deep cultural differences between Indians and whites, and to undermine, and even kill, their sworn enemies among the tribes. While Black Hoof stressed the common humanity of Indians and whites, Tenskwatawa believed that Indians "ought to live agreeable to our several customs, the red people after their mode and the white people after theirs." During the winter of 1805, Tenskwatawa founded a multiethnic religious community at Greenville, Ohio, based on this principle of separation from Americans. In "dream[s] to God," the great spirit instructed Tenskwatawa to establish a village "towards the big fort where the peace was concluded" at the Treaty of Greenville in 1795. According to Richard McNemar, an ambassador from the Shaker village of Union, Ohio, who visited the Prophet in 1807, the residents of Greenville built a "large frame house" at the center of the village, surrounded by "57 smoaking [sic] cottages." The council house became a sort of Indian United Nations, where the Shawnees made "provision[s] to receive and instruct all from the different tribes that were willing to be good." Tenskwatawa and Tecumseh drew support from war chiefs and other unvanquished American Indians across the Old Northwest. Main Poc of the Illinois Potawatomis, Blackbird of the Potawatomis near Fort Dearborn, and Little King of the Ottawas and Chippewas from L'Arbre Croche in northern Michigan became influential members of the resistance movement. By 1807, Greenville was "the Mecca of the new religion" that swept across the Old Northwest in the face of American aggression. The Shawnee Prophet blamed the despondency and hopelessness among American Indians on those chiefs allied with the United States. Tenskwatawa explained that "the great spirit told him to separate from . . . wicked chiefs and their people."[35]

Soon after the Prophet's vision, in March 1806, residents of Greenville accused supporters of the United States in Ohio and Indiana of witchcraft. Chief Tetapachsit, a Christian Indian allied with neighboring Moravians among the White River Delawares, was among the first to be killed. His outspoken support for the Americans angered Tenskwatawa and many of the young people among the Delawares. For one thing, Tetapachsit had signed the Treaty of Greenville. It was also rumored that he participated in the alcohol trade. According to the Prophet, Tetapachsit and others like him were to blame for the loss of traditional Indian cultures in the Old Northwest. Moravian missionaries recalled that in the moments before his death "we saw ten Indians with their faces painted black, some on foot, others on horseback . . . with the old chief Tedpachsit." The Prophet's Delaware adherents then "built a fire near our place, struck the old chief on the head with a hatchet and threw him into the fire." Rife with symbolism, Tetapachsit's gruesome death near the Moravian mission demonstrates that Tenskwatawa's witch hunts targeted individuals who remained firmly opposed to his movement rather than those who were ambivalent about his power. In the end, sixteen people lost their lives in a similar fashion.[36]

According to Hendrick Apaumat, a Christian Indian from New York working on behalf of the United States, Tenskwatawa gave "a tomahawk to his followers to destroy all those who have shut their ears against his religion."[37] Yet the Prophet had a wider range of religious and political goals than Apaumat suggested. By focusing on widespread problems across Indian country, the Shawnee Prophet attempted to unite people around reforms rather than kinship ties. Tecumseh and the Prophet exploited generational differences by challenging the older leaders of the Delawares, Shawnees, Wyandots, and Miamis, thereby facilitating the rise to positions of authority of younger warriors who believed that warfare might expel American colonizers. Reformers asked their supporters to take power away from hereditary leaders such as Tetapachsit who had allowed evil to proliferate by permitting themselves to become pawns of the Americans and the Moravians allied with them. Their strategy made sense. As members of the Kispokotha division, most of Tecumseh and Tenskwatawa's intimate kinsmen lived too far away to be of much help. Consequently, the Shawnee brothers challenged their supporters to imagine a new, pan-Indian community. In a speech to Harrison in August 1808, Tenskwatawa proclaimed that his supporters "were once different people, they are now but one."[38]

While limited in effectiveness and scope, the witch hunts focused a great deal of attention on Tenskwatawa and the people of Greenville. American officials overestimated his influence and began to fear a two-front war in which Indians from west of the Mississippi and militant villagers from the Ohio country would unite to destroy the white settlements between them. Reports from the West confirmed their suspicions, as Americans noted a "Potawatomi runner" from the Meramac River in Missouri carrying wampum to the tribes east of the Mississippi. Rumors of a far-reaching Indian conspiracy were so pervasive that William Hull, then governor of Michigan Territory, attempted to prevent any eastern tribes from communicating with their western kinsmen.[39]

Tecumseh and Tenskwatawa struggled to find a balance between the parochial interests of Indian villagers and the dire need, as they saw it, for reform and resistance in Indian country. Leaders of revitalization movements in the Great Lakes had always exploited the diversity inherent in this parochial world to their own advantage. Kinship relations between members of different tribes helped make alliances possible. For example, the warrior Shabonee was born into the Ottawa tribe but later married a Potawatomi woman. Shabonee became an important leader among his wife's people and recruited many Ottawas and Potawatomis to the resistance movement.[40] American spies noted that Ottawa and Potawatomi supporters ignored many of the Prophet's mandates. But Harrison and Hull focused their energies on the commonality of belief and practice as described by the Shawnee Prophet rather than the diversity within the movement.[41]

While American officials strove to undermine the Greenville community, members of a neighboring sectarian religious movement were drawn to the spiritual awakening (as they saw it) happening there. The United Society of Believers in Christ's Second Coming, or Shakers, met with members of the Greenville community on several occasions early in 1807, at a time when William Kirk was busy establishing a mission at Wapakoneta. Driven from New York and out of favor with neighboring whites, the Shakers had much in common with the Indians at Greenville. The Shakers saw the people of Greenville as misunderstood martyrs persecuted for their apocalyptic assessment of Indian life in the Old Northwest. They believed that the Greenville community had "suffered great persecution, both from the whites & Indians, & have all manner of evil spoken of them, as we have had, & we think by the same false spirit." The Shakers were convinced that both groups shared access to "good spirits" through visions. They searched incessantly for evidence of these good spirits in others, assessing people's spiritual character wherever they went. In March 1807, on their way to Greenville, they stopped at Lewistown and met with Captain John, the village chief. The Shakers decided to move on quickly after concluding that "we could feel nothing in him or any of the people that felt like the spirit of God."[42]

Proceeding on to Greenville, Shakers Richard McNemar, Benjamin S. Youngs, and David Darrow were greatly impressed by the order and size of the community. More important, the Shakers believed that "the spirit we felt there brought on our minds a very striking & solemn sence of what God was doing in the earth." Greenville's population and the concomitant size of its structures easily outstripped the strength and size of the Shakers' village near the Ohio River in Adams County, Ohio.[43] The Shakers forged a religious rather than a material bond with the Indians at Greenville. Spurred on by the Cane Ridge, Kentucky, revival in 1801, Shaker membership had increased markedly. Shaker practice was built around the belief that they were an "advance guard or the intercessory remnant whose example and prayers would ultimately lead all men into blessedness" at the time of the Second Coming of Christ. The Shakers' belief in sexual abstinence, personal testimonials of faith, group dances, and public confession appealed to the residents of Greenville.[44]

Like the Shakers, the Prophet focused particular attention on marriage, sexuality, and social relationships within Indian communities. Across the Great Lakes, the culture of violence between Indians and whites bled into relationships within Indian communities. Unequal sex ratios caused by incessant warfare contributed to the abuse of women, who became dependent on the remaining male survivors. Men married multiple wives and demanded more labor and deference from them. Indian women faced increasing violence from their husbands for "not paying proper attention to her work," being unfaithful, and failing to have children. To counter these trends, Tenskwatawa encouraged his followers to enter into monogamous unions. He asserted the right of Indian husbands "to punish her with a rod" when dissatisfied. However, the abuse was to be limited so that when "the punishment was over, both husband and wife, was [*sic*] to look each other in the face and laugh." Tenskwatawa also chastised Indian women for marrying white men. Intermarriage with whites, in his view, had confused the boundaries between non-Indian and "genuine Indian" communities.[45]

Despite these connections, the Shawnee Prophet forced the Shakers to declare their attitude toward his movement before common religious ground could be forged. With Peter Cornstalk as his interpreter, the Prophet expressed little interest in speaking with them because "the ministers of the white people don't believe what he says." Benjamin Youngs replied that, "we are not of those kind of ministers, we are a people separated from them by the work of the *great spirit,* they count us as foolish too & speak against us."[46] He reassured the Prophet by emphasizing their peripheral status among their American neighbors. Youngs and his companions hoped that a partnership between the two like-minded communities might assist them in their shared struggle against their enemies—people they hoped to mollify and prepare for the Second Coming. A friendship developed only after assurances that the Shakers conceived of community in terms of access to the Great Spirit rather than race. In fact, Youngs and his fellow Shakers were quite different than any other religious society encountered by the Shawnees. Their willingness to treat Indians as equals, and to allow the people of Greenville to remain independent from their church, was unique among missionary endeavors in the nineteenth century. As radical religious outsiders, the two groups overlooked the obvious differences between them, believing that they were "all brothers of one family, united to the good spirits above."[47]

Religious convictions aside, Tenskwatawa recognized his community's need for material support. The Shakers responded with both produce and agricultural implements, angering neighboring settlers who feared recent additions at Greenville from the Michigan, Illinois, and Wisconsin territories. By September 1807, they had provided a grindstone, fifty bushels of wheat and rye, and other goods, including meat and salt. Youngs insisted that "we have sent it for the present relief of those, and those only, who love the good spirit of peace and hate the spirit of war."[48] But American hostility toward both the Greenville community and Union Village forced the Shakers to abandon their support. Surrounded by enemies, Tenskwatawa found his position in Ohio more and more untenable.

Despite the generosity of the Shakers and the execution of several key pro-American chiefs, Tenskwatawa failed to attract substantial numbers of young people from the tribes around Greenville. Three years of witch hunts among the accommodationist tribes of Indiana and Ohio had little success. Older influential chiefs such as the Wyandot leader Tarhe (also known as the Crane) joined forces with chiefs Black Hoof and Little Turtle. Born near Detroit in 1742, Tarhe fought alongside the British until the Battle of Fallen Timbers. Since that time, Tarhe had attempted to create a lasting peace with the Americans and to limit the influence of militants. In fact, in 1808 Tarhe saved the lives of four Wyandot women targeted for death by the Shawnee holy man. Tarhe and others like him forced the Prophet to shift his energies to the north and west.[49]

The western Potawatomi chief Main Poc, who was just beginning to experience the ill effects of white settlement in the Illinois country, offered hope to Tenskwatawa's struggling movement. In November 1807, Main Poc traveled east from his village on the Kankakee River to meet with the embattled Shawnee visionary. He stayed at Greenville for several weeks. Both men agreed that leaving Greenville provided the Prophet the best means to spread his religious and political goals to potential supporters outside of Ohio and Indiana. Main Poc persuaded Tenskwatawa to relocate his village 120 miles to the northwest of Greenville near what is now Lafayette, Indiana. Soon thereafter, Tenskwatawa and approximately eighty of his followers founded the village of Prophetstown. Between 1808 and 1811, the two leaders increased the size of the movement from fewer than one hundred adherents to close to one thousand supporters.[50]

Main Poc and Tenskwatawa chose the new site carefully. Located at the juncture of the Tippecanoe and Wabash Rivers, Prophetstown was accessible to Indian towns north and south of the village, and it also sat astride an east-west route that many of the western tribes followed on their way to visit the British in Canada at Amherstburg. Prophetstown's population was in constant flux, as young men and tribal leaders of diverse Indian groups came and went in search of war plans and supplies.

Prominent members of western tribes, including Main Poc, attracted more and more people to Prophetstown. Blackbird, a Potawatomi chief from southern Michigan, also became associated with the Prophet because he saw the "White Devil with his mouth wide open ready to take possession of our lands by any means whatever." On August 5, 1812, Blackbird and another Potawatomi leader named Mad Sturgeon led approximately 600 Potawatomi warriors in the famous siege of Fort Dearborn. The political and military objectives of the Prophet's vision of Indian reform became more important as the diversity of tribes increased. Tecumseh believed "that all the remaining Indian land belonged to no particular tribe, only to all the Indians in general."[51] Prophetstown provided a meeting place for Indian people interested in revitalizing their cultures or simply finding a way to stop the white advance.

Tenskwatawa's influence over the multitude who assembled at Prophetstown was far more limited than some accounts suggest. Main Poc, for one, disagreed with many of the basic tenets of Tenskwatawa's teaching. In fact, Main Poc was a notorious drinker who often used the drug for effective visions. American officials were slow to recognize Prophetstown's divided leadership. However, the Northern Superintendent of Indian Affairs, William Clark, understood the shared authority of its leaders and referred to Tenskwatawa and Main Poc together as "the Indian Prophets."[52]

Clark spied on Main Poc's negotiations with the Winnebagos, Kickapoos, and Sacs in Illinois and Wisconsin, fearing the Potawatomi leader's ability to wage a massive war "against the frontiers of this country." Tribes even farther west, including the Ioway and Meskwaki (Fox) Indians, responded to Main Poc's call. William Wells, the Indian agent at Fort Wayne, resorted to bribery between 1807 and 1811 to sway Main Poc from the British to the American orbit. Main Poc got the better of Wells, however, and accepted supplies from both the British and the Americans.[53]

Main Poc's influence proved to be a mixed blessing. The Potawatomi war chief's actions were often personally or tribally motivated. His refusal to give up alcohol and end his raiding against the Potawatomis' traditional enemies, the Osages, undermined the movement. Harrison and the governor of the Illinois Territory, Ninian Edwards, used Main Poc's intransigence against Tenskwatawa and Tecumseh. The Americans blamed the Shawnee brothers for the violence in Illinois and dismissed their portrayal of Prophetstown as a pacifist religious community. More important, Harrison and Edwards questioned their claim to speak for militants across the Old Northwest. Nevertheless, the Shawnee Prophet believed that Harrison would support him because he "preach[ed] the word of God to the Indians."[54]

Tenskwatawa had to face the inescapable reality that he and his supporters remained dependent on the United States. Dependency on the Americans stretched his diplomatic abilities, as he appealed to militants who hoped to reject American aid and the culture that came with it. Palpable evidence of American power in the region remained obvious. In June 1808, Harrison sent an envoy, John Conner, to investigate reports of stolen livestock attributed to Prophetstown. As trader to the White River Delawares, Conner surely remembered Tetapachsit's death in 1806. His frustration with the Shawnee holy man is evident in the letter he composed to William Wells. Conner believed that more than twenty horses, along with slaughtered cattle and pigs owned by whites, had been stolen. He estimated that approximately 130 warriors from the Shawnees, Potawatomis, Chippewas, and Winnebagos were living at Prophetstown.[55]

A determined group of Miami and Delaware leaders redoubled their effort to kill the religious movement through a wave of bad press. The brutal witch trials that took the lives of several of their allies remained fresh in the minds of Little Turtle, Black Hoof, Owl, and other pro-American Indian leaders in Ohio and Indiana. The confederacy at Prophetstown had created an inner civil war within Indian villages across the Great Lakes that threatened the ability of accommodationists to remain in the Old Northwest. Soon enough, Indian and American spies flooded Harrison with news about the community. In a letter to Henry Dearborn, Harrison reported that an unidentified "intelligent man" had observed the residents of Prophetstown "engaged in what they term religious duties." The problem, in Harrison's view, was that "their prayers are always succeeded by or intermixed with warlike sports, shooting with the bow, throwing the tomahawk, or wielding the war club." The marriage of religion and war at Prophetstown prompted Harrison and his Delaware and Miami allies to "defeat the measure [Prophetstown] at any risk."[56]

Wells claimed that the Prophet was powerful enough to intimidate any white man into giving him what he wanted. "If he only looked at a white man," Wells claimed, they would be rendered defenseless. Wells's caustic remarks stemmed from his allegiance to the Miami chief Little Turtle, who had adopted Wells after taking him captive. Wells's warnings to Harrison initially failed to produce the military action against Prophetstown he desired. Nevertheless, he did succeed in creating a climate of fear surrounding the Prophet that infected white settlers in the area for years to come. As long as the population of Prophetstown remained small, however, Harrison considered the village more of a nuisance than a serious military threat.[57]

Aware of his detractors and his vulnerability to American attacks, the Prophet sent an emissary to Vincennes in June 1808. In a subsequent speech, the unidentified representative told Harrison that the "Great Spirit has told us that our conduct is not right; that we ought to live in peace upon the land he has given us." He also urged Harrison to ignore slanderous reports about Prophetstown. They had been "much misrepresented," he claimed, by the "bad reports you have heard." Later that August, the Prophet visited Vincennes and reaffirmed his friendship with the United States. He also asked for more supplies for his followers, a request Harrison honored. Unknown to Harrison, Tecumseh had already left for Amherstburg, Ontario, in mid-June, requesting aid for Prophetstown and closer military ties between the young confederacy and the British.[58]

Tecumseh met with a number of important British officials at Amherstburg that summer, including the deputy superintendent of Indian affairs, William Claus, and an Indian agent and trader, Matthew Elliott. Representatives of the Potawatomi, Sac, Huron, Chippewa, and Ottawa tribes, including the Ottawa chief Little King, also met with the Shawnee war chief. The Ottawas became a particularly important addition to the confederacy. Indeed, the Chippewas, Ottawas, and Potawatomis traditionally believe that they were originally one tribe. In the early years of the nineteenth century, kinship ties linked them together and fostered shared religious beliefs as well. American observers described Little King's brother, Le Maigouis (the Trout), as "the Herald of this new religion" in the North. Little King and the Trout were from L'Arbre Croche (Cross Village), on northern Lake Michigan, whose residents had been allied with the French during Pontiac's Rebellion in 1763. In fact, a number of British prisoners of war were murdered there before the British defeated Pontiac and his followers. Now the Ottawas and Chippewas joined with Tecumseh and the Shawnee Prophet by calling for Indian unity and resistance to further land sales. By fall 1808, Little King led more than three hundred Ottawas and Chippewas to Prophetstown. Like Main Poc and the Potawatomis, they joined the movement through the encouragement of local religious leaders who urged them to meet with Tenskwatawa at Prophetstown.[59]

New recruits at Prophetstown exhausted the meager supplies of corn, and British and American aid was not enough to meet the needs of the burgeoning population. New recruits were younger warriors who hoped to restore gender roles that were appropriate to the mixed hunting–agricultural economies of the past. Accordingly, they "rejected any Indian adoption of American agricultural methods and gender roles." In fact, the Prophet believed that the Americans wanted to make "women of the Indians." But such declarations would have to wait. Conditions were so desperate that an unnamed follower conceded that "we are now not ashamed to work and make corn for our women and children." But still there was not enough corn. Starvation hit the community hard over the winter. Disease soon followed, taking the lives of Little King and approximately 160 of his supporters. Curiously, only five Shawnees died. The northern tribes interpreted the deaths as a sign that Tenskwatawa had used his power against them. The 180 surviving Ottawas and Chippewas left Prophetstown the following spring without waging a single battle against the settlers. Ottawa and Chippewa survivors could not ignore the disease's preference for their own people. Village loyalties proved more enduring than the Prophet's brand of pan-Indian nativism.[60]

Tenskwatawa and Tecumseh's claims to speak for all the Indians were often frustrated by the Algonquian belief in dispersed authority—that like-minded individuals could disassociate themselves from a given movement or leader when they wished. Like Main Poc, the Ottawas and Chippewas insisted on making independent decisions, frustrating the Shawnees' efforts to control the movement. In fact, Ottawa and Chippewa survivors remained convinced of Tenskwatawa's bad intentions and organized a war party against Prophetstown in June 1809.[61]

While most American officials remained ambivalent about the residents of Prophetstown, American Indian opponents of the revitalization movement became more strident. William Hull feared that inter-tribal warfare might engulf the settlements and attempted to stop the Ottawas and Chippewas from attacking Prophetstown. He warned the northern tribesmen that "the Shawanoese were under the protection of the United States, and we should consider hostilities against them the same as against us." The Territorial Governor of Michigan was also eager to assert American sovereignty over the Upper Great Lakes. Using the kinship language of "fathers and children," Hull reminded the Ottawas and Chippewas "that if the Shawanoese had done them an injury they must represent it to their Great Father the president of the U.S." He foreshadowed the years ahead, to a time and place void of British influence in which Indians would live under an unquestioned American state.[62]

The Territorial Governor mediated an agreement between the Shawnees at Prophetstown and the Ottawas and Chippewas at L'Arbre Croche in which both sides pledged to avoid interfering in each others' affairs. But more importantly, the untimely demise of Little King and his followers dealt a heavy blow to the confederacy. The level of Ottawa and Chippewa support for Prophetstown never surpassed that of the winter of 1808–1809. In fact, many northern tribesmen would not return to Prophetstown until April 1810, after the Treaty of Fort Wayne and a new round of land cessions. Once again, Tenskwatawa and Tecumseh redirected their recruitment to the Kickapoos, Winnebagos, and Potawatomis. The importance of the western tribes grew markedly.[63]

The Treaty of Fort Wayne, concluded on September 30, 1809, confirmed the suspicions of the warriors at Prophetstown. The treaty ceded more than three million acres of land along both the southern Indiana-Illinois border and east-central Indiana. Following the treaty, Main Poc, Black Bird, Tecumseh, and others believed that armed resistance provided the only means of preventing American settlements on tribal lands. A reported 956 Delaware, Potawatomi, Shawnee, Miami, and Eel River Miami tribesmen participated in the treaty. Most had seen enough bloodshed and British inconsistency to resist joining forces with Tenskwatawa. Peace advocates among the St. Joseph Potawatomis, including Five Medals and Kesis, avoided the treaty grounds because they "feared retaliation by their younger warriors." Nevertheless, the friendly Potawatomi chief Winemac joined with Little Turtle of the Miamis and Captain Anderson of the Delawares and signed the treaty. Cooperation with the Americans bolstered their prestige with Harrison, but it drove a powerful wedge within Indian communities. Between May 1809 and June 1810, Prophetstown nearly doubled its population when another three hundred villagers joined the movement. The treaty confirmed the Prophet's claim that the Americans intended to "push the original people into the Great Lakes."[64]

Incessant violence and land cessions had accelerated the "geographic diffusion" of Midwestern tribes such as the Potawatomis, Shawnees, Kickapoos, and Delawares between 1795 and 1810. One Potawatomi chief named Gomo, whose village was located north of Peoria along the Illinois River, complained to Ninian Edwards about the situation. He criticized American policy-makers, remarking that "since our intercourse with the whites, there are almost as many chiefs as there are young men." The Potawatomis, he explained, "had all lived in one large village" years ago. By 1810 the Potawatomi people were scattered across Wisconsin, Illinois, Indiana, and Michigan in a series of autonomous towns. Following Gomo's speech to Edwards, another Potawatomi leader from eastern Illinois named Little Chief spoke for still more tribesmen who were struggling to remain neutral as the battle lines hardened between Prophetstown and the United States. According to Little Chief, the Shawnee Prophet, "the man who talks with the Father of Light," blamed the Potawatomis, Chippewas, and Ottawas "for not listening to him." Little Chief chastised Edwards for failing to respect their desire to avoid the conflict altogether. The neutral tribes were now "like a bird in a bush, beset, and not knowing which way to fly for safety."[65]

Not surprisingly, violence erupted across the midwestern frontier following the Treaty of Fort Wayne. American travelers concealed their identities by disguising themselves as French traders in order to avert bloodshed. In May 1810, an emboldened Tenskwatawa directly challenged Harrison's authority. He warned the governor that "his people should not come any nearer to him, that they should not settle on the Vermillion river—he smelt them too strong already." Upon learning of Indian attacks on settlers, Americans carried their rifles with them at all times. The flow of new emigrants onto the Indian lands ceded by the Treaty of Fort Wayne all but ended.[66]

But the threat of violence within Indian communities was far more severe. Tenskwatawa urged the young men at Prophetstown to open a new round of witchcraft trials and execute the older chiefs who had sold their lands or simply refused to support him. Little Turtle of the Miamis, Leather Lips of the Wyandots, and Gomo of the Potawatomis were specifically targeted. Later that spring, a dozen Delawares and at least five Wyandots were murdered by their kinsmen. On June 1, 1810, Leather Lips was killed in his village along the Scioto River, twelve miles from modern-day Columbus. Leather Lips opposed the confederacy at Prophetstown and had signed the Treaty of Greenville on behalf of the Wyandots. His executioners—Wyandots from the Sandusky River—forced Leather Lips to kneel beside a shallow grave, where they tomahawked him before an audience of his followers. Two weeks after his execution, Harrison conceded that many of the Wyandots were now under the influence of the Prophet.[67]

Swift reaction to the wave of killings followed. Groebles, a Piankashaw chief from the Little Wabash River in southern Illinois, pleaded with Harrison for a new tract of land beyond the Mississippi. He complained that "he heard nothing but the cry of war—that he was an old man and did not wish to have any share in it—that he wanted to retire to a place of safety."[68] Great Lakes Indians still viewed the lands west of the Mississippi as a haven from bloodshed, despite increased white settlement there and similar reports of witchcraft among Algonquian emigrants. Many treaty signers, including Groebles, felt compelled to move as their hold on power in their home villages weakened. Land cessions thus became a devil's bargain for the Americans. Harrison had forced his allies to sign over more than 56 million acres of land to the United States by 1805 alone. Additional land cessions between 1805 and 1809 contributed to the fragmentation of the peaceful alliances, as peace advocates struggled with each other over diminishing hunting grounds and resources distributed by the United States.[69]

Some village chiefs benefited from American partisanship. By 1804, Black Hoof and neighboring peace advocates among the Miami and Delaware "had positioned themselves . . . into the chief conduits for the passage of U.S. annuities to Indians." Black Hoof, unscathed by the witchcraft trials, managed to persuade an estimated eight hundred Shawnee villagers at Wapakoneta to remain in the alliance with the United States. Respect for the Shawnee chief among the Maykujay and Chalagawtha divisions at Wapakoneta, in addition to the generous redistribution of federal annuities to his people, contributed to their allegiance to the Americans.[70]

The concentration of American wealth and power in the form of treaty annuities paid to the Wapakoneta villagers had real consequences for Prophetstown and the many other Shawnee villages that maintained a neutral or antagonistic stance toward the United States. The U.S. Indian agent for Wapakoneta, John Johnston, put it simply. In his opinion, "there is no part of this country now where 500 men can subsist ten days at a place on what the woods may furnish." During the spring of 1810, villagers at Prophetstown planted approximately 200 acres of corn and also raised some cattle. Harrison estimated that Prophetstown supported no more than 400 warriors, but that over 3,000 supporters could be found within thirty miles of the community. Without American help, the Shawnee brothers could not concentrate a fighting force of more than 1,000 warriors at Prophetstown from 1808 to 1811.[71]

Fears of war across the Great Lakes forced Indian men to remain at their villages in order to defend the fields planted by the women. William Burnett, a Scots-Irish trader along the St. Joseph River in Northern Indiana, observed that Indian hunters "continually imagine that the Americans are coming upon them." The war mood settling in on both sides of the frontier became so pronounced that men "neither routinely nor regularly left for their wintering grounds." Bereft of American support, and hemmed in by more than 345,000 white people living in the Great Lakes region by 1810, Prophetstown's warriors increased their dependence on Indian women as food providers—a trend that began with the fur trade. As male hide hunters ranged great distances in search of fur-bearing animals, Indian women created the food surpluses necessary to sustain Indian villages. Steady increases in corn acreage in 1810 and 1811 indicate that women comprised at least a third of the villagers. Indian women, as the primary farmers and food suppliers within the pan-Indian alliance, enabled hundreds of warriors at Prophetstown to remain at the site from 1810 until the Battle of Tippecanoe on November 7, 1811.[72] Paradoxically, warriors who became invested in the revolutionary innovations of pan-Indianism found themselves increasingly dependent on both the United States and Indian women. The goal of pushing back American settlers could not be realized unless the Prophet's followers sacrificed the winter hunt and focused their energies on recruitment and strategy.

Heightening tensions between Prophetstown's warriors and the Americans forced the Wapakoneta Shawnees to redouble their commitment to the American alliance. Black Hoof, along with other peace advocates, including Tarhe, attended two major peace conferences with American settlers, in August and December 1811, to assuage the fears of their white neighbors. The Wapakoneta Shawnees also provided spies and scouts to the Americans during the war. Black Hoof even fought against the combined British and Indian forces on the Americans' behalf. Other Wapakoneta Shawnees, such as Logan, a mixed-blood Shawnee, gave his life in an attempt to convince Harrison of the Shawnees' loyalty to the United States. Two of Logan's children, John and William Perry, carried on their father's work in the war by serving as scouts for the Americans.[73]

Neither the nativists at Prophetstown nor Harrison wanted peace. And as tensions mounted, the antagonism from both camps polarized the dialogue and made accommodation impossible. Buoyed by their increased numbers, and incensed by the latest land giveaways, the warriors finally took action along the frontier. The greatest violence took place in the Illinois country. Several Potawatomi leaders, including Main Poc, Turkey Foot, and Matchoquis, attacked American settlers. The murder of a small party of pioneers by Sac Indians particularly enraged Ninian Edwards. In that incident, Sac warriors stole several deerskins and other articles from the frontiersmen's camp. During the lengthy pursuit that followed, the Sacs waged a preemptive strike against their pursuers, ambushing the frontiersmen and killing four. One other man was stabbed several times and left for dead in the brush. In a much larger engagement in the fall of 1810, Main Poc led over 170 Sac, Kickapoo, and Potawatomi warriors across the Mississippi against the Osages. Wounded in the attack, Main Poc survived with the help of the British at Fort Malden.[74]

Main Poc had preempted the Shawnee brothers' authority and undermined their efforts to recruit new members, but Harrison blamed Prophetstown for the bloody turn of events. Unfazed, Tecumseh boasted during a visit to the British that fall that the wave of recent attacks showed that "the warriors now manage the affairs of our nation." As a member of the Kispokotha division, which supplied war chiefs to the entire tribe, Tecumseh recognized that power was shifting from village to war chiefs. "We sit at, or near, the borders where the contest will soon begin," he added confidently. Recent delegations of more than 1,100 Winnebago, Sac, and Meskwaki warriors at Prophetstown bolstered the Shawnee leaders' hopes that tribesmen from the western Great Lakes had chosen to ally themselves with the confederacy.[75]

Tecumseh's bold assertions, and the increased violence between Indians and whites, convinced Harrison of the need to strike Prophetstown. Harrison's army, composed of U.S. infantry and militia units from both Indiana and Kentucky, began its march toward Prophetstown on September 26, 1811. From Vincennes, they proceeded northward along the Wabash River. On October 3, near what is now Terre Haute, Harrison paused for nearly three weeks to build a fort that would bear his name. Harrison's army of more than one thousand men reached Prophetstown on November 6 after another nine days of marching. Tecumseh's absence on a recruiting trip among the Creeks and Cherokees gave Harrison a decided advantage. Buckling under pressure from the warriors in his camp, the Prophet reneged on his promise to Tecumseh to appease Harrison and the Americans. Instead, they would fight the Americans. Tenskwatawa promised the men that the white man's bullets would not harm them and that many American scalps would soon hang in their lodges.[76]

In the early morning of November 7, Indian warriors fought in the short skirmish that became known as the Battle of Tippecanoe. White Loon, a Wyandot-Shawnee warrior, and Stone Eater, a Kickapoo warrior, directed between 250 and 450 warriors against Harrison and his army while Tenskwatawa "spent the early morning in ritually seeking the aid of the Master of Life." The battle ended after nearly two hours of bayonet charges and sniper-fire from both sides. Superior numbers and arms dispersed Prophetstown's warriors. By midday, most of the warriors had escaped across the marsh lining the battlefield.[77]

Although Tenskwatawa was not in the battle, the Indians' measured defeat mortally wounded the Shawnee visionary's credibility. As Prophetstown emptied, calls for his execution grew louder. The Prophet's medicine had proved ineffective against American firepower: twenty-five to thirty-six warriors lay dead on the battlefield. Indian warriors had killed about sixty-two Americans and wounded 126 others. But despite heavy American casualties, support for the Prophet vanished. Tenskwatawa blamed the defeat on his wife, who had failed to tell him that she was menstruating during the battle. The Shawnees and other Eastern Woodland tribes strived to separate feminine and masculine powers, particularly during a woman's menstruation, which they associated with the height of a woman's reproductive power. Warriors and hunters avoided women in this state for fear that women's power to create life might destroy their ability to take life. But the Prophet's erstwhile allies dismissed his attempt to blame his wife for the failure of his own spiritual power. The Kickapoos lost eleven warriors in the battle and were in no mood to provide shelter to the Prophet. Like the Kickapoos, the Winnebagos threatened to kill Tenskwatawa for giving them the false hope that his medicine would protect them in battle. Disgusted with the Shawnee holy man, members of the confederacy returned to their villages to fight a guerrilla war against American settlers on their own terms.[78]

American hatred for Indians, which had grown since the Battle of Fallen Timbers, doomed the wounded warriors remaining in and around Prophetstown. Immediately following the engagement, a group of Kentucky volunteers shot and killed one man as he crawled toward safety. The Kentuckians quickly scalped the warrior and divided the scalp into four pieces. An eyewitness claimed that "such was the fate of nearly all the Indians found dead on the battle ground."[79] According to the eyewitness, both the "treachery of the Indians" and "the bloody scenes of the battle" justified the dismemberment of the Indian dead.[80] The American desecrations did not go unnoticed. Some of the Indian survivors returned to the site, exhumed the American dead, and scalped them in retaliation for the soldiers' acts.[81]

On November 8, Harrison's troops marched into an empty Prophetstown. They found between 100 and 200 abandoned lodges lining the Wabash River, in addition to considerable food supplies. Ironically, the corn and beans the villagers had struggled for so long to stockpile helped the beleaguered American troops survive in the aftermath of the conflict. Sorely lacking supplies, the soldiers had been forced to eat horse meat for five days before the battle. The precious commodities the Prophet and the diverse members of his confederacy had tried so desperately to protect now sustained their bitter enemies.[82]

The Battle of Tippecanoe did not end Harrison's "Indian problem" in Indiana and Illinois, but it effectively ended Tenskwatawa's short tenure as leader of the Indian confederacy. Members of the confederacy no longer respected the Prophet. More important, angry groups of defeated warriors fanned out across the frontier, committing depredations against American settlements. Tippecanoe became the prelude to the larger, deadlier battles of the War of 1812. Organized Indian opposition to white settlement was anything but over. Pan-Indian opponents of the United States survived the Shawnee visionary, demonstrating that the power of the movement transcended the charisma of one leader from 1805 to 1811.[83] Indian resistance did not recede until decisive American victories at the Battle of Fort Meigs, Ohio, on July 21, 1813, and Tecumseh's death at the Battle of the Thames in Canada on October 5, 1813.

Prophetstown's tumultuous rise to prominence in the Old Northwest, and its sudden dissolution in 1811, offers a compelling example of the logistical and organizational obstacles faced by pan-Indian visionaries such as Tecumseh and Tenskwatawa. Hostility between Indians at Prophetstown and their kinsmen who were opposed to the confederacy define both the importance and the limitations of tribal bonds. Tecumseh and Tenskwatawa were part of a struggle to retain Indian lands that was larger than any one leader, yet powerful enough to be sustained in dispersed communities across the frontier. No single leader, village, or ideology became the epicenter of Indian resistance to American expansion. Communal bonds in the Old Northwest were too strong to relinquish power to any one man or any one vision.

The Shawnees and their neighbors stood at a crossroads after the Battle of the Thames. The defeat of the pan-Indian alliance signaled a larger American attack on the connections between Native peoples in the Great Lakes and impacted Indian–white relations for years to come. American officials now asked Tecumseh's survivors—Black Hoof and the Wapakoneta Shawnees—to assist the United States in tearing down the diverse world of parochial, multiethnic villages that had defined the "middle ground" since the early eighteenth century. American officials hoped to construct politically unified Indian nations, led by chiefs with the authority to cede land to the expanding United States.

2. The Ohio Shawnees' Struggle against Removal, 1813–1833

On July 23, 1813, in an apparent fit of boredom, Ensign William Schillinger got on a horse at Fort Amanda, Ohio, and rode several miles to the Shawnee town of Wapakoneta. Schillinger, located south of the major theaters of the war, spent most of his days making ammunition and defending the fort from would-be attackers who never materialized. Relations between the soldiers and the people of Wapakoneta were friendly, driven in part by the important role played by Shawnee scouts in the success of the American war effort. In his diary, Schillinger recorded that he "took a survey of the Indians gardens or farms (for they know no difference between their farm or Garden)." What he saw inspired both envy and revulsion in the young officer, for he had eaten very little beyond salted pork and the occasional deer or turkey brought in by the hunters in his regiment. Schillinger witnessed a profusion of "vines, such as Pumpkins, Water & Musk mellons, cucumbers, beens [*sic*] of various kinds, growing among their corn which was planted without any kind of order." But the Shawnees' worst offense, according to Schillinger, was that "the work is principally all done by the squaws."[1]

Both the perceived disorder of the Shawnee gardens and real differences over gender roles drove the soldier's critique. The Shawnees did not raise cash crops, such as wheat, that were typical of the Ohio frontier. Also absent is any mention of fruit trees and livestock, particularly pigs and cattle. Simply put, Schillinger was struck by the distance between American and Algonquian agricultural practices. But he was especially disturbed by the dominance of Shawnee women in the agricultural sphere. Both Indian and American women on the frontier raised "kitchen gardens" complete with vegetables meant for home consumption. But American women did not tend the majority of the acreage under cultivation on the typical farm. Moreover, the vegetables they raised, including onions, potatoes, turnips, lettuce, and cabbage, distinguished their gardens—and the food they consumed—from their Indian neighbors. Schillinger confirmed his belief in the primitiveness of Shawnee culture by focusing his attention on American farms worked by men and Indian gardens cultivated by women.[2]

Americans who visited and lived among the Shawnees echoed this soldier's confusion regarding the important role played by Indian women in agriculture and trade and in building camps, preparing skins, cutting and hauling firewood, and cooking. At the same time, Americans voiced their disdain for Shawnee men who seemed to be interested in little more than "the chase and war pursuits," while they casually ignored the agrarian values on which most American men obsessed. Americans linked these gender differences to the oppression of Indian women. John Johnston, the Indian agent at Piqua, Ohio, was convinced that "nothing can be more degrading[,] servile or menial than the condition of their females in the married state" even though Indian women "look upon such things as their appropriate duties."[3]

Shawnee men were equally troubled by the gender roles imposed with increasing force by American missionaries and government officials. Agricultural practices—and the gender differences associated with them—became one of the primary means by which both Shawnees and Americans defined themselves personally and collectively as they attempted to live among each other between 1813 and 1833.

When Schillinger returned to Fort Amanda later that evening, messengers alerted him to the combined British and Indian siege of the Americans' Fort Meigs, approximately eighty miles to the northeast. Soldiers commanded by Green Clay lifted the siege, but the Americans continued to battle against warriors led by the Potawatomis, Winnebagos, and Chippewas. Skirmishes between militants and American troops occurred regularly to the north of Wapakoneta, complicating attempts by the Ohio Shawnees to remain neutral. By February 1814, the Shawnee Indian agent John Johnston compelled the peaceful Shawnees and their neighbors to move from neutrality to armed support for the American war effort. Johnston told the Shawnees, Wyandots, Senecas, Miamis, Potawatomis, Ottawas, and Kickapoos that for the Americans, "war is our trade and you cannot live quiet and take no part in it." He went on to explain that if the Shawnees and their neighbors refused to fight, they would be considered enemies of the United States.[4]

In response, additional Shawnees volunteered for the Americans. Some of the men, including François Duchoquet, were the children of French fathers and Shawnee mothers. Duchoquet and others, working as hired hunters, stepped in to make up for the soldiers' inability to track and kill large game. Still more Shawnees worked as scouts and interpreters. Many of these young men were the children of hereditary leaders. Fighting alongside the Americans enhanced their ability to win leadership roles in the tribe in the future. Combat-tested friendships with American soldiers facilitated their role as mediators across cultures, an important element of chiefly authority in the postwar Midwest.[5]

Relationships between Shawnee hunters and scouts and American soldiers and settlers raise important questions about the limits of cultural pluralism on the American frontier. As border combatants, Shawnees and settlers had become sworn enemies between the mid-1770s and 1794. Since that time, an increasingly sound Shawnee and American alliance centered at Wapakoneta challenged long-held frontier assumptions about American Indians. Schillinger, Johnston, and Quaker missionaries such as Joseph Rhodes and Henry Harvey remained either ambivalent or strongly opposed to a racial quarantine between Indians and whites. However, victory over the British in the West bolstered the confidence of American settlers and led to a deeper investigation of the cultural differences between Indians and Americans. The editors of the *Niles Weekly Register* articulated one of the more common brands of Indian hating by arguing that enemy tribes "must be brought to a sense of justice . . . they must be *Jacksonized,* as the saying goes in the west." While future president Andrew Jackson's belief in Indian removal and pacification through violence was popular, it is also true that a small but vocal group of Jackson's critics emerged in the Old Northwest. The Shawnees thus struggled to find Indian and American allies in a region divided over Indian identity and perceived racial differences between Indians and whites.[6]

Regardless of American points of view on the subject, the Ohio Shawnees firmly opposed relocation west of the Mississippi. In August 1816, some Shawnee scouts and leaders within the tribe, including John and William Perry and Black Hoof, left their villages near present-day Lima, Ohio, on a 200-mile journey to Lexington and Bourbon County, Kentucky, to visit with friends from the army and to see the country. Black Hoof and the Perry brothers hoped to build on their friendships with American soldiers and foster a new era of openness and cooperation.[7]

The tour through his former hunting grounds must have been bittersweet for the aged chief Black Hoof, who for most of his life had tried to thwart American settlement in Kentucky and Ohio. Despite serving as an American ally in recent years, he continued to face indignities. He had even been shot in the face by an American soldier unconvinced of his trustworthiness. Still, Black Hoof decided to make the journey upon the request of a Kentuckian whose life he once saved in the decades of conflict between the settlers and Shawnees. The most esteemed leader of the Maykujay division was an "honored guest" in the Bluegrass region of central Kentucky.[8]

Younger Wapakoneta Shawnee leaders such as John and William Perry generally agreed with Black Hoof's perspective, but their lives had not been defined by the conflict between colonial powers and their native allies in a larger struggle for control of the Ohio Valley. Born at the dawn of American dominance in the Old Northwest, the sons of the Shawnee war chief Logan understood the tour through Kentucky quite differently. Both chose to follow Black Hoof's path of accommodation with the Americans. They enlisted at Fort Laramie, Ohio, and enabled an American company of Rangers "to know the friendly Indians from those who are not so." In fact, their father, who also signed up to fight for the Americans, was killed in a skirmish with the Potawatomis. The *Niles Weekly Register* later reported that the Perry brothers had "always conducted themselves with faithfulness and gallantry." For the Perrys, working as scouts was not simply a means of improving relations between the Shawnees and Americans. Enlisting in the American army allowed younger Shawnee men to achieve status in their villages at a time when traditional outlets for prestige through warfare and hunting were declining rapidly. Grateful Americans fueled the optimistic notion that a long-overdue era of peace and stability was about to begin in the Ohio country.[9]

Challenging many of their opponents' assumptions, the Ohio Shawnees and their neighbors planned for a future in Ohio. Along with another 1,600 Seneca, Delaware, Ottawa, and Wyandot Indians, Ohio's Indians were now confined to the northwest corner of the state. The land they occupied was the last to be settled in the state, in part because of the challenges associated with draining the swampy and wooded lands south of Lake Erie along the Maumee River and its tributaries. Methodist, Baptist, Moravian, and Quaker missionaries worked with the tribes after the war. Among the Wyandots, the African American preacher John Stewart and a circuit-rider named James Finley helped the tribe dominate the news coverage of Ohio Indian progress toward American notions of civilization. Their command of English and participation in the grain and cattle trade contributed to the Wyandots' popularity among philanthropists.[10]

Americans on the western frontiers generally considered those Indians who remained to be sad hangers-on, vanquished relics of another era. Members of the Democratic Party such as Thomas Hart Benton of Missouri dismissed Indian efforts at remaining in their homelands. In a speech before the U.S. Senate in 1824, Benton echoed the sentiments of Lewis Cass and Andrew Jackson, complaining that the Indians "must know that . . . the power of the state is against them; and that, sooner or later, they must go." Population imbalances encouraged Benton and his colleagues to promote Indian removal. At the time Benton made his remarks, there were an estimated 2,350 American Indians in Ohio, with another 11,579 in Indiana and Illinois. Indian people in the Old Northwest lived among solid American majorities at the conclusion of the war. In 1815, nearly 69,000 settlers lived in Indiana Territory, while more than 300,000 had settled in Ohio.[11]

But Tecumseh's survivors struggled to remain despite overwhelming differences in population and resources. From the perspective of the American Indians who remained there, removal beyond the Mississippi was not an alternative. Allies of the Americans, including Little Turtle of the Miamis, died in the war along with Logan and several other Shawnees in hand-to-hand combat with their enemies. They had shed their own blood for the Americans, and most believed that in the process they had earned a place for themselves behind the frontier. Coexistence with whites was the only means of survival, and as such, the Shawnees rejected the binary racial and ethnic division between Indians and whites advocated by Benton, Cass, and their supporters. Black Hoof had witnessed the advancing American settlements for decades. He reminded the Indian agent Johnston that his people "were arrived at the point, beyond which they could not go, that when they looked over the Mississippi they saw the White people moving there as fast as in former times they spread themselves over Kentucky and Ohio." The Shawnees tied their survival to their ability to live as useful neighbors amid their former enemies.[12]

Americans demanded deep changes in tribal leadership in exchange for a place in Ohio. In addition to the transformation of gender roles, Indian agents made clear that they hoped to terminate the multiethnic, "Ohio Indian" identities of the eighteenth century. Johnston and the Fort Wayne Indian agent, Benjamin Stickney, dedicated themselves to the establishment of separate tribal governments in the Old Northwest. Both men used treaties to consolidate authority around leaders who had remained loyal to the United States. According to Stickney, tribes allied with the British in the late war "should not hereafter be permitted to exercise any separate government . . . to kindle a council fire" within the boundaries of the United States. Government officials found willing partners in Black Hoof and his Wyandot, Delaware, Ottawa, and Seneca allies, who hoped to increase the power of their villages. These village chiefs competed with rivals scattered across what is now Arkansas, Missouri, Indiana, and Ohio for control of American treaty annuities and acknowledgment as the national leaders of their respective tribes. Ohio Indian leaders used their rapport with the Americans as leverage against village chiefs with whom they competed. In exchange for their support, Black Hoof expected nothing less than acceptance in Ohio as a separate, though economically and politically supportive, minority of the population. While many whites at the time believed that removal was inevitable, the Ohio Shawnees worked toward a future in Ohio.[13]

Outward signs of affection between Kentuckians and Shawnees in 1816 belied the economic and physical hardships triggered by ongoing warfare. Neighboring whites destroyed their property and sometimes killed the livestock of the 840 Shawnees at Wapakoneta, significantly weakening economic reforms initiated by the Shawnees. Black Hoof frankly admitted that "the war took everything from us." Government annuity payments arrived sporadically, if at all, during the war. At the same time, farming became unreliable as Shawnee women no longer felt safe working in the fields outside of their villages. Denied the fruits of the American victory, the Wapakoneta Shawnees again bartered with their recent enemies, the British, and went on long winter hunts, far beyond their recognized lands, to feed and clothe their children.[14]

Refugees from other tribes suffered even more as the war stagnated agricultural production and made hunting more difficult. Family bands from the Southeast and New England strained the resources of the Ohio tribes. Indian agents in the postwar Old Northwest determined access to government annuity payments by the tribes' geographic location and their loyalty to the United States. Nanticoke, Conoy, and Creek Indians in Ohio did not receive treaty money and, deprived of their own land, were no longer able to support themselves through farming and hunting. In a letter to the secretary of war, Black Hoof complained that "many other Indians . . . come here . . . they are poor and we have to divide with all." Recognized tribes, including the Shawnees, Wyandots, Delawares, Ottawas, and Senecas, had to share precious resources with members of unrecognized tribes. A coalition of leaders, including Walker of the Wyandots on the Sandusky River, Black Hoof, and Civil John of Lewistown, reminded the secretary of war that he had promised to "do every things that would be of assistance to us," including "having our land divided from the other tribes." American policy-makers used tribally controlled annuity payments and the harsh reality of postwar poverty to isolate Indians into tribal categories. Under the American regime, recognized tribes were compelled to exclude refugees from village membership and to establish specific boundaries over village-owned lands.[15]

The American government's main liaison to the Shawnees in Ohio, John Johnston, looked in vain for a solution as refugees drifted further into poverty. Native people disassociated from their original tribes and excluded from white society suffered terribly, underscoring the importance of federal recognition for a tribe's survival as dependency on the United States deepened. Johnston recognized his own impotence, believing that "little can be done with naked hungry and expectant savages."[16]

The Shawnees, Wyandots, Delawares, and other pro-American tribes in the region pressed on in spite of these setbacks. They adopted a strategy for retaining their homelands premised on the transformation of their economies and renewed support for hereditary leaders whose diplomatic skills confirmed their prominence among both their American and Indian neighbors. Shawnee men took advantage of new opportunities created by American schools, stock raising, and employment as interpreters, hunters, and diplomats. They used these new avenues for advancement to answer their American critics and consolidate the power of the Maykujay division as leaders of the emerging Shawnee nation.

By 1814, there was a remarkable degree of consensus among the Ohio Shawnees. With Tecumseh dead and his brother Tenskwatawa exiled in Canada, Black Hoof had few serious rivals and enjoyed the widespread support of his people. Weeks before Black Hoof's tour of Kentucky, the Ohio Shawnees united to bring about a successful harvest that both pleased and surprised visiting Quakers. In August 1816, the Quakers marveled at the Shawnees' ability to raise a crop without horse-drawn plows. Two years after Schillinger's visit, the Shawnees harvested 250 acres of corn and other vegetables. Shawnee women worked the village-owned fields, using hoes to clear irrigation canals and free the corn rows of weeds.[17]

Black Hoof also embraced neighboring whites willing to assist the Shawnees in bringing crops to harvest. Quakers from the village of Mount Pleasant, Ohio, took the lead, constructing a mill at Wapakoneta worth $1,600. On the Ohio frontier mills were used to grind grain into meal or flour, to cut timber, and to process wool and flax. At Wapakoneta, the Quakers constructed the mill to involve Shawnee men in agricultural labor. In a complimentary letter to the secretary of war, James Ellicott and Philip Thomas, Quaker representatives from the Baltimore Yearly Meeting of Friends, reported that "the chiefs furnish promptly from day to day, any number of young men that may be wanted to aid in such work . . . about the Mill." Traditionally, Shawnee women converted corn into bread or hominy by grinding it with a pestle in a wooden mortar called a *botaga*. With the completion of the mill in 1816, Shawnee men became involved in the production and sale of cornmeal and flour to newly arriving settlers in need of provisions.[18]

The Quakers appealed to the Shawnees because they concentrated on the tribe's material needs, unlike other denominations primarily interested in conversion and the afterlife. The Great Lakes tribes understood that the presence of missionaries was a powerful symbol of their desire to remain at peace with their American neighbors—a shared endeavor that both the Shawnees and Americans referred to as "The Gold Chain that ties our hands." The Shawnees tried to keep the chain alive, but the original meaning of the metaphor had changed. Ohio's Indians no longer helped to define the rules for interaction as Americans arrived and dictated the terms of survival. They understood that cooperation with missionaries signaled their commitment to the new American era. In 1816, Quaker James Ellicott happily reported that "the Indians have been at all times disposed to furnish every assistance in their power" to the missionaries.[19]

But Quaker missionaries, like their Methodist and Baptist competitors, used gendered understandings of work on the midwestern frontier as their template for the cultural transformation of Indian societies. Under the missionary Joseph Rhodes, who arrived during the summer of 1817, the Quakers implored the Shawnees to break their communal fields into family-run plots worked primarily by men rather than their women and children. Thus, the Quakers' emphasis on male labor and the nuclear family posed a direct challenge to the unity of Shawnee families and villages. The Shawnees had traditionally lived in communal villages and their fields had been tended by women. If they embraced the Quakers' plans, Shawnee men would be forced to shift from their time-honored role as "life-sustaining killers" to the female world of food production associated with the vagaries of the plant world.[20]

Symbolically, this transition threatened to emasculate Shawnee men, yet the white settlers surrounding them would continue to mock them if they refused to go along. But Shawnee men were worried about far more than being made fun of by their American neighbors. In 1824, as Quakers became more aggressive in implementing these changes, Black Hoof told C. C. Trowbridge that "Shawnee men have never been in the habit of assuming the dress and performing the duties of women." To do so might violate the interdependent but separate roles assigned to women and men when the world began. Black Hoof went on to explain that the "Great Spirit had already furnished them with a religion suited to their nature and capacity" and that "they thought it best for each [Shawnees and Americans] to keep the ways which the Great Spirit had given them."[21]

The Shawnees expressed their beliefs through a number of important rituals, but the spring and fall Bread Dances continued to be the most important of them all. The Bread Dances marked the transition between the seasons and provided religious sanction for interdependence between the sexes. According to Thomas Wildcat Alford, the first Shawnee to record a tribal history in 1936, the fall Bread Dance was a "prayer of gratitude . . . to the Great Spirit

. . . and a petition for an abundant game season." In both the spring and fall Bread Dances, men were chosen to hunt game animals ranging from deer to squirrels. Women were also chosen to provide corn bread and to process the wild game killed by the men for the ritual. In the past, patrilineally related family bands left their large summer villages to hunt after the fall Bread Dance. Only the very old and young were left behind at the summer villages. Women and children assisted the men by establishing austere camps along creek and river bottoms. The wigwams they constructed were large enough to house the entire family throughout the long winter months. Women and children admonished the men to leave the camp for extended periods of time in search of deer, buffalo, bear, turkey, and panthers. To do otherwise would bring shame upon Shawnee men. According to a Shawnee woman interviewed during the summer of 1935, "good hunters were always away, so their women raised the corn by themselves."[22]

The productive capacity of Shawnee men was vital to survival from the fall to the spring. By late December, as the men's attention shifted from big game to smaller fur-bearing animals, women played a vital, though secondary role: processing the skins, gathering firewood, and cooking the meals for their families. From February to March, women and men worked more closely together making sugar from the sap of maple trees.

Most Shawnees returned to larger villages such as Wapakoneta and Hog Creek by late March. Reunited as a community of interrelated kin, leading Shawnee women then called a meeting and organized a Bread Dance by mid-April. The spring Bread Dance celebrated the reproductive powers of women and marked the beginning of the agricultural season. Shawnee women carefully selected leading men to kill game for the ritual in order to sanctify the reunification of the Shawnee people and to bless the upcoming agricultural season. The Bread Dance was a prayer of thanksgiving and renewal that reaffirmed the distinctive, communal values of the Shawnee people.[23]

Following the spring Bread Dance, a leading woman from each village began the agricultural season by planting the first kernels of corn in her garden. Important rituals could not take place without corn. And the Shawnees attributed feminine qualities to the crop. One Shawnee woman frankly stated that corn was "just like a woman; if she doesn't oil her hair it sticks out; if the kernels aren't greased, the corn will have short pointed leaves and be curled up and burned."[24] The continuing importance of these beliefs in the twenty-first century punctuates the difficulties men faced in the early nineteenth, as Quaker missionaries and government agents asked them to abandon religiously sanctioned gender roles as a demonstration of their commitment to the American civilization program.

Names given to Shawnee children shortly after birth also reflected traditional gender roles and deeply ingrained male and female identities in traditional Shawnee society. Anthropologists have found that Shawnee names reflect the separate, but interdependent roles of women and men. Women's names usually end with "*hši* (to recline or to be in a situation of action) and *pama* (to look at something animate)." In contrast, "common masculine endings include *škaka* or *okaka* (one who is in action or situation through his feet), *pawi* (to stand), *he* (to walk, to move by means of feet or wings), *hšimo* (to voice, having voice) *pto* (to run)." The feminine endings imply sedentary observation, the masculine endings movement and action.[25] Despite the cultural reshuffling under way in the early republic, men continued to occupy a symbolic position in the tribe outside of the camp circle as hunters and warriors beyond the agricultural sphere occupied by women. Changes demanded by Americans thus threatened to transform Shawnee identity. Missionaries and Indian agents wanted to turn male and female tasks upside down, contradicting the dominant status enjoyed by Shawnee hunters since the fur trade had increased the importance of hunting three centuries earlier.

The Shawnees and their neighbors were now being asked to change course once again, only now the proposed changes no longer complemented traditional tasks. The American civilization program particularly threatened Shawnee women, who were asked to adopt what they viewed as alien and demeaning tasks. Quaker missionaries attempted to move Shawnee women out of the fields and into the home, where they would learn "domestic arts," common among many white women in the nineteenth century. The Quakers intended to restrict and redefine the cultural geography of the Shawnee people. According to the Quaker plan, men would be brought in from the forests to the fields, while women would be moved from the fields to the home. There they would milk the cattle, spin and weave cloth, repair and clean clothing, make soap, and cook and preserve food. The newly established reservations of northwestern Ohio confined Ohio's Indians to their summer villages and gave Quaker missionaries leverage within their communities.[26]

The Ohio Shawnees' commitment to the Quakers and their subagent, John Johnston, remained strong in spite of the dramatic changes they proposed. Quaker missionaries focused on changing Indian villages rather than individuals, and as a result, they did not threaten kinship ties by creating a rigid divide between believers and nonbelievers. Members of the Society of Friends believed that conversion to Christianity involved "a gradual, protracted process" rather than an "instantaneous act." In this way, Quaker missionaries touched the lives of most Shawnee families rather than a select group of believers. The Friends interpreted "the inestimable blessing of civilization" to mean the acquisition of practical skills, including "agricultural pursuits, the mechanical arts, and household economy"—all skills necessary for survival while coexisting with frontier whites. The Quaker program best resembled the goals articulated by Black Beard more than fifteen years earlier. Ranching and education, he believed, might resurrect the Shawnee economy and improve their chances of remaining in the Old Northwest.[27]

The Quaker missionary Joseph Rhodes involved the Shawnees in the American brand of agriculture by recruiting Shawnee laborers to work on his model farm. Chiefs and missionaries alike understood that providing laborers for missionary farms demonstrated the tribe's commitment to the success of a mission. And missionaries designed their model farms as educational laboratories where American Indians could see an American-style farm in operation and work with the agricultural equipment common among settlers in the area. The resulting traffic of Shawnee laborers nearly overwhelmed Rhodes's wife Martha, who had to feed thirty-six Shawnees after her husband requested some help with the headgates of his farm. Joseph Rhodes reported that he had "never had so large a company" over for dinner. Shawnee laborers helped Rhodes with everything from clearing land to running the mill.

A deeper investigation of Rhodes's diary reveals a great deal of reciprocity between the Shawnees and their would-be civilizers. In July, Rhodes received news that Black Hoof intended to slaughter a cow and harvest the wheat crop the Shawnees had planted. The Quaker missionary rushed off to the chief's residence and witnessed more than twenty Shawnees harvesting a half-acre of wheat on the chief's lands. Always eager to please, Rhodes "showed them how to reap which they were anxious to know . . . likewise how to put up a shock, which there was great room for amendment." Black Hoof's men appreciated the Quaker's advice on harvesting wheat and shocking it into organized rows for gathering. Rhodes seemed pleased as well, for he remembered that "the good old Chief gave me a good piece of meat [and] I returned to my cabbin [*sic*] well satisfied." In his time at Wapakoneta, Rhodes exchanged information, material goods, and labor with the Shawnees.[28]

The Wapakoneta Shawnees helped Rhodes in myriad ways, but they were less willing to accept his advice on new crops intended to replace the corn, beans, and squash that had sustained them for centuries. By 1817, the Shawnees had planted some wheat, but Rhodes recorded little success with other crops. According to Rhodes, one of his closest Shawnee neighbors offered "a great many excuses" for his failure "to clear a turnip patch." On a more intimate level, the Shawnees supported Rhodes when his wife became ill later that August. Rhodes reported that throughout her sickness, he and his wife had received "not so much as the scratch of a pen" from members of the Ohio Yearly Meeting of Friends. Thirty miles from the nearest settlement, he acquired medicine from a Native healer at Wapakoneta and employed Shawnee runners in notifying family members of his wife's illness. Rhodes recorded that "all the chiefs of that nation" visited him the day after Martha Rhodes died. Clearly grateful for their support, Rhodes acknowledged that "we are wonderfully supported in our lonesome abode."[29]

Shawnee leaders and their children benefited the most from Quaker missionaries and government agents such as John Johnston. In fact, missionaries and agents created jobs for well-connected Shawnees and allowed some to avoid the more wrenching changes taking place among their people. John Wolf, a subchief at Wapakoneta and a scout for the Americans in the War of 1812, accompanied Johnston on his seasonal visits to the Indian villages of northwestern Ohio for more than twenty years; he set up camps between August and September and cooked as Johnston met with the various tribes in his subagency. Wolf's support for Johnston secured his own status as an important leader at Wapakoneta and provided food and clothing for his family while many of his kinsmen went hungry. Yet some of his Indian neighbors ridiculed Wolf and referred to him as "Johnston's negro" during their travels together. Wolf was clearly bothered by the name-calling. Johnston recalled that on some occasions Wolf became belligerent toward him while drinking, telling Johnston that he "must get another negro for he would be my negro no longer." Johnston dismissed his complaints, preferring to believe that hard drinking had caused them. Johnston did not question the strangeness of hiring a Shawnee chief as his servant as he traveled across the Shawnees' former homelands. Wolf continued working for Johnston despite these protests and even named his son after the Indian agent. The friendship between the two remained strong well after removal. Years later, in 1846, Wolf wrote to Johnston from Kansas pleading with his old friend from Ohio to write a letter to his son, then fighting his own battle with alcoholism. Wolf hoped that his son would "hearken to you and leave off whiskey."[30]

However demeaning the jobs were, Johnston was almost exclusively interested in the reformation of Shawnee men. Since 1810, the War Department had provided money for the employment of American laborers on village grounds. Johnston had high hopes for these male laborers because he mistakenly believed that the Shawnees had formerly relied almost exclusively on hunting. He was convinced that "labouring men is much wanted to instruct them in farming" now that "the wild game is gone."[31] Both the Quakers and Johnston used model farms and model laborers to convey American values. Close cooperation between missionaries and agents was not uncommon in the early nineteenth century. In fact, Johnston and his superiors, such as Lewis Cass, "considered missionaries to be the paid agents of the government."[32]

Shawnee advocates of American reforms had long recognized useful ways of participating in the new agricultural economy developing in the Old Northwest. Younger Shawnee men, 147 individuals at Wapakoneta and Hog Creek alone, needed both a way out of poverty and avenues toward prestige in their communities. In this way, Shawnee leaders and the missionaries who supported them hoped to turn their attention inward, toward the village. Some Shawnees believed "that they have no alternative, but [to] abandon their habits, and apply themselves to agriculture."[33] American officials stood behind this clique within the tribe and tied government assistance to the establishment of individual homesteads. In a letter to George Crohan of the War Department, Johnston reported that "many families are moving out from the towns and settling on their lands; to such I hold out inducements of ploughs, hoes, etc."[34]

Cash-poor and with few alternatives, some Wapakoneta Shawnees accepted this kind of material assistance and were pulled from the villages that were the foundation of Shawnee culture. Unlike the Quakers, Johnston promoted individualism and private property among the Shawnees. He feared the continued existence of a cohesive Shawnee community because he anticipated a backlash from land-hungry Ohioans who wanted access to Indian lands and improvements. Consequently, Johnston worked toward the devolution of Shawnee kin ties and their gradual acceptance as individual yeoman farmers in rural Ohio.[35]

Black Hoof soon faced Indian challengers as well. Rumors of the Prophet's return to the Wabash began circulating as early as November 1815. In reality, ever-increasing numbers of Tenskwatawa's former Kickapoo, Potawatomi, and Winnebago allies rejected the Prophet and had abandoned their refugee camps in Canada by the summer of 1817. They preferred rehabilitating their old villages along the Tippecanoe River on their own terms. But their arrival in Indiana spread alarm throughout the remaining villages of the Old Northwest. American officials strengthened Black Hoof's hand by insisting that Tenskwatawa must submit to Black Hoof's authority and reside at Wapakoneta if he chose repatriation. Not surprisingly, the Prophet refused and remained in Canada. Nevertheless, American allies feared being confused with returning militants in the event of violence with settlers. They expected calls for their removal to resurface.[36]

Joseph Rhodes soon reported that a group of Potawatomis had harassed Shawnee women at work in their fields and had threatened to "surround their town and kill all their men." Similar threats continued in the months before a new round of treaty negotiations scheduled that fall. Throughout July and August, Rhodes worried about being caught in the middle. He believed that "there is 5 or 6 nations that are combined together to distress the Shawnees, as they are counted rich" because of their cattle, horses, and healthy fields of corn. Economics does not fully explain the possibility of violence. Rather, word had spread across Indian country about the Americans' desire for another treaty regarding what remained of Indian land in northwestern Ohio. Not surprisingly, defeated warriors who had fought alongside the British in the War of 1812 blamed pro-American chiefs and their newfound authority for the anticipated land cession.[37]

To be sure, decades of collaboration with representatives of the United States allowed the Wapakoneta Shawnees to become important power brokers among the enduring Ohio tribes. Since 1795, Black Hoof had been an important intermediary between the government and the Wyandots, Ottawas, Delawares, and Miamis of Ohio and Indiana. The Wapakoneta chief conducted a tour of these neighboring tribes in the summer of 1817 to lay the groundwork for the Treaty of Fort Meigs. Armed with "proper instructions," Johnston granted Black Hoof the power to establish the terms of the formal treaty negotiations to be held later that fall. Johnston's superiors, including Lewis Cass, were determined to negotiate with individual tribes rather than multitribal conglomerates. Nevertheless, Black Hoof persuaded Johnston to invite the leading members of all of the affected tribes to the treaty negotiations. Black Hoof warned Johnston that "the Wyandots will feel reluctant without their presence."[38]

Concluded in September 1817, the Treaty of Fort Meigs ceded northwestern Ohio to the United States and established reservations for the remaining Wyandot, Seneca, Shawnee, and Ottawa tribes. More important, the treaty made explicit the American strategy of using treaty annuities to reinforce the power of pro-American chiefs and the villagers they represented. "The chiefs and their successors" in each of the remaining tribes now had the legal right to distribute reservation lands to tribal members listed on the treaty schedule. Treaty stipulations granted fee-simple land patents to chiefs. Black Hoof, Wolf, John Perry, and other subchiefs gained a tract of ten square miles surrounding Wapakoneta, while Captain Lewis, Civil John, the Turtle, and other Shawnee and Seneca chiefs gained a tract of forty-eight-square miles at Lewistown. Piachtha, Onowaskemo, and other subchiefs of the Hog Creek Shawnees received a twenty-five-square-mile tract adjoining the Wapakoneta reservation. Chiefs now controlled tribal resources and distributed them to their supporters. This change provided coercive power to chiefs and improved their ability to speak on their peoples' behalf. The Treaty of Fort Meigs allowed American Indian leaders to become mediators between American officials and rank-and-file members of their tribes.[39]

Lewis Cass, more than any other government official in the Old Northwest, executed the government policy of creating so-called paper chiefs throughout the Great Lakes region. As governor of Michigan Territory from 1813 to 1831, he negotiated sixteen treaties with Great Lakes tribes. Both Cass and his lieutenants—Indian agents—became directly involved in tribal politics and handpicked leaders with whom they could deal. In just one example of the process, Cass chided Menominee leaders at the 1827 Treaty of Butte des Morts (Hill of the Dead) for their failure to appoint a chief who could negotiate for the entire tribe. According to Cass, the Menominees were "like a flock of geese without a leader. Some fly one way & some another." On the day following his speech, he chose one of several village leaders, Oshkosh, as the "Grand Chief" of the Menominee Nation.[40]

Similarly, the Shawnees' long history of decentralized authority and the incessant movement of tribal members between villages frustrated Cass. The tribe's peripatetic and egalitarian political structure contributed to competition between prominent individuals. Serious rivalries for power occasionally emerged that developed into larger, pan-Indian resistance movements that threatened village chiefs and antagonized colonizers. Referring to Tecumseh's vision of pan-Indian resistance to American expansion, Cass argued that "once admit an Indian confederacy founded on an acknowledged community of interest, and we need be troubled with no more Indian negotiations. We should never procure another acre of land." Concentrating power in the hands of a limited number of tribal chiefs thus facilitated American efforts to relocate Great Lakes tribes beyond the boundaries of the United States.[41]

Treaty-makers also granted chiefs control over yearly annuity payments. For the Shawnees this meant that Black Hoof now received the $2,000 (later $3,000) annually provided to the tribe at Wapakoneta. This last element of the postwar treaties angered Shawnees west of the Mississippi who were then a majority of the tribe, as well as those Shawnees who had supported Tecumseh and Tenskwatawa in the War of 1812. Black Hoof and the Maykujay division now controlled the tribe's purse strings as dependency on the United States deepened. The Wapakoneta Shawnees' long-standing commitment to a new American order in the Old Northwest began to have serious consequences for those Shawnees who wished to remain free from their authority.[42]

Black Hoof had reached the summit of his power as the "Grand Chief" of the Shawnee people by 1817. Yet he had arrived at this dominant position by eschewing his role as a village chief and accepting an imposed fiction as the "Grand Chief" of an emerging Shawnee nation. Other Shawnee villagers beyond the Mississippi were far removed from the lands dominated by the United States and thus did not participate in this increasingly lopsided conversation about leadership and power. In fact, the first federal treaty between the United States and the Western Shawnees took place in 1825. Algonquian leaders long accustomed to working with diverse villagers now had to reconcile Ohio's multiethnic political culture with the new, tribally focused sentiments of American officials and a select group of paper chiefs. But even as the Wapakoneta Shawnees responded to American pressure and cut ties with neighboring villages, their ability to coordinate actions with other Great Lakes tribes remained invaluable to the United States.

Hereditary leaders such as Black Hoof recognized that American policies were intended to erode the influence of descent-based leaders who challenged American plans for them. He and his contemporaries reinforced their hereditary claims to power by educating their children in American schools, securing property for their families, and conducting activities designed to perpetuate the esteemed position of their families. Black Hoof sent his son along with two other children from prominent families to an American school despite the fact that it was nearly thirty miles from Wapakoneta. These children later became influential leaders after the Shawnees were removed to Indian Territory. Land grants to the children of prominent Shawnee leaders, including 640 acres to Nancy Stewart, daughter of the late Shawnee chief Blue Jacket, also reinforced their power. American policy-makers used this combination of land grants, education, employment, and diplomacy to establish a small number of leading families in each of the remaining Great Lakes tribes. By 1830, the United States funded fifty-two schools and served more than 1,500 Indian students. The overwhelming majority of these schools and students were located east of the Mississippi River.[43]

Those with access to the resident missionaries and agents enjoyed better conditions, while the less fortunate had to rely on the patronage of their kinsmen. Quaker missionary Henry Harvey noted that 40 percent of the money earmarked for improvements to reservation lands went to a handful of Shawnee chiefs. Less than five Shawnee leaders at Wapakoneta and Hog Creek controlled nearly half of all Shawnee assets between 1815 and 1832.[44] Treaty commissioners furthered their influence by paying chiefs who attended treaty negotiations. These tactics contributed to the increasing dissonance between tribal chiefs and the rank-and-file members of the tribe they claimed to represent.

Wapakoneta continued to be the dominant village of the Shawnee tribe between the War of 1812 and the Indian Removal Act. However, the Treaty of Fort Meigs organized the Ohio Shawnees into three separate political units located at Hog Creek, Wapakoneta, and Lewistown. While village leaders at each locale controlled their own village's resources, American policy-makers increasingly pitted village chiefs against each other in a contest for control of the tribe as a whole. In the 1818 Treaty of St. Mary's, negotiators demonstrated their commitment to the creation of tribal governments when they divided the Seneca/Shawnee village of Lewistown into separate communities organized along tribal lines. The treaty states that "the north half of the said tract shall be reserved for the use of the Senecas who reside there and the south half for the use of the Shawnese who reside there."[45] American officials used treaties to step up their campaign to homogenize Indian villages along tribal lines.

As this map indicates, Lewis Cass and John Johnston partially succeeded in dividing the Native American population of northwestern Ohio into distinct tribal categories. Drawn by Rachel Easley and Eric Anderson.

Postwar treaties entitled Indians to the use of ceded lands until American settlers bought it from government-run land offices. American officials thus waited to let ever-increasing numbers of settlers diminish the Shawnees', Wyandots', and Delawares' willingness to remain in Ohio. Cass confidently asserted that "as our settlements gradually surround them, their minds will be better prepared" for removal. The Shawnees and their neighbors regularly hunted and trapped on the ceded lands following the treaties of 1817 and 1818. Trading centers such as Vincennes, Indiana, catered to Shawnee, Delaware, and Miami hunters from the northern border of Ohio and Indiana well after the war. Morris Birkbeck, an English Quaker who later published a diary of his travels in the Old Northwest, reported that "considerable numbers" of Indians traveled to Vincennes "to trade fur for skins." Birkbeck was clearly surprised by the "motley assemblage of inhabitants and visitors" there, including a Shawnee hunter who was "well remembered . . . for the trouble he gave during the late war."[46]

The Great Lakes tribes resisted government efforts to confine them to their reservations, what one scholar describes as "slums in the wilderness." The Shawnees and Senecas were particularly notorious for leaving their summer villages at Wapakoneta, Hog Creek, and Lewistown during the winter months. Promising hunting grounds and maple groves remained northwest of their towns, along the rivers and streams of Hamilton and Madison Counties in Indiana. Indian agents acknowledged the ongoing viability of hunting and struggled to separate Indian hunters from angry settlers who failed to distinguish between Indian allies and enemies in the late war. Increasingly monochromatic views of Indians resulted in part from the simple reality that most Americans in the region were not born in either Ohio or Indiana. They knew little about their Indian neighbors.[47]

This mixture of ignorance and contempt sometimes led to violence. In May 1824, American settlers perpetrated one of the worst incidents of frontier violence when they massacred nine Seneca and Shawnee Indians in Indiana as they rested in their winter hunting camp. Surprisingly, three of the murderers were hanged for their crimes. The convictions marked the first time that Americans were found guilty of murdering Indians in Indiana. But the Indians' victory in court was fleeting because American settlers impatient for Indian removal staunchly supported Andrew Jackson in the elections of 1824 and 1828. He articulated the dominant perspective on the remaining Great Lakes tribes. Jackson insisted on a racial quarantine between Indians and Americans because he preferred an "extensive Republic, studded with cities, towns, and prosperous farms, embellished with all the improvements which art can devise" to a "country covered with forests and ranged by a few thousand savages."[48]

Indian agents struggled to meet the demands of well-placed public officials who called for an end to hunting and a stricter adherence to the American civilization program. Johnston, for one, pleaded for time, and assured Lewis Cass that he was "using every ascertion [*sic*] to induce them to break up their villages and scatter over their Reserves on detached farms after the same manner of the whites."[49] While the Ohio tribes remained committed to the American alliance, they rejected the abandonment of long-held cultural and economic practices.

The Wapakoneta Shawnees tried to reach a compromise between cultures by incorporating stock raising into the tribal economy. Raising cattle and hogs became a substitute for Shawnee hunters disheartened by the very real possibility of violence if they left their reservations. Moreover, the tribe's proximity to Cincinnati, then one of the country's largest cattle and hog markets, gave the Shawnees confidence that their investments were well suited for the changing Ohio frontier. Between 1818 and the late 1820s, the Wapakoneta chiefs spent more than a third of their annuity on cattle. Neighboring whites closely monitored these purchases. Most applauded the investments, believing that the livestock would "contribute to the comforts of these children of the forest." Indeed, Shawnee farms differed little from the homesteads surrounding them. If anything, their farms were larger and more prosperous than their non-Indian neighbors'. Most recent migrants to Ohio owned farms averaging less than 150 acres. The typical midwestern farmer owned between five to fifteen head of cattle and cultivated an average of sixty acres.[50]

American Indians remained the largest per capita landholders in Ohio despite losing approximately 4.2 million acres in the Treaty of Fort Meigs and a considerable amount of their autonomy during the early nineteenth century. The Wapakoneta Shawnees controlled 19,200 acres of land in 1818, while neighboring Wyandots, who had the largest reservation in Ohio, controlled 85,680 acres of land. Wise investments by tribal leaders created prosperous reservation farms. Jealous American settlers then turned to the destruction of Indian property. Sandusky River Wyandots repeatedly complained about illegal hunters and stolen honey. It was not uncommon for the Ohio tribes to discover "hogs shot down . . . and in other cases a half, or quarter of the animal taken off and the rest left to the great loss and vexation of the Indians." Settlers regularly wreaked havoc on Indian homes and property while they were away on their winter hunts. Some settlers destroyed Indian improvements to break their morale and intimidate them into leaving the state. Yet the terror and intimidation failed to break their attachment to their lands.[51]

Isaac Harvey and William Hadley, two Quaker missionaries working among the Shawnees at Wapakoneta, defended the Shawnees' reserves by purchasing some of the land surrounding their reservation. The Baltimore, Ohio, and Indiana Yearly Meeting of Friends set aside money for the purpose so that Shawnee farms vulnerable to attack might be protected. Unlike contemporaries such as the Baptist missionary Isaac McCoy, who joined Jackson and called for an "Indian Canaan" in the West, the Quakers defended the Shawnees' right to remain in Ohio.[52] Yet Quaker beliefs regarding Indian removal and slavery became even more unpopular among neighboring settlers, many of whom hailed from Virginia and Kentucky and reviled abolitionists.[53]

John Johnston also came under attack for his sympathetic attitude toward the Ohio tribes. Members of the Monroe administration, particularly Secretary of War John C. Calhoun, placed Johnston under increased scrutiny. Johnston pleaded with Calhoun for "the privilege of dealing with the Indians in my own way." Between 1820 and 1832, Calhoun and others chose instead to force Johnston to spend most of his time responding to myriad accusations, ranging from nepotism and fraud to simply being "unfriendly to the removal of the Indians."[54]

In spring 1820, Black Hoof and Captain Lewis asked to meet with President James Monroe in Washington, D.C., when they became aware of Johnston's diminishing prestige. The Shawnees also wanted to challenge several provisions of the Treaty of St. Mary's. In the 1818 treaty, the Shawnees had relinquished their land patents for the three reservations centered around Wapakoneta in exchange for a far less legally binding arrangement in which the government "reserved [the reservation] for the use of the Indians . . . unless ceded to the United States." Treaty negotiators persuaded the Shawnees to sign the treaty after substantially increasing the size of their reservations. However, the treaty limited the tribe's legal rights to the land by removing their land patents. From Black Hoof's perspective, the Shawnees' tenuous grip on their reservation required President Monroe's intervention. Johnston believed that most of their complaints could be adjusted from Ohio, but he conceded that "I will have no peace until a deputation from my Indians is permitted to go to Washington."[55]

Shawnee leaders recognized the Quakers' vital role as mediators between important American institutions and their own people at a time when the Ohio Indians' access to Washington's power brokers had decreased markedly. Black Hoof had corresponded with Thomas Jefferson during his presidency, and had worked closely with William Henry Harrison in the War of 1812. But the era of the "Great Father" passed from existence for Black Hoof and his contemporaries in postwar Ohio. Accordingly, representatives from the Wapakoneta, Hog Creek, and Seneca/Shawnee reserves first stopped in Baltimore on April 11, 1821. The Shawnee chiefs asked P. E. Thomas, an important member of the Baltimore Yearly Meeting of Friends, to set up a meeting with Calhoun. Thomas agreed and, along with two other Friends, accompanied the Shawnees to Washington. During their stay in the nation's capital, Black Hoof, Wolf, John Perry, Colonel Lewis, and an unidentified Hog Creek chief negotiated several land claims and made plans for spending the Shawnee annuity that year. In addition, the Shawnee chiefs attempted to win land patents for the heirs of Shawnee warriors killed in the War of 1812. Individual land patents became a successful strategy for neighboring Miami and Potawatomi Indians, who used land set aside for individuals as de facto reservations after their reservation lands were sold. Calhoun refused most of what they requested. Nevertheless, Quaker assistance allowed them to gain access to the secretary of war. The Shawnees also gave Thomas most of their 1821 annuity and asked him to purchase livestock and other goods for the tribe in Cincinnati.[56]

Neither Johnston's pleas to the secretary of war nor Black Hoof's visit to Washington prevented Ohio governor Ethan Allen Brown from continuing to press for Indian removal. Removal advocates described the Ohio Indians as morally depraved and blamed them for the slow economic development of the state. Johnston conceded as much to his opponents, acknowledging that "the cases are not rare where I have to give them money to pay their Tavern bills." Complaints of drunken Indians committing crimes against white homesteaders near their reservations became pervasive and encouraged Brown and other partisans of forced migration. Some corresponded with Johnston and called upon the agent and his wife at their home in Piqua, Ohio. In February 1824, Will Oliver, a removal advocate and ally of the governor, spoke directly with Johnston and protested that the Wapakoneta Shawnees "have received the most prominent situations in the country" and that their use of prime real estate "operate[s] to retard the improvements of the country." According to Oliver, Johnston assured him that the Shawnees were "prepared to sell."[57]

Most Americans failed to blame the tavern-keepers whose grog shops bordered reservation lands for the real and imagined social malaise of reservation life. And unfortunately, Capt. John Perry, one of Black Hoof's secondary chiefs, contributed to off-reservation violence. In July 1827, while drinking at a tavern in Piqua, Ohio, Perry stabbed several customers, including the editor of the local newspaper. The day after the incident, a delegation of Shawnee chiefs requested a public meeting with the people of Piqua. Wewellipu, the speaker for the tribe, placated the townspeople with a vivid description of Perry's remorse concerning the incident. He also stated that the Shawnees had "held an assembly of all our people" to suppress whiskey drinking among their people. Finally, he continued, "we have so much communication and trade" with the people of Piqua that the Shawnees "wish to live in friendship with our white brethren." Piqua's residents agreed to dismiss charges against Perry in exchange for Shawnee promises to pay the expenses of the men wounded in the attack.[58]

Random violence between Indians and whites throughout the 1820s diminished Shawnee dreams of remaining separate from, but affiliated with, their American neighbors in Ohio. Many believed that both Indians and whites would be better off living in separate worlds. Even Johnston, who once imagined integrated settlements of Indian and white yeoman farmers, now called for the removal of the Ohio tribes. Citing the poor condition of the Delawares remaining in Ohio, Johnston conceded the "dreadful effects on the Indians of the increase of the whites on the continent from the contaminating influences of the white man." His critics believed that "the Indians in Ohio could never be removed out of the state" while he was agent. Yet unlike neighboring whites, Johnston claimed to have altruistic rather than economic motives for removal. In a letter to Governor Brown, Johnston explained that "I am as anxious as any man to move the Indians from a sincere regard for them."[59]

By the mid-1820s, the Quakers had become the Ohio Shawnees' last remaining allies. Quaker missionaries did their best to generate positive publicity for the tribe, reporting that attendance at the mission school doubled between 1822 and 1823. Many Shawnee boys worked on the Quakers' farm as well. Calls for their removal only redoubled Shawnee efforts to defend their reservation. By 1824 most of the Ohio Shawnees lived on individual homesteads rather than in the center of their towns.[60] In contrast, Johnston, who corresponded regularly with public officials in Washington, continued to file negative reports about the Shawnees and their commitment to the American civilization program. In a letter to Calhoun, he confirmed the secretary of war's suspicion that "the Shawanoese and Delaware are altogether unfit to be intrusted [*sic*] with the management of money."[61] Paradoxically, both Johnston and the Quakers cultivated dependency on Americans and their institutions even as they admonished the Shawnees to disavow their tribal loyalties and conform to the yeoman-farmer ideals of Jeffersonian democracy.

Lewis Cass continued to interfere with the Shawnees' internal affairs as the tribe's removal from the state became more certain. In 1824 Cass betrayed Black Hoof by allowing Tenskwatawa to return to Ohio in order to promote removal. In an ironic twist of fate, Tenskwatawa once again rose to prominence. As a de facto removal agent, his mission required diminishing Black Hoof's authority as an opponent of forced relocation. In light of recent attacks on their improvements, some Shawnees believed they had no other choice but to follow their kinsmen and voluntarily emigrate from Ohio. In September 1826, to the consternation of Black Hoof, Tenskwatawa persuaded 250 Shawnees at Wapakoneta to abandon their village and remove west of the Mississippi.[62]

Undeterred, the remaining Shawnees maintained their opposition to removal and even attempted to turn the loss of so many of their people into a political gain. In an apparent nod to the changing political climate of Ohio in the late 1820s, the Shawnees took to the presses. In July 1828, the *Piqua Gazette* published a religious debate between Wewellipu, a younger subchief and speaker for the Shawnees, and Harry Hoot, a Wyandot Indian-turned-Methodist Indian missionary. Hoot and other Wyandot evangelicals traveled to Wapakoneta to proselytize among the Shawnees. Firmly rejecting their efforts, Wewellipu countered that the Quakers "are the only real peacable people that we can find." Moreover, the Shawnee speaker argued that unlike other whites, who invariably betrayed the Shawnees' trust and turned against them, "they [the Quakers] do not change."[63]

The Shawnees maintained their independence from the Wyandot Methodists. Nearly half of the 700 Wyandots remaining in Ohio attended a school established by the Methodists where they received instruction from Wyandot class leaders. Clearly disappointed by the Shawnees' firm rejection of their preaching, the Wyandots admonished the Shawnees to "Try all you can to do better" so that "when we leave this world, we will all go to one place, however we may differ here." Wewellipu was clearly annoyed with Hoot's condescending assessment of Shawnee society. He countered that the Shawnees "know we cannot remain here without changing our habits and customs." Moreover, most Wapakoneta villagers felt optimistic about the prospects for change given the fact that their "bad people have all gone to the West and left us." Wewellipu's thoughts on the Wyandots and Methodists may have been misguided, however, for the Wyandots were the last tribe removed from Ohio in July 1843.[64]

Ohio Indians had all demonstrated a real commitment to the American civilization program by the 1820s. Their successful adjustment to Ohio's new agricultural economy, based as it was on stock raising and corn and wheat production, set off an important debate about the ramifications of Indian sovereignty—and their acceptance as distinct communities—after American dominance had been established. Many Ohioans, including residents near the Seneca/Shawnee reservation of Lewistown, became increasingly bothered about the possibility of Indians leaving their reservation communities entirely and integrating themselves into American towns. In 1829, residents of Bellafontaine composed a letter to Governor Allen Trimble, complaining that "a number of the inhabitants are but little better than the Red Brethren around us." The petitioners wanted the Ohio governor to stop fellow townspeople who have "told them that they are entitled to all the privileges of the white male inhabitants of our country . . . which is no small grievance to the honorable part of this community."[65]

As American Indians made compromises regarding cultural and economic practices, it became increasingly difficult for the "honorable" citizens of Logan County to distinguish between off-reservation Indians and non-Indian residents of the state. The citizens of Bellafontaine used fuzzy notions of perceived racial differences, ranging from dress and the kind of homestead one occupied to rumors about an individual's parents, to exclude people from elective office and other forms of participation in the state's economic and political system. Those Indians who remained on the reservations were not considered citizens of the United States and were denied the right to vote or to testify against whites in court.[66]

Some Ohioans fought against increasingly popular racial ideologies and advocated a more inclusive and pluralistic racial and political culture. A memorial from "The Ladies of Steubenville, Ohio" attempted to shame white male voters into a more charitable perspective on Ohio's Indians. The memorialists admitted that "*there are times* when duty and affection call on us to *advise* and *persuade* . . . our husbands and brothers." Determined to fight the removal of Ohio's Indians, the ladies of Steubenville argued that the Shawnees and others possessed an "*undoubted natural right*" to their lands in Ohio.[67]

Black Hoof's death ultimately accomplished what Lewis Cass, Tenskwatawa, and innumerable removal advocates could not. Quaker missionary Henry Harvey aptly memorialized Black Hoof in 1831 when he wrote that "he was always an advocate for his own nation" and that "he was of such an age that recollections carried him back" to Shawnee dealings with William Penn in eighteenth-century Pennsylvania. His funeral assumed an even greater significance than the old chief would have wanted. Covered in a blanket and wrapped in calico, belts, and ribbons, Black Hoof was buried after Shawnee hunters returned from a two-day long hunt in which they killed deer and turkeys for a large feast to be held after the funeral. John Perry, the middle-aged man who had accompanied Black Hoof on his victory tour through Kentucky in 1816, led the funeral procession. Though much younger and less experienced than Black Hoof, John Perry became the Ohio Shawnees' head chief.[68]

The transition in leadership from Black Hoof to Perry marked the beginning of a new era in Shawnee life. Regardless of their differences, Black Hoof,

Tecumseh, and Tenskwatawa had spent the majority of their lives fighting American expansion. Tecumseh was killed in the process, and while Black Hoof and Tenskwatawa eventually advocated for peace, both men had arrived at their position after enduring decades of violence and out-migration from Ohio. In contrast, John Perry and others like him learned of these struggles through stories rather than hard experience. As a young man, he had fought alongside American soldiers in the War of 1812. Perry and others like him had gained prestige through channels opened by Americans, first in war and later through churches and schools created by settlers.

American traders and speculators wasted no time in pressing Black Hoof's survivors for the dissolution of their Ohio reservations. James B. Gardiner, the government treaty negotiator, outlined the Shawnees' fate if they continued to reject removal. In addition to their having to pay taxes exclusively "for the benefit of the white people" and being required to work on public roads, the government would no longer intercede on the Shawnees' behalf in cases of violence between Indians and whites. Gardiner warned the Shawnees that "they might be beaten or killed by white men" and that "no matter how many Indians [were] present—unless they could prove it by a white man, they had, or would have, no remedy." Bereft of legal participation or protection, most Shawnees understood Gardiner's words to mean that the unceasing cycle of terror and violence they had been subjected to for so many years would continue. Gardiner then told the Shawnees that they should "always listen to the advices of white people, because they were wiser than the red people, as the red people were wiser than the blacks." In response, Wewellipu repeated Black Hoof's sentiments about the joint creation of Indians and whites in America. Wewellipu focused on the common humanity of men rather than on perceived racial differences. The Shawnee speaker countered that he believed that "all men were created alike." Bereft of Black Hoof's leadership and threatened with certain violence if they remained, the Wapakoneta Shawnees signed a removal treaty in fall 1831.[69]

Like the Shawnees, the ladies of Steubenville placed the blame for Indian removal squarely on the shoulders of the "honorable part" of Logan County and the public officials who represented them. Nevertheless, the Wyandots, Delawares, Senecas, Ottawas, and Shawnees who remained behind the frontier are consistently remembered for their failure to grow toward the American civilization program. Unlike their neighbors to the southeast—members of the Five Tribes who struggled against removal in a series of highly public court cases—the Ohio tribes campaigned quietly for a continuing place in the Old Northwest. Most of the Great Lakes tribes that were eventually forced out of the state had already made significant concessions to the white agricultural frontier surrounding them. Prophetically, they believed that there was no end to the cycle of treaties and land cessions in the face of white settlement. After the removal treaty had been signed, Wewellipu reiterated his belief that the Shawnees had been cheated by the same men who had promised the tribe a permanent place in Ohio in exchange for the adoption of a new way of life. Turning to Gardiner, Wewellipu reminded Gardiner that the Shawnees "have good homes here" and that it had taken "an abundance of labor and pains to make them." Speaking for Ohio's Indians, Wewellipu placed responsibility for removal on the American settlers surrounding them.[70]

Between 1827 and 1833, the Ohio Shawnees joined many of their kinsmen on a united tribal reservation in Indian Territory. Their departure closed a chapter in their long struggle against American expansion. The ultimate failure of their efforts led to renewed conflict among the Shawnees—a people long accustomed to village-based leadership in a multiethnic Indian and white world. But the ties forged between the Ohio Shawnees and the federal officials and missionaries who had worked among them helped them establish a dominant position in the West. By persistently defending their lands, the Ohio Shawnees experienced both crushing defeat and new opportunities for the future, including a preordained role as the leaders of the new Shawnee nation in the West.

3. A Third Way to a Separate Ground: Rethinking Indian Resistance on the Trans-Mississippi Frontier, 1780–1830

In 1934, a Shawnee named Thomas Wildcat Alford, who was then seventy-four years old, tried to explain why his tribe had split into two peoples, both geographically and ideologically, during the American Revolution. According to Alford, Algonquian-speaking peoples began immigrating beyond the Mississippi long before the Indian Removal Act of 1830 made these migrations official U.S. policy. His ancestors resisted the temptation to leave the Ohio country between the conclusion of Pontiac's War in 1763 and the Battle of Point Pleasant in 1774. After Point Pleasant, a conflict in which the British claimed victory, many Shawnees reconsidered and met in a series of "secret councils" designed to assess "the power of the English." Then a rift developed between the Thawegila and Chillicothe Shawnees; the two descent groups responsible for supplying national leaders for the tribe. They disagreed as to whether the wars against the English should continue. Both sides believed "that the future welfare of the Shawnee nation . . . in order that it might survive," hung in the balance. But the Thawegilas were convinced that continued warfare for the Ohio country was futile. They refused to continue the fight. Increasing numbers of Piqua and Kispokotha Shawnees, along with some Chillicothes, joined the Thawegilas and began abandoning their homelands. Significantly, most of the Kispokothas—the descent group responsible for warfare—turned their energies to helping the Thawegila and Piqua Shawnees carve out a space for themselves and their allies on the trans-Mississippi frontier. Only now their opponents, tribes indigenous to the region such as the Caddos, Quapaws, and Osages, stood in their way. The Kispokotha, Thawegila, and Piqua Shawnees left behind members of the Maykujay and Chillicothe divisions, Shawnees with whom they could not agree. By the early nineteenth century, Alford's people, the Western Shawnees, had reorganized the relationship between the five Shawnee descent groups, and had presided over a schism in the Shawnee nation whose legacy is palpable to this day.[1]

Alford published his views on the schism in *Old Chillicothe: Shawnee and Pioneer History: Conflicts and Romances in the Northwest Territory,* a book authored by a local historian named William Galloway. A resident of Chillicothe, Ohio, in the heart of what had been Shawnee land along the Scioto River, Galloway collected historical documents and interviewed descendants about life on the eighteenth and nineteenth century Ohio frontier. The author was obsessed with family lore. One of his ancestors, John Galloway, had made a name for himself fighting the Shawnees. And in the curious transmission of myth and history across generations, family storytellers claimed that Tecumseh had courted John Galloway's daughter, Rebecca, until their romance fell apart because of the famous Shawnee's unwillingness to give up his Indian ways. William Galloway collected and transmitted history in this context.[2]

Galloway lived in a town named after the Chillicothe Shawnees, a reflection of this descent-group's prominence in south-central Ohio. Nevertheless, he did not interview contemporary Chillicothes in writing his history. Instead, Galloway consulted Alford, who was then the most prominent Shawnee of his age. Alford was widely recognized for his achievements as a student at the school for African American freedmen that, to a far lesser extent, doubled as an Indian boarding school, Hampton Institute. His later efforts as an educator and advocate of the Dawes General Allotment Act further enhanced his reputation. He had been born in 1860 along the banks of the Canadian River in central Oklahoma, far from Galloway's hometown. The son and grandson of prominent Shawnees, Alford belonged to the Piqua division of a people who ultimately became known as the Absentee Shawnee Tribe. Between 1825 and 1863, his people had earned their name because of their absence from reservation lands set aside for the Shawnee people in modern Kansas. They had refused to join their fellow tribespeople, choosing instead to ally themselves with an agglomeration of tribes who shared their unwillingness to be confined on tribal reservations, where missionaries and government agents hoped to assimilate them into an alien American value system.[3]

Thomas Wildcat Alford was in an awkward position. He was an Absentee Shawnee whose people had supported neither Tecumseh nor Black Hoof. Now he was asked to tell their story to another person interested in Indians who had achieved mythic status in American popular culture—a man whose family was intimately connected with the most famous of all Shawnee warriors. Indian men who had fought to the bitter end such as Tecumseh fascinated Galloway. Those who abandoned Ohio, as Alford's ancestors had, were not going to be part of his story. But in yet another ironic twist to their relationship, Galloway asked Alford to help tell the story of Chillicothe, a descent-group and, later, an American town, that his people had forsaken. Like many Shawnees before him, Alford had to provide information to a man who had defined his interests and objectives far from central Oklahoma. If Alford hoped to tell the story of *his* people, he would have to be subversive about it. He partially succeeded. While most of *Old Chillicothe* covers the stock characters of frontier Ohio, there are moments where Alford manages to tell the Western Shawnees' side of the story. Frustration with Galloway may have motivated Alford to publish his own history, *Civilization and the Story of the Absentee Shawnees,* two years after the publication of *Old Chillicothe.* Alford believed that the Western Shawnees had been largely forgotten by government officials and historians alike since documentation of their history "is quite scanty . . . because they are peacable [*sic*]." Consequently, "the government always neglected or ignored their interests."[4]

Alford remembered the move from east to west as a crucial decision regarding Shawnee culture, the survival of the Shawnees' distinctive ceremonials, and the gender roles associated with them. The Western Shawnees hoped to continue a way of life that they believed was no longer possible in the East. As British and, later, American dominance became certain, the separation of the Shawnee people derived from the reality of cultural imperialism rather than the certainty of military domination. Nevertheless, American settlers caught up with these voluntary emigrants. By the second decade of the nineteenth century, Alford's people again faced the crisis that they had hoped to evade during the Revolution. Yet unlike their relatives in the East, western Algonquians lived on the uneasy fault line between Spanish, and, later, Mexican Texas and the United States. As options narrowed in Missouri and Arkansas, new opportunities in the Spanish borderlands beckoned. While western Algonquians struggled with new landscapes and new enemy tribes, they attempted to craft an ingenious response to the well-known goals of American policy-makers.

By the first decade of the nineteenth century, the Western Shawnees boasted a majority of the tribe. For rank-and-file Algonquians originally from the Great Lakes, the movement of so many people overshadowed Tecumseh's revitalization movement and undermined his rival, Black Hoof, and his quest for a lasting peace with Americans. Indeed, most of Tecumseh and Black Hoof's prospective supporters turned a deaf ear to the stark options they outlined, voted with their feet, and permanently abandoned the Ohio country. Thousands of American Indians from east of the Mississippi joined Alford's Shawnees and voluntarily migrated from the Great Lakes region.

These widespread migrations became a third reply to American expansion in the pivotal years between Tecumseh's efforts in the first decades of the nineteenth century and Andrew Jackson's Indian Removal Act in 1830. Their motives for leaving and their eventual support for a pan-Indian proto-state on the Missouri–Arkansas frontier are relatively unknown to students of American Indian history, particularly when compared with the familiar divide between militants such as Tecumseh and those who advocated peaceful resistance such as Chief John Ross and the Cherokees.[5]

The diversity and sophistication of American Indian responses to American expansion has a long and complicated history that can only be recovered by moving beyond widely recognized spokespersons for tribal and pan-Indian resistance such as Tecumseh. In short, Alford's struggle with Galloway—his effort to tell the little-known story of Algonquians in the West—is an ongoing one. Alford recognized that historical requiems for Tecumseh reveal more about Americans' fascination with "the last gasp of Indian resistance" than about the hard but no less courageous efforts of the vast majority of Indian people.[6]

The genesis of the Absentee Shawnee people is worth examining for what it reveals about the ongoing Shawnee commitment to local, multiethnic alliances west of the Mississippi River. Between 1780 and 1830, a third group of Shawnees heavily influenced the creation of a multiethnic Indian state. Their efforts further complicate any attempt at creating a fixed Shawnee political and cultural identity. Indeed, Shawnees helped craft a distinctive synthesis of tradition and innovation in the West. The Western Shawnees were one of more than a dozen Algonquian-, Iroquoian-, and Muskhogean-speaking peoples from the east who dominated large stretches of Missouri and Arkansas between the 1780s and the conclusion of the War of 1812. Lands in Arkansas and Missouri offered a popular alternative to Indians confronted with American aggression in the eastern half of the United States. Tribes such as the Shawnees, Delawares, Cherokees, and Creeks came together in this borderland. They reinvented Tecumseh's pan-Indianism by applying his vision of resistance and Indian unity to increasingly popular legal and political concepts employed by the Cherokee constitution builders to the southeast. Emigrant Indian leaders supported American policies even as they hoped to preserve their distinctive ways of life. The emigrant Indians were neither militant nor peaceful, and their efforts complicate our understanding of Indian removal and the roles played by American Indians in the process. By the mid-1820s, these western emigrants asked the United States to recognize a sovereign confederacy of Indian tribes in the West—the first, and last, multitribal, sovereign alliance of tribes originally from east of the Mississippi River.[7]

Close examination of the myriad multiethnic villages of Missouri and Arkansas offers a compelling window into the lives of ordinary Shawnees and their neighbors in this pivotal period in their history. Wide-ranging coalitions of tribes, from the Delawares and the Shawnees to the Cherokees and Kickapoos, exploited the ambiguous boundaries of the region in an effort to preserve their autonomy.[8] This wide geographic zone, stretching from the confluence of the Arkansas and Mississippi Rivers to the southeast and from the Missouri and Kansas Rivers to the northwest, offered the promise of cultural sovereignty for thousands of emigrant Indians from the eastern United States. Resident tribes, such as the Osages, Quapaws, and Caddos, fought against the emigrant tribes and the colonizers with whom they were allied. Farther south, emigrant and resident Indians along the Red River competed with one another, often cooperating with Spain, and later Mexico and Texas, for regional dominance. The emigrant tribes exploited these competing claims to their own advantage, creating an autonomous space for themselves in this contested zone.[9]

While their eastern kinsmen worked with missionaries and established tribal governments modeled after the United States, western migrants developed a kind of Indian republicanism, a loose form of political and military affiliation in which participants retained a mixed allegiance to both their tribe and the alliance. Voluntary removal to lands west of the Mississippi became the preferred alternative for many eastern tribes struggling to find ways of coping with American expansion. Between the 1780s and 1815, some tribes had clear majorities in the West, while others had significant minorities in the region. In 1825, the Indian agent, explorer, and close friend of Lewis Cass, Henry Rowe Schoolcraft, estimated that 11,579 Indians remained in Indiana and Illinois. In contrast, he estimated that Missouri and Arkansas Territory had a combined Indian population of 18,917. The population disparities are particularly startling for the Shawnees, Delawares, and Kickapoos. Schoolcraft further refined his figures, noting that there were 1,383 Shawnees, 2,200 Kickapoos, and 1,800 Delawares, as compared to the 800 Shawnees and 80 Delawares living in Ohio. Finally, he estimated that 6,000 Cherokees lived in Missouri and Arkansas.[10]

By the early 1820s, what had begun as small-scale alliances between related tribes developed into a much larger coalition that sought independence from, yet collaboration with, the United States. With the support of twelve tribes and a combined population conservatively estimated at 14,000, alliance members had the numbers to promote their interests among both Americans and their Indian opponents farther west.[11]

Of course, alliances between tribes, both militant and peaceful, have stretched across tribal, linguistic, and geographic lines for centuries.[12] What sets this political movement for a sovereign confederacy apart from earlier pan-Indian efforts is its large size, its distinctive blend of traditional and progressive political ideas, and the way in which its leaders inverted American goals to suit the needs of thousands of emigrant Indians. Like Tecumseh, Black Hoof, and their supporters, alliance members consciously reinvented themselves between the American Revolution and the first two decades of the nineteenth century. However, their motives for immigrating and the peoples they encountered along the way shaped their distinctive responses to the United States.

The Shawnees and Delawares, who began migrating beyond the Mississippi in the 1780s, used their esteemed position among their Algonquian neighbors to become central figures in the Indian republic. The Shawnees were particularly close to the Delawares and Kickapoos. In fact, an elaborate intertribal kinship system linked them together. The Shawnees referred to the Delawares as grandfathers and often deferred to them in public councils. Similarly, Shawnees called the Kickapoos "first brothers." The Kickapoos and Shawnees also recalled a time before the arrival of Europeans when both tribes were united as one. As Algonquian speakers, the Shawnees, Delawares, and Kickapoos shared a similar dialect intelligible to all three tribes. Other Algonquian tribes, including the Miamis and Ottawas, were included in this elaborate kinship system between tribes, but the historic, linguistic, and kin ties binding the Delawares and Kickapoos to the Shawnees were stronger than any other.[13]

In the West, the Shawnees became essential mediators between European colonizers, Algonquian-speaking tribes, and their Creek and Cherokee neighbors. The Shawnees enjoyed longstanding kin ties with the southeastern tribes. Mixed marriages were common. Even Tecumseh's mother was a Creek. The Shawnees' Algonquian neighbors certainly noticed the affinity, and named the tribe "Shawnee," or "southerner" in recognition of their long-standing relations with tribes below the Ohio River. Extensive Shawnee settlements among the Yuchis, Creeks, and Cherokees fostered distinctive dialects and ceremonial practices among these Shawnee villagers. Alford's grandfather, Kishkalwa, lived among the Creeks in Alabama for much of his life, until neighboring Shawnee and Creek villages left for Missouri in 1785. The Shawnees also allied themselves with the English in Carolina as early as the 1680s. Former Carolina governor John Archdale appreciated their assistance, writing that the Shawnees "continued [to be] good Friends and useful neighbors to the English." As a boy, Alford remembered that the Absentee Shawnees "were associated in their councils with . . . the Tallihassee Town of Creeks, the Delawares, the Piankashaws, and the Kickapoos."[14]

Economic and kin relationships with Europeans also played a vital role in the decision to move. Louis Lorimier, a French trader who was married to a métis woman who was part Shawnee, had been loyal to Great Britain during the American Revolution, and he persuaded many Shawnees to move across the Mississippi after the Battle of Fallen Timbers in 1794. Originally from Canada, Lorimier had operated a trading post near Wapakoneta since 1769. George Rogers Clark, with the assistance of John Galloway, in 1782 sacked Lorimier's trading post for his role in outfitting Shawnee warriors then fighting against Kentuckians for control of the Ohio Valley. His position, along with those Shawnees, Delawares, and Kickapoos closest to him, became untenable. Accordingly, Lorimier moved west, helped the Shawnees obtain a twenty-five square mile land grant from the Spanish, and secured exclusive trading privileges with the Shawnees and allied tribes as a result of his efforts. Under Lorimier's direction, emigrant Indian warriors became mercenaries for the Spanish crown. They defended Spanish, and later French, outposts from Osage attack. Regular conflicts with the Osages accelerated the alliance between the emigrant tribes. Mixed bands of warriors, who had migrated west for similar reasons, worked together to defend European settlements and to protect their access to western hunting grounds. Emigrant Indians thus chose what they believed to be the lesser of two evils in the 1790s. Continual warfare with tribes such as the Osage seemed a more desirable alternative to the ongoing bloodshed and cultural changes demanded by Americans to the east.[15]

The Shawnee emigrants—who typically moved in family bands, with disparate political alliances and cultural practices—established seven villages just beyond the Mississippi. Modern Cape Girardeau, Missouri, became the population center, with three outlying villages south of St. Louis. Two additional villages were established farther south, along the St. Francis River, near the border with Arkansas. Jimmy Rogers, a white captive-turned-village chief, established another village west of St. Louis on the Meramec River.[16]

Located within the original Spanish land grant, the Cape Girardeau villages encompassed twenty-five miles of prime farmland between the flood plains of the Whitewater River to the west and the Mississippi River to the east. The richness of the soil and the proximity to French and Spanish traders made the region around Cape Girardeau an ideal settlement for most Shawnee emigrants. By 1815, William Clark estimated that 1,200 Shawnees, 300 of whom were warriors, lived fifteen miles north of Cape Girardeau along Apple Creek. French traders, including Lorimier and Pierre Menard, who later became an Indian agent for the United States, heavily influenced the villagers who lived there. Explorer Stephen Long noted in 1817 that the Apple

Creek Shawnees "have very little acquaintance with the English language, and appeared reluctant to use the few words they knew." Like their French kinsmen, it was not uncommon for these Shawnee villagers, particularly the métis, to own slaves and large numbers of livestock. Shawnee interaction and intermarriage with French traders such as Lorimier also made French the most commonly spoken European language.[17]

Emigrant tribes reconciled old ways and new ways in the West by settling villages and creating new practices that were Native-led and -organized. Shawnees celebrated the Green Corn Dance, or Busk, a ceremony that is typically associated with the Creeks, in early July. S. C. Turnbo, yet another local historian and chronicler of the Arkansas frontier, remembered that settlers were sometimes invited to Shawnee dances. According to Turnbo, "if whites were present they would invite them onto the floor to dance with them. If they accepted the Indians would make sport of their awkwardness." Survival in Missouri, Arkansas, and Texas required that smaller tribes such as the Western Shawnees engage both colonizers and their Indian neighbors in a dialogue meant to improve the emigrants' chances of survival in the West. Some American traders remained essential. But more often Shawnee villagers became closely associated with other emigrant tribes.[18]

Most Western Shawnees remained wedded to hunting and agriculture into the nineteenth century. Hunting parties sometimes formed new villages after finding lands rich with game. Some never returned to the "big shawneetown" along Apple Creek, forming smaller villages along the St. Francis and elsewhere.[19] Shawnee women maintained their traditional control over the planting of crops, gathering nuts and roots, and processing animal skins. While their cabins and kitchen gardens resembled those of their white neighbors in style, communal fields worked by the women revealed a deep commitment to traditional gender roles. Differences between the Shawnees and their American neighbors became even more extreme during the winter months, at the height of the hunting season. Naturalist and travel writer John James Audubon spoke to these differences after Shawnee hunters invited him on a winter hunt in 1810. Audubon and the Shawnees crossed the Mississippi River into Tennessee. Shawnee women then landed the boat on shore and struck out on their own. "The squaws," according to Audubon, ". . . proceeded to search for nuts, whilst the *gentleman* hunters made the best of their way." Clearly pleased with the outcome, Audubon bragged that "the trees around our camp looked like butchers' stalls." More than fifty years later, Alford remembered that his mother and father had carefully separated the economic tasks associated with men and women. The move west was undertaken, in part, to preserve the Shawnees' traditional gender roles, clearly separating

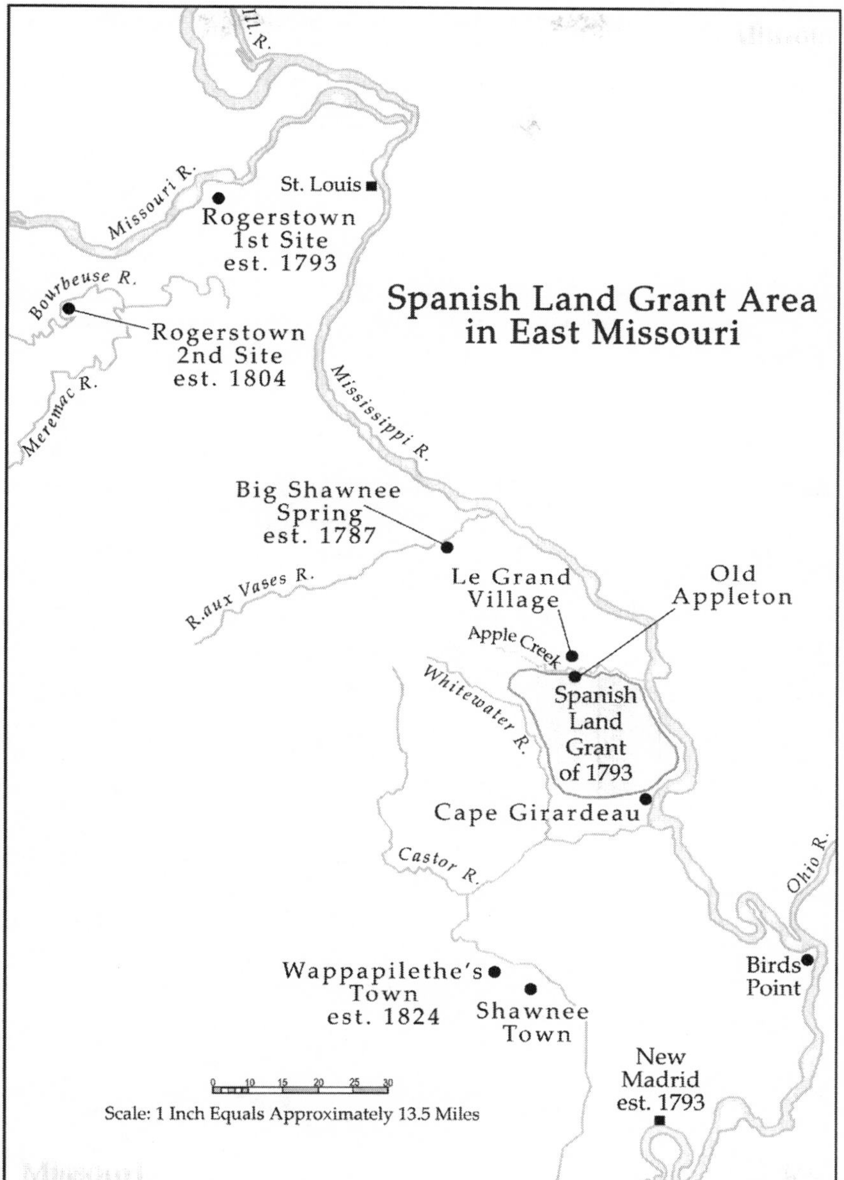

The Shawnee communities of southeastern Missouri before American settlement swept the Shawnees and their allies from the region. Drawn by Luwanna Reed and Leann Barber.

them from their eastern counterparts who began implementing the gendered reforms advocated by missionaries.[20]

In contrast with the Cape Girardeau communities, Rogerstown was much smaller and closer to the American political and cultural orbit. Captured and later adopted in 1778 by the famous Shawnee of the Chillicothe division, Chief Blackfish, Jimmy Rogers became a well-known village chief. Nathan Boone remembered that his father, Daniel, sometimes visited the Shawnees at Rogerstown, where they reminisced about Chief Blackfish and their struggle for the Ohio country. Unlike Boone, who went on to help George Rogers Clark destroy Blackfish's town in Ohio, Rogers married Blackfish's daughter and helped lead the Shawnees to the West.[21]

Not surprisingly, the Rogerstown Shawnees anticipated the American advance into Missouri and initiated a series of economic and educational reforms, such as the incorporation of domesticated livestock into their economy and the establishment of interracial schools. Villagers at Rogerstown made these changes free from the direct supervision of federal Indian agents. These reforms were the logical outcome of their long relationship with their Spanish, French, and American neighbors. The Rogerstown Shawnees worked closely with a host of ethnic outsiders, particularly Americans and neighboring Delawares. Like the Ohio Shawnees, the children of prominent men, including Jimmy Rogers' son Lewis, attended the Choctaw Academy in central Kentucky. Lewis Rogers went on to become a leading figure among the Missouri Shawnee villagers in Kansas after removal, while one of his sisters helped to seal ties with the Delawares by marrying one of their leaders, Cohun.[22]

The reforms initiated by the Rogerstown band addressed the need for balance between time-honored economic pursuits in Missouri and cooperation with American settlers. In 1817, John Mason Peck, a Baptist preacher in Missouri, established a school at Rogerstown that catered to both Indians and whites. Peck did not seem to mind the interaction between Indian and white students at the school. He acknowledged that the students "were at their books in school hours, and engaged with the bow and arrow and other Indian pastimes, during intermission." Western Shawnee villagers supported themselves without the benefit of treaty annuities, which were delivered exclusively to the eastern Shawnees at Wapakoneta. According to Jedidiah Morse, a leading geographer and Congregational minister who toured the region in 1822, four of the wealthiest Shawnee men in the village helped to pay for the school. The Rogerstown Shawnees raised the rest of the money through the sale of cattle and hides. Peck marveled at the "little farms" cultivated by the Shawnees and at their consistent ability to bring in "the best cattle to [the] St. Louis market."[23] The Rogerstown band managed to combine hunting throughout the winter with stock raising and other agricultural pursuits in the summer.

Farther south, the St. Francis River bands were perhaps the most diverse and isolated from European colonizers. They made the most of the swampy, generally undesirable terrain surrounding New Madrid, continued hunting and trading, and avoided extensive contact with colonizers. The New Madrid earthquake of 1811 devastated the Mississippi and Ohio Valleys and made the region even less desirable to American settlers. Rivers flowed backward for a time, sinkholes emerged, and settlers abandoned the epicenter in southeastern Missouri. Tremors continued in the spring of 1812, making the American settlements virtually uninhabitable. The bottom lands along the rivers soon became a haven for mosquitoes, a nightmare for farmers, and an ideal place for Indian people in search of a reprieve from whites. One of their few white neighbors, Samuel G. Hopkins, a sympathetic advocate perhaps driven by his desire for trading privileges with the St. Francis villages, wrote that "it seems as if providence in commiseration of their misfortunes had directed them hither, where white men will not live; and where there is just enough of fish, fowl, and game to minister to their subsistence." Small numbers of Creeks and Delawares banded together with the Shawnees on the St. Francis, and their primary benefactors were the Western Cherokees. Some domesticated livestock, coupled with whatever game they could kill, was used to obtain cash or barter for additional food and clothing. Thomas Nuttall, the botanist and travel writer, met two parties of Shawnee hunters in the region, one of whom purchased gunpowder from him with money acquired from the fur trade.[24]

As Indian communities moved west, their allegiance to their eastern kinsmen faded. In fact, Indian migrants consciously sacrificed land and kinship ties for a chance at cultural sovereignty in the West. Paithuckoosaw, a Missouri Shawnee leader, reminded American leaders that "there [was] now but little feeling of blood & friendship" between the western branches of the tribe and their eastern counterparts. Like Paithuckoosaw, Western Cherokee leaders asked the president of the United States for "his permission to establish a separate and distinct government . . . and to dissolve all obligations which they have been heretofore under to the Cherokees who reside east of the Mississippi."[25] Village chiefs and the leaders of subsidiary bands surrendered much of their power in order to survive as part of a much larger alliance.

Nevertheless, some eastern Shawnees, including Tecumseh, attempted to restore fading kinship ties with their western kinsmen prior to the War of 1812. Tecumseh traveled to Missouri twice, in the summers of 1809 and 1810, in order to recruit warriors to the pan-Indian resistance movement led by him and his brother. Both trips failed. The multilayered identities of the Western Shawnees made reconciliation and coordination between Shawnees east and west of the Mississippi impossible. Even Tecumseh's sister, Tecumpease, married a French fur trader in St. Genevieve, Francois Maisonville, despite her famous brother's objections. Both Tecumpease, and the Western Shawnees more generally, rejected Tecumseh and Tenskwatawa's militancy as well as their ban on mixed marriages.[26]

By the early nineteenth century, French fur traders and their métis children acted as intermediaries between tribes and American officials on the lower Missouri River. The enduring twenty-five-year partnership between Lorimier and Pemanpich was not uncommon among the Missouri Shawnees. Pemanpich's children used their mixed ancestry to live on in Missouri after their less fortunate Shawnee kinsmen were forced further westward. Lorimier granted Pemanpich and their six children his estate, slaves, and other property after his death in 1808, making them some of the wealthiest Missourians in the antebellum period. But the significance of these marriages reached beyond the monetary rewards granted a few Shawnee children. Frenchmen, their métis children, and white captives among the Missouri Shawnees helped the emigrant Indians navigate the confusing milieu of competing colonial powers and tribal adversaries.[27]

The Western Shawnees' rejection of Tecumseh was unusual in that many tribesmen to the north and west of Prophetstown, primarily from the Kickapoos, Potawatomis, Winnebagos, and Ottawas, provided enthusiastic support for the confederacy. The western emigrants shared familial bonds and cultural practices with Tecumseh and his supporters in Indiana Territory. But these ties were not strong enough to break their commitment to peace with the United States. As Chief Lewis Rogers of the Rogerstown Shawnees frankly put it, his people realized that their "children would not live well or happy while at war with the whites."[28] Nicolas de Finiels, a French engineer and traveler who served the Spanish crown, admired the Shawnees' ability to adapt to the changing colonial circumstances on their own accord. In 1803, most Shawnees rejected Christian missionaries and the wide-ranging cultural changes that came with them. He observed that "the impatience and inflexibility of the [French] missionaries . . . doomed their efforts to failure." Finiels believed that the "free man of nature reacts when something is forced upon him but yields unwittingly to everything that is not demanded of him."[29] The plurality of cultures coupled with the absence of a dominant power beyond the Mississippi deprived the emigrant Indians of the incentives necessary to join with Tecumseh and other Indian militants to the east.

Years of intermarriage and cooperation between various colonizers and these multiethnic villagers failed to quell Americans' doubts about their loyalty to the United States between the time of the Louisiana Purchase and the conclusion of the War of 1812. With Indian attacks no longer a threat in Ohio, Indiana, and Illinois, many settlers crossed the banks of the Mississippi. Missouri's white population increased from 10,000 in 1804 to 25,000 by 1814.[30] A familiar cycle of settlement and harassment soon began in Missouri and Arkansas. These semiautonomous communities terrified most American settlers, who associated Indian self-help with armed rebellion.

The emigrant tribes experienced a devastating loss of life and property in the second decade of the nineteenth century. Between 1811 and 1814, the Apple Creek Shawnees reported a loss of over sixty-five hogs, forty-nine cattle, and forty-eight horses. Upon his return from the winter hunt earlier that spring, the Apple Creek chief, Wapapilethe, found his house "had been broken open, and what I had left in it was all gone." The destruction visited upon the villages of eastern Missouri weighed heavily upon the Shawnees. Wapapilethe personally knew the white man who had settled illegally on his land and had robbed him and his people, but Indians in Missouri were barred from testifying against whites. Legally powerless, the Apple Creek Shawnees complained that "the whites do not steal these things merely for their value, but more to make us abandon our land and take it for themselves."[31]

Another Shawnee man was beaten and evicted from his farm by a white man who coveted his land and improvements. In spite of overwhelming evidence, as well as protests from the Shawnees and Pierre Menard, the county judge refused to prosecute the man responsible and allowed the statute of limitations for his crimes to pass. These assaults led to the massive dislocation and relocation of emigrant Indians. Between 1815 and 1819 alone, the Shawnee population of southeastern Missouri plummeted from 1,200 to 400. Farther south, the Western Cherokees experienced similar problems. They moved west from the Arkansas border with Tennessee to the north bank of the Arkansas River, between present-day Little Rock and Fort Smith. Their horrifying experiences in the postwar years confirms historian John Mack Faragher's argument that Missouri and other frontier states "use[d] squatters as a club to beat emigrant Indians into submission."[32]

Several village chiefs traveled north along the Mississippi River in the fall of 1815 to meet at Portage des Sioux with the northern superintendent of Indian affairs, William Clark; the territorial governor of Illinois, Ninian Edwards; and the influential St. Louis trader, Auguste Chouteau. They complained that American attacks on their villages had intensified since the end of the war. Wapapilethe bitterly remarked that attacks upon the Shawnees' livestock and improvements had increased even though "our behavior has been such that no honest white man can have any cause to find fault with us." American settlers particularly targeted wealthy Shawnees who had amassed livestock and property in anticipation of American dominance in the region. Most Shawnees owned livestock, but several tribal members owned more than two hundred head of cattle, hogs, and horses.[33]

Federal officials tried to mediate a solution. In a letter to Secretary of War William Crawford in October 1815, Clark, Edwards, and Chouteau argued that "the uncommon sobriety and general good conduct" of the Delawares and Shawnees warranted the creation of a joint reservation in western Missouri. All three men had spent the early years of their lives fighting the larger confederacies of which these tribes were a part. Ninian Edwards, for one, battled with Potawatomis and Kickapoos allied with Tecumseh throughout the War of 1812. Yet only a year later, all three believed that manageable alliances between tribes such as the Delawares and Shawnees made sense for Missouri. Unlike government officials in Washington, D.C., western officials had a closer and more nuanced view of alliances and believed that they could sometimes be used to promote peace.[34]

Clark and his compatriots did not doubt the veracity of the Shawnees' complaints, citing their unwillingness to join Tecumseh and remain neutral in the War of 1812 as reason enough to give them the same legal protections afforded to American settlers. And Amos Stoddard, the federal official charged with managing the American takeover of the Louisiana Territory, promised that all Spanish land titles would be validated by the United States. To that end, William Clark visited the city recorder's St. Louis office in 1816 to verify the Shawnees' title to their lands in and around Cape Girardeau. To the consternation of the Missouri legislature, William Clark found the original title, dating from January 4, 1793, guaranteeing their legal right to the Missouri lands. James Caldwell, the Speaker of the Missouri House of Representatives, urged Clark to invalidate the Spanish title so that "the richest and most fertile part of the Counties aforesaid" might be opened to settlement.[35]

The emigrant tribes continued to suffer despite Clark's discovery of the land grant and his willingness to defend them from Missouri legislators. His influence steadily declined as settlers interested in agriculture rather than the Indian trade moved in and occupied Indian lands. Between 1808 and 1818, farmland in and around St. Louis had increased in value from approximately fifty cents an acre to twelve dollars an acre, and recent migrants, the overwhelming majority of whom were Americans, played a major role in the skyrocketing land values. American squatters unable to purchase expensive land poured onto the Indian settlements below St. Louis. Then territorial governor William Clark ordered Alexander McNair, the head of the territorial militia, to remove squatters from government and Indian lands, but McNair refused. The differences between McNair and Clark came to a head when both men ran for governor after Missouri became a state in 1821. Clark was lambasted as both pro-Indian and antisquatter, while McNair gloried in his defense of squatters and his unsympathetic attitude toward the state's Indian population. McNair defeated Clark in a landslide. Attacks on Shawnee settlements worsened as state officials such as McNair brought a new political reality to Missouri.[36]

William Clark's steady exit from prominence as the co-captain of the Lewis and Clark expedition and champion of Jeffersonian ideals in the West was part of a much larger shift at work in American Indian policy. Federal Indian policy between 1789 and 1815 was designed to extinguish Indian cultures through the steady assimilation of Indians into American society. Jeffersonians believed that the cultural divide between Indians and whites, spelled out in the Enlightenment notions of savagery and civilization, mattered far more than racial phenotypes. According to historian Reginald Horsman, policy-makers of the revolutionary generation "lacked any sense of cultural relativism. The different ways of life that they discovered were not regarded as simply different, they were regarded as wrong." For example, Clark made clear that those Indians who refused to adapt to the changing economy would be forced from their lands by cycles of indebtedness and land transfers. But American Indians who adopted the trappings of Christianity and the yeoman farmer ideal would be allowed to remain as citizens of the United States.[37]

William Clark's defeat in the gubernatorial election of 1820 signaled the close of the Jeffersonian era in Indian-white relations. Advocates of the slow but steady assimilation of American Indians gave way to strident, anti-Indian policy-makers. Local politicians, emboldened by frontiersmen hungry for Indian lands, lost patience with Jeffersonian policy-makers. Small-scale Indian removals—some voluntary, some not—began almost immediately, as Americans increasingly ignored Indian land titles and legal protections. By the early 1820s, a new brand of uncompromising racial supremacy came to dominate political life in Missouri.[38]

Even the smaller Shawnee, Delaware, and Creek villages in the swampy, mosquito-ridden country along the St. Francis River came under siege by proponents of the new racial order. Multitribal hunting parties frequently came into contact with American homesteaders along the Missouri-Tennessee border. New settlers complained about the Indians' burning of grasslands near their homes and the frequent trespass of Indians on their farms. In early

April 1820, two Indian and American bands of hunters crossed paths just east of the Mississippi River and exchanged gunfire. The gunfight resulted in the death of one settler and the injury of another. Local militia members pursued the Shawnee and Creek hunters involved in the shoot-out into Tennessee, but the Indians managed to elude them. A man named Captain Walker of Winchester, Missouri, held two St. Francis leaders as prisoners until those involved surrendered themselves at the New Madrid jail. Both men eventually turned themselves in; both soon died at the jail under questionable circumstances. One member of the militia, Stephen Ross, admitted that a crowd of whites "whose curiosity had led them to visit the jail" killed one of the Indians involved. Ross doubted that Governor Clark would approve of his "conduct and the conduct of those engaged in this affair."[39] Unlike the men involved in the Shawnee/Seneca massacre on Deer Lick Creek, Indiana, in 1824, no one was prosecuted for their murders. Even those Shawnees inhabiting the most inhospitable regions of the territory faced declining control over their lives by 1820.

Most American residents of Missouri and Arkansas viewed Indians with contempt and attempted to force them beyond the western rim of settlement. The deaths of the Indian hunters foreshadowed a larger conflict over sovereignty that involved a struggle for land as well as legal control. Politicians viewed semiautonomous Indian communities within state boundaries as a threat to state sovereignty. Sen. Thomas Hart Benton of Missouri, a member of the Committee on Indian Affairs and outspoken advocate for states' rights, argued before the Senate that "the existence of separate communities, within its bosom, and independent of its laws, is a palpable evil, an anomaly in government." In this context, federal officials were not given the coercive powers necessary to curb settlers from abusing Indians, and state officials loathed the enforcement of laws designed to protect Native Americans.[40]

The emigrant tribes moved to the Ozark mountains bordering Arkansas. Soon enough, western Missouri regressed into violence as Indian refugees from eastern Missouri fought with American squatters who refused to acknowledge their right to the land. Finding and cultivating food was not easy in the Ozarks. The rocky and wooded terrain was not suited for large-scale corn production, and war with the Osages made it increasingly difficult for the Shawnees to tend the harvest. The situation became desperate. Matthew Adams, a migrant from Kentucky and Indian trader from Ste. Genevieve, observed that the Shawnees "have been for a considerable time in a suffering situation . . . their children skinning off the bark of trees and making use of sap. Procuring roots, weeds, & c. which their chiefs told me was their only alternative to support life." In a cycle painfully familiar to most American

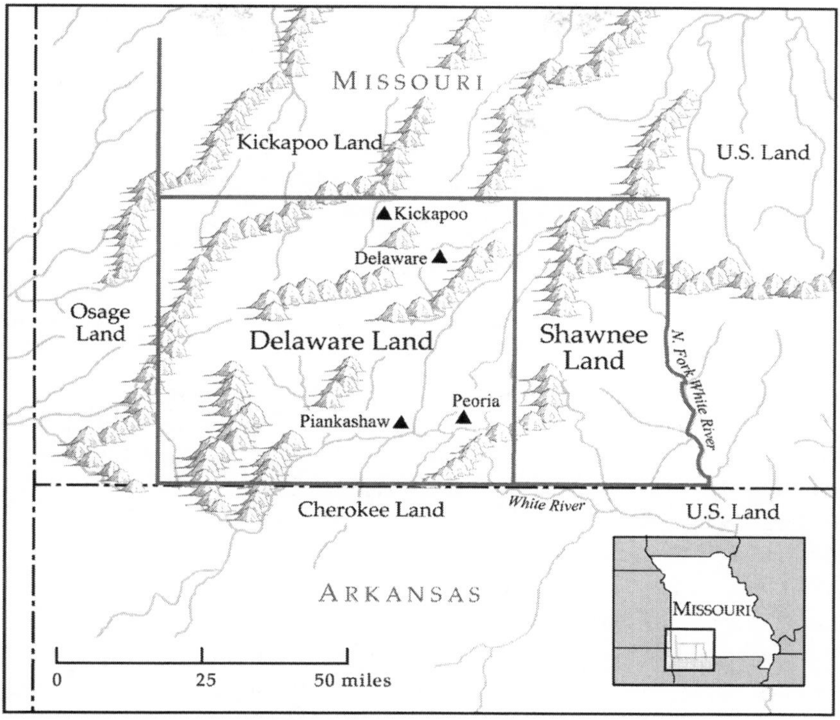

William Clark created reservations for the refugee emigrant Indians that were not recognized by the U.S. government. The Shawnees and their more powerful neighbors, including the Western Cherokees, dreamed of linking these reservations together into an Indian state. Drawn by Dave Marincic, Paul Bailie, and Michael Treve.

Indians since large-scale contact with colonizers, the Shawnees began a new round of migration and removal, then subsistence and poverty. American settlers destroyed the Shawnees' economy with alarming speed following the conclusion of the War of 1812.[41] The dislocation of Shawnees, Delawares, and Kickapoos from eastern Missouri forced these villagers to disperse into smaller, impermanent settlements, where they scratched out a tenuous existence from vacant lands along the eastern boundary of Osage territory. Former residents of the Shawnee villages in southeastern Missouri had become a people without a country.

But the Shawnees and their neighbors did not submit to the Americans. To the contrary, they developed a revolutionary response to rapacious settlers and the politicians who defended them. They chose to come together in an even larger alliance than they had known before the war. State politicians soon complained that "remnants of tribes" had coalesced into a diverse "river population." These "stragglers from different nations" were sometimes called a republic. More often, Indian agents lumped them together as "White River" or "Red River" Indians. Regardless of Americans' confusion regarding their identities, their combined settlements stretched from the north bank of the Arkansas River to southwestern Missouri. As such, neighboring whites in Missouri, Arkansas, and Texas described them as formidable warriors and threats to state and national sovereignty. Stephen Austin, for one, feared them. The problem, according to Austin, was that "they have never acknowledged themselves as conquered."[42]

American officials soon found out that conquest mattered. Led by an expanding population of Western Cherokees, members of the alliance proposed a "union of tribes" along the Ozark frontier. Cherokees such as John Jolly, Tahlontuskee, Tekatoka, and Quatawepea, or Captain Lewis, of the Shawnees, hoped to create "one great family" of emigrant Indians.[43] Between 1818 and 1825, leaders of the alliance scattered details of their plans in written correspondence, wampum, and intertribal conferences stretching from Arkansas to Washington, D.C.

Cherokee proponents of an Indian state offered an alternative to political fragmentation and dependence on the United States. Chickamauga Cherokees, who later became known as "Old Settlers," began migrating westward during the time between the Treaty of Holston in 1791 and the more aggressive land treaties of the early nineteenth century. Like their northern counterparts, the Old Settlers resisted the radical changes proposed by Americans. Some ventured westward in search of an alternative to Jefferson's assimilationist program.[44]

However, Western Cherokees did incorporate significant cultural innovations into their daily lives, including the use of Sequoyah's syllabary and the adoption of written laws. George Washington and Thomas Jefferson encouraged the development of tribally run legal systems so that diplomatic ventures with Indians could run through recognized leaders and tribal governments modeled after the United States. The first written law of the Eastern Cherokees was drafted in 1808. By 1820, the Western Cherokees had followed suit with their first laws against stealing property, primarily horses. The Old Settlers employed a light horse company—Indian policemen of sorts who patrolled Cherokee territory regularly beginning in 1820 to enforce their newly codified legal system. Written laws now regulated Cherokee life east and west of the Mississippi.[45]

Tribes such as the Cherokees began to abandon the familiar markers of ethnicity—language, kinship, and ritual—in exchange for rules of conduct and citizenship based on the new legalisms of the age. Ironically, the transition from Jeffersonian Indian policy to what became known as Jacksonian Indian policy adversely affected these tribes just as they incorporated American legalisms into their government. The Cherokees were becoming a state at the precise moment that the United States sought to undermine the sovereignty of Indian tribes by forcing American Indians to submit to federal authority.

Previous scholars of the emigrant Indian confederacy have argued that the confederacy's main purpose was the destruction of their Osage enemies.[46] Certainly, dominance over the Prairie-Plains tribes was essential to the confederacy's goals. The Cherokees, Shawnees, and their allies had been waging an incessant war with the tribes native to the region since their arrival in the eighteenth century. But emigrant Indian leaders also hoped to unite more than twenty thousand Indian people to achieve a balance of power with the Americans. In this way, recent Indian migrants became far more than mercenaries-turned-militants whose primary goal was defense against the encroachment of European and American settlements.

The forced migration of Kickapoos, Delawares, Shawnees, Piankashaws, and Peorias into the northwestern Ozarks laid the groundwork for an increasingly desperate struggle with the Osages over diminishing resources. In June 1821, Missouri Indian agent Richard Graham reported that "a party of Osages last month destroyed a village of the Cherokees & murdered 110 souls, men women & children of the cherokees & a Delawar family—it is also reported that 10 white men were killed by same party." The emigrant Indians and a handful of their white neighbors whose subsistence patterns resembled their Indian neighbors understood the importance of defeating the Osages. Graham, Stephen Long, and other government observers noted that settlers in the Ozarks nearly always sided with the multitribal members of the republic against the Osages. Graham, Clark, and the secretary of war worried that white and Algonquian involvement in the Cherokee-Osage conflict might create a widespread, bloody war throughout the West.[47]

Consequently, government officials did their best to keep whites out and to limit the number of Algonquian participants as much as possible. In fall 1821, Major William Bradford, commander of Fort Smith, assured Secretary of War John C. Calhoun that he had separated Americans from a retaliatory war party of the emigrant Indian tribes. He put the Americans on notice and told them that he would order "the civil authority in force against them" if they did not remain behind. Graham matched Bradford's efforts among the Delawares.[48]

In spite of their efforts, William Clark predicted that a "General Indian War" would take place sometime in 1822. According to one American official, the young men of the Missouri Delawares seemed "like blood hounds in the leash." Clark and others believed that "the Osages will be destroyed" without the protection of the United States. Graham feared the power of an alliance between the Cherokees and their Algonquian neighbors, and worked to divide the republic by separating members of the Algonquian alliance from the Iroquoian-speaking Cherokees who spearheaded the Osage campaigns. The Shawnees, Kickapoos, and Piankashaws typically followed the Delawares in both war and diplomacy. According to Graham, "if any Delawars have been killed, that nation will form a coalition with the Cherokees & draw with them the Shawnees."[49]

Manipulation of tribal annuity payments offered one means of social control for government agents such as Richard Graham. The struggle he initiated over the distribution of money to the Osages, who ceded land to the United States in 1808 and again in 1818, offers yet another example of American intervention in Indian leadership in order to achieve goals set by policy-makers in Washington. Graham pursued an end to the wars of the early 1820s by consolidating the Osage bands into a national unit for the purpose of distributing annuities. The St. Louis Indian agent argued that this was the best strategy for pacification of the Osages. However, he warned that "the long separation of this nation has given distinct views and feelings to the three bands and in many respects they act as different nations." The Osages had split into three autonomous bands by the late eighteenth century: the Little Osages to the north along the Missouri River, the Arkansas band to the south along the lower Verdigris River, and the Big Osages along the upper Osage River. Osage chiefs balked at Graham's consolidation strategy, choosing instead to remain autonomous. But Graham, as distributor of federal treaty annuities, held the upper hand. Graham assured John C. Calhoun that the Osages would submit to the government plan, writing that "I expressed to them that I was now their agent & in the future their annuities should be delivered to the chiefs collectively without any reference to their village rights and if they did not meet me collectively as the Osage Nation they would not receive their annuities."[50]

By distributing treaty annuities to individuals he regarded as "national" leaders, Graham upset power relations between previously autonomous villages. Both the Osages and their Algonquian enemies now had to contend with an inner civil war over dwindling resources. White River subagent John Campbell spelled out Delaware feelings regarding annuity payments and the increasing class divisions upsetting their villages. Campbell stated that "the poor Indians complain to me constantly and state they get little or nothing that the big fish eat all the little one's up in the division."[51] This competition signaled a two-pronged threat to Indian life in Missouri. American settlements disrupted village-based economies just as the need for American money necessitated the merging of villages into tribal or national governments. The long-cherished independence that had originally motivated the Algonquians to move west became a luxury.

Graham's bold diplomacy did not render all competing tribes dependent on the United States. The threatened loss of government funds placed the Delawares in a difficult position, while the Shawnees, who had already been denied annuity money and were still without land in the West, faced no such dilemma. But all Algonquian emigrants stood at a crossroads in the 1820s. The Creeks, Cherokees, and Choctaws were valued allies who had offered the Algonquians land and access to hunting grounds in exchange for loyalty. Together, the southern tribes were as strong numerically as the Americans, particularly in Arkansas. Sacrificing the Cherokee alliance in exchange for government annuities carried with it the loss of land, security, and autonomy for the smaller Algonquian bands in the West.

Graham targeted the Delawares as the primary cause of continued warfare among the Algonquians. In a letter to Calhoun in November 1821, Graham predicted that he "should affect without difficulty a good understanding between the delawares Shawanees Kickapoos and Osages," but has "been disappointed in the Delawares." Captain Anderson, the Delaware leader who had lived in Indiana until 1818, when the Treaty of Fort Meigs required that his people leave the state, balked at Graham's peace proposal. As the newly minted spokesperson for the Western Delawares, Anderson told Graham that it would be impossible for his warriors to avoid hostile encounters with the Osages while they were away on the winter hunt. Graham countered with a dark threat: "If any Delawares take up the tomahawk and goes to war against the Osages I will stop their annuity payments and withdraw their traders from them."[52]

Graham soon realized that threatening to cut off rations and ammunition worked against both American and emigrant Indian plans. Pierre Menard stepped in and tried to broker a settlement amenable to both sides. Menard reminded Graham that additional migrants from Ohio were now in central Illinois and "are naked and starving and will be unable to join their friends in time to raise a crop, if they are not assisted." The French trader-turned-Indian agent did not stop there. Secretary of War John C. Calhoun wanted Indian agents to encourage the eastern tribes to move west. Graham's heavy-handed tactics might halt the voluntary immigration of the Ohio tribes who had once hoped to join their kin beyond the Mississippi.[53] After 1815, increasing pressure from American settlers and federal policy-makers quickened the violence between the tribes in Missouri, Arkansas, and East Texas. Voluntary migrants became cautious and held on to their lands in the East as news of warfare and starvation in the West reached their villages.

Ongoing warfare with the Osages, and government interference in their efforts, forced the western Shawnees and their neighbors to decide between their allies, Indian and white, in the West. Some, such as the Rogerstown community, worked closely with missionaries and limited their military involvement with other tribes. But most Shawnees remained committed to their Algonquian allies. Their continued alliances and interest in an economic system that could not be contained in a tightly bounded reservation zone circumscribed the government's plans for them.

Negotiations between the Osages and their Algonquian enemies revealed the inner workings of the emigrant Indian alliance. A temporary peace between the tribes negotiated in September 1822 required that in the event of "any difficulty . . . between the Osages and any of the Delawares Grand Children, the adjustment of it is to be left to the decision of the Delaware nation." As "Grand Children" of the Delawares, the Shawnees, Kickapoos, Weas, Peorias, and Piankashaws accepted a subordinate kinship position and ceded significant political power to the Delawares: the ability to negotiate directly with the federal government and their Indian enemies.[54] Meanwhile, both the Delawares and Osages agreed that any further problems between them should be mediated by Graham and other federal officials. American officials now had the means to intervene in the Osage–Algonquian dispute. However, kinship-based alliances between the Algonquian tribes prevailed, as Americans recognized that Algonquian channels of authority had to be used to meet American objectives.

The peace treaty also led to the creation of tribal reservations for the Delawares, Shawnees, and Kickapoos in southwestern Missouri. Occupied between 1820 and 1825, the reservations drawn up by William Clark were never formally granted to the Shawnees and their neighbors through treaty. Algonquian refugees had been without a clear patent to their lands since the 1803 Louisiana Purchase. Moreover, the new reservations were already compromised by white settlement. Consequently, Captain Anderson and the Delawares asked that the squatters attracted to the lead mines along the White River be removed as soon as possible. Moreover, Graham's land treaty provided the tribes with far less than they expected. As one Delaware put it, "you have placed us in a small hole." A government surveyor, John Sullivan, confirmed their complaints, observing that "the Delaware and Shawnee lands are generally very mountainous, rocky & unfit for cultivation, except the small bottoms, most of which are subject to frequent inundation."[55]

Nevertheless, the new reservations brought emigrants originally from both north and south of the Ohio River closer together. Bordered by the western Cherokee reserve to the south; Osage lands to the west, near modern-day Carthage and Neosho, Missouri; and bounded on the east by the towns of Western Plains and Mountain Grove, the emigrants shared a large expanse of land. And despite the fact that the Americans designed tribally bounded reserves, the emigrants built villages outside of the land allotted to them. For example, contemporary maps indicate that the Piankashaws, Peorias, and Kickapoos settled on the Delaware reserve by 1824. Even a band of Shawnees led by Quatawepea, or Colonel Lewis, lived on the Cherokee Grant just south of the Algonquian reservations in north-central Arkansas. The Algonquian alliance survived, as tribal reservations became multitribal commons. They persevered in their commitment to autonomy through alliances.[56]

The geographic concentration of so many newcomers and tribes native to the region meant that warfare between them would inevitably continue. By 1823, some 8,000 "well disciplined and armed" Algonquians were poised to destroy the 8,500 Osages who remained. Along with the Cherokees, the alliance's combined population reached 14,000.[57] The allied tribes waged war with the Osages because they understood that a western outlet to hunting grounds was essential if they were to remain free of American dominance. They also recognized that they would have to open their lands to newly arriving emigrants connected with the current members of the alliance. Cherokee leaders made clear that "if . . . strangers . . . come into our country [they] are to be fed from our table."[58]

Emigrant Indians used their long experience with colonizers to their own advantage. As invaders of Osage lands, the Cherokees and their allies developed a strategy of reporting alleged Osage abuses to the Americans and then demanding "country in payment for the various losses we have experienced."[59] The Cherokees soon controlled most of north-central Arkansas and part of Missouri by adopting tactics that had been used against their own people by Americans farther east.

Spurred on by the success of this strategy, the allies became de facto removal agents. Those who were once recruited westward by colonizers were now drawn to the Ozarks by advocates of the sovereign Indian confederacy. Between 1823 and 1825, alliance members sent white wampum belts to nineteen tribes in the East. Their purpose, according to a council of Shawnees and Cherokees, was "in relation to their removal to the West and occupying a country convenient to each other for the purpose of union and support of regulations calculated to govern the whole . . . promote the culture of the earth and a tendency to civilization."[60] The size of the emigrant populations tripled, as promises of hunting grounds and freedom from American settlers spread eastward.

In this way, the emigrant Indians cooperated with the Monroe administration's goal of removing Indians from the eastern United States. Yet the confederacy they proposed created a fascinating conflict of interest for the Americans. The emigrant tribes made the federal government's quest for Indian assistance with removal contingent on the sacrifice of the United States' equally powerful desire to be completely sovereign over the Indians and the land within its borders. Leaders of the confederacy proposed a compromise. In exchange for a sovereign but allied Indian state, the emigrants would promote removal and incorporate newcomers from east of the Mississippi.

Many of the Algonquian advocates of the Indian state who migrated to the Arkansas/Missouri border had fought with the Americans in the War of 1812, only to be discouraged by popular postwar sentiment regarding Indians. One such man was Colonel Lewis. Lewis was a Shawnee village chief who had lived alongside Black Hoof and the Wapakoneta Shawnees following the Battle of Fallen Timbers. Born in approximately 1766, Lewis traveled to Washington, D.C., on several occasions and corresponded with government officials until his death in 1826. Like other Indians on the Ohio frontier, Lewis had learned much from American officials and settlers, particularly their views on race, Indian cultures, and American policies toward Indians. In an 1816 letter to President Monroe, Lewis articulated his understanding of American attitudes toward his people and their response. Lewis spoke of his desire for a "future state" that his people could only obtain after Americans taught "our young people the arts of the whites." He believed that this prospective Indian state would "render our living less precarious as well as less burdensome to our friends the white people." Finally, he acknowledged that the eventual incorporation of Christianity and American customs was "absolutely necessary to procure those advantages" for the Shawnees and their allies. Indeed, Quatawepea modeled himself after American settlers in Ohio by accumulating property to such an extent that he became "unpopular with his tribe." Nevertheless, Lewis abandoned his Ohio village and took his plans for an Indian state to the Cherokees.[61]

The Chickamauga Cherokees who settled in Arkansas shared Lewis's perspective on Indian-white relations. One such man, Tooantuh, or Spring Frog, had fought with Andrew Jackson against the Red Sticks, a branch of the Creek Confederacy then allied with Tecumseh. Born in 1754, Spring Frog abandoned his village along the Tennessee–Georgia border after the War of 1812. Once in Arkansas, Spring Frog and others like him worked closely with Shawnees who were less well known, such as Paithuckoosaw. Paithuckoosaw was also born in the Southeast, and he developed close associations with tribes from the region before migrating beyond the Mississippi. His long geographic and linguistic résumé enabled him to "reconcile . . . differences between tribes or individuals."[62] All three men had considerable experience with American officials ranging from Thomas Jefferson to Andrew Jackson. They understood American policies perhaps better than William Clark did. And they had been betrayed by American allies in war. Members of the western alliance wanted to create an Indian state that would not be subject to the whims of American leaders.

The clearest description of this protean state comes from Colonel Lewis, the Shawnee leader. According to Lewis, the allied tribes had three main goals. First, their "Great Council" wished to promote removal now that Indians in Indiana, Ohio, and New York had nowhere to hunt and were constantly harassed by white farmers and whiskey salesmen. As a result, they became determined to "give Indians forming this Council a settlement by which they may exact and enforce their own laws and regulations." Lewis added that leaders of this Indian state would have coercive authority, an innovation that had not yet supplanted less authoritarian notions of leadership among the emigrants. According to Lewis, the confederacy would have the ability to enforce laws "on those nations who may be disposed not to listen to reason and justice." Finally, they hoped to receive "teachers and husbandmen" in order gradually to give up hunting and become farmers. Toward this end, council members arranged for a meeting of their eastern and western kinsmen at Wapakoneta, Ohio, in 1823. They hoped to gain wide acceptance for both removal and their sovereign confederacy, and then carry their request forward to Washington, D.C., for official approval. Nineteen delegates were sent from the various tribes, including two each from the Cherokees, Delawares, Kickapoos, Wyandots, Miamis, and Ottawas, as well as one from the Potawatomis, Weas, and Peorias.[63]

Federal officials in the West, including William Clark and Richard Graham, lent their enthusiastic support to delegates from the alliance. In fact, Graham accompanied the delegation to Washington in February 1825. Washington newspapers such as the *Daily National Journal* reported that "a movement [has] begun, upon the plan now before Congress, for bettering the condition of our Indians, by Indians themselves." Alliance delegates, bolstered by the enthusiasm of Clark and others, believed that Secretary of War Calhoun would ultimately support their efforts. Cherokee delegates addressed Calhoun as their "brother," a startlingly egalitarian use of kin terms in the era of the "Great Father."[64]

Calhoun refused to sponsor their plan for an Indian state, despite the fact that members of the council desired "a settlement by which they may exact & enforce their own laws and regulations necessary towards the agricultural life." Unimpressed, government officials insulted the republicans even further by demanding that the Cherokees cede some of their land to the United States.[65] American ultimatums made clear that their proposal, based as it was on the establishment of a government and economic system resembling the Americans' assimilationist program, would not be enough. Movement toward American notions of "civilization" did not carry with it an acceptance of Indian autonomy. Colonel Lewis and his allies discovered that in the West, as in the East, "civilization" was a fig leaf for a naked land grab.

Calhoun's aggressive calls for additional land cessions also revealed important conflicts between government officials east and west of the Mississippi. Both Clark and Graham, his principal lieutenant, had encouraged the emigrant alliances. They opposed the creation of separate agencies for Indian tribes in the West. To their mind, peace was easier to maintain through multi-tribal negotiations than separate conversations with individual tribes. Accustomed to cooperative, semi-autonomous villages in the West, Clark, Graham, and the trader and Indian agent, Pierre Menard did not feel the same urgency to disband confederacies as did their counterparts in the East. Members of the confederacy had been led astray by the false promises of federal officials out of touch with the majority opinion on the proper course of Indian affairs.[66]

But the rejection of the confederacy also revealed sharp differences between the tribes now separated into eastern and western divisions. Eastern tribes, including the Ohio Shawnees, rejected the western plan because they feared the loss of their distinctive identity and leadership. Ohio Indian agent John Johnston exacerbated these fears, telling the Ohio tribes that if they joined the alliance "you will be gone forever, and never be talked to any more as a nation." Moreover, Black Hoof, the Wapakoneta village chief who hosted the intratribal meeting, remained opposed to removal. Black Hoof used his own long experience with American expansion to guide him. He believed that such removals would not cease and that the Shawnees must adjust to life surrounded by American settlers in Ohio.[67]

Finally, and perhaps most importantly, Calhoun and state politicians from Missouri and Arkansas became increasingly uncomfortable with the relative autonomy of the alliance within the borders of the United States. American policy-makers wanted a subordinate entity for American Indians. Calhoun, for one, attempted to control the alliance's war with the Osages, demanding that "if injuries have been done by the Osages to the Cherokees attonment *Must* be made for them, but the Cherokees must not go to war for that purpose. They *Must* look to the government for redress." The Cherokees and their Indian allies resisted American efforts to control the war and the Indian nations within their boundaries. They argued that "they have never been treated other than as part of the Cherokee Tribe, enjoying their own laws and customs, the only guide known to them."[68] Nevertheless, Arkansas Governor George Izard lobbied against the confederacy. He believed that the alliance was developing a "plan of insurrection" that involved the defeat of the Osages and the subsequent conquest of American settlements.[69]

In yet another stroke of irony, American officials adopted the Indians' dream of a pan-Indian state and transformed it into official policy. In the 1830s men such as Calhoun and Benton joined Andrew Jackson in trumpeting the idea of an Indian Territory in the West—a land free from white settlement that might become an "Indian Canaan." The Baptist missionary Isaac McCoy, who worked as a lobbyist for the Jackson administration, argued that the region would be free of white settlements and that a pan-tribal government would evolve under the benevolent supervision of Christian missionaries.[70] McCoy even fantasized about the name of this faux Indian state, dubbing it "Aboriginia." McCoy's pan-Indian state never materialized. But Indian Territory did become a culturally quarantined zone that segregated Indians from whites and was heavily supervised by many of the government officials who had helped undermine the confederacy. Indeed, McCoy's revised concept of an Indian state helped justify removal and the creation of the Indian Territory.

With the creation of Indian Territory in 1825, the Shawnees and many of the tribes with whom they were allied confronted the reunification of their people for the first time in their recorded history. The United States created tribal reservations in the West, an innovation that required the destruction and consolidation of autonomous American Indian villages in Missouri, Arkansas, and the eastern United States. After more than fifty years of separation, removal treaties concluded in 1825, 1832, and 1833 mandated that the Shawnees, Delawares, and related tribes unite in modern Kansas. Alford's people refused and carried their dreams of independence still further west, into Texas and Mexico. In contrast, Indian emigrants to the West who reunited with their kinsmen because of Indian removal often had to accept subservient positions within the new political order on their reservations. Architects of the Indian Removal Act attempted to correct centuries of localism within tribes. But in their attempt to recreate "national" tribal governments, they initiated a deeper, and more protracted competition between members of villages east and west of the Mississippi that have consumed tribal affairs for years to come. Alford dealt with the consequences of this policy in his own lifetime. In his opinion, the struggles of the Absentee Shawnees in the twentieth century stemmed from the fact that they were neither militant resisters nor simple advocates of peace. Even Alford, who wrote the first history of the Shawnees by a Shawnee author, wondered whether his work, and, by extension, his people's history, would be taken seriously. In the conclusion of *Civilization and the Story of the Absentee Shawnees,* Alford maintained that what he had written "was all nonsense to the government," despite the fact that his was the first "real, inside history of the Shawnees."[71]

4. The Nexus of Faith and Power on the Reservation, 1830–1845

Graham Rogers, the head chief of the Shawnee nation in the late 1860s and a descendant of the Missouri Shawnees at Rogerstown, recalled a transitional moment in Shawnee history that had catapulted him and his family to positions of power. In an interview with the nineteenth-century historian and chronicler Lyman Draper, Rogers equated removal to Kansas with the onset of a system of national merit-based leadership. According to Rogers, "The Shawnees changed their system of government—used to have tribal organization [Shawnee divisions]—now select the ablest & best men without regard to tribes." Rogers and his kinsmen benefited from the dissolution of hereditary leadership roles based on "tribes" or tribal divisions. His grandfather was a white captive-turned-village-chief along the Meramac River in Missouri, and, as an ethnic outsider, lacked the divisional affiliation required of tribal chiefs. Numbering approximately 130 persons at its height, the Rogerstown Shawnees were quick to incorporate stock raising, American schools, and Protestantism into their daily lives. Yet these reformers were not entitled to traditional leadership roles based on patrilineal descent and divisional affiliation prior to removal. Before 1830, the Rogerstown Shawnees rarely spoke for or acted with the rest of the tribe. Once in Kansas, these heretofore marginal villagers emerged as "national" Shawnee leaders.[1]

Many Shawnees vigorously disagreed with Rogers' triumphant view of the changes in Shawnee leadership. Dispossessed of land and prestige since the 1830s, Rogers's opponents accused the "ablest & best men" of bringing ruin to the tribe in their quest for power and the reformation of descent-based leadership roles. According to an Absentee Shawnee informant interviewed by Erminie Wheeler-Voegelin in the 1930s, "the mekoce [Maykujay] went broke in Ohio . . . sold all his land and had nothing, then he came to Kansas with the rest of the Shawnee." The Maykujay then promised "not to be appointed as any sort of business man (a chief) and he promised to abide by the rules of Oawikila, pekowi, kispoko, calakaaOa and spito [Thawegila, Piqua, Kispokotha, Spito]." The Maykujays ultimately broke their promises to the members of the other divisions and intermarried with them, undermining the integrity of the descent groups in the process. As a result of the reservation system, and the Maykujay's actions, individuals with hereditary rights to leadership positions found traditional pathways to power contested by men such as Rogers. For Voegelin's Absentee Shawnee informant, the Hog Creek and Wapakoneta Shawnees who arrived in Kansas in 1833 and 1834 were largely to blame for the tribe's postremoval troubles. Ultimately, mixed-blood leaders "divided this land in Kansas . . . cut the reservation in half . . . and . . . took allotments again, just as [they] had in Ohio."[2]

These divergent perspectives on the transition from hereditary leaders with village-based authority to the elected officials of the new Shawnee nation illustrate the deep-seated suspicion between villagers after removal. Yet suspicions between villagers were nothing new. It took the arrival of missionaries and the geographic consolidation of the Shawnee people to transform mistrust into concrete political consequences. Indeed, alliances between missionaries and elected leaders ultimately determined who would dominate the new Shawnee nation.

While some Shawnees lost control over their lives since the creation of the Shawnee reservation, others believed that the new order brought lasting benefits to tribal members. There was some truth to this feeling of loss of control. By the middle 1840s, a coalition of Rogerstown and Hog Creek Shawnees became the national leaders of the tribe despite the fact that their combined populations remained a minority of the Shawnees.

Both Draper's and Voegelin's informants described the Kansas period as a time in which tribal leadership roles were turned upside down—an era in which the weak became strong and the strong became weak. Between 1825 and 1833, four major Shawnee bands located in both Missouri and Ohio merged together as a tribe in what is now Kansas.[3] Their long history as independent groups had come to an end. By the mid-1830s, approximately 2,500 Shawnees and another 10,000 of their Indian neighbors north of the Ohio River transformed themselves from autonomous, multiethnic bands into ethnically and politically consolidated nations modeled after the United States.[4] Perhaps no other period in Indian–white relations, save initial contact with Europeans, created such sweeping cultural and political changes among the Algonquian-speaking tribes east of the Mississippi. The reservation system imposed tightly controlled national regimes upon the removed tribes. In the Indian Territory, sharply defined tribal boundaries fueled the political consolidation of the emigrant tribes. In this way, reservations forced the emigrant tribes to dismantle both their traditional systems of governance and their alliances with members of other tribes and bands. National governments emerged under pressure from Americans who worked with a handful of elites in each tribe to undermine traditional leaders and the multiethnic villages that had sustained them. Dependent now on government annuity payments, the Shawnees and their neighbors became embroiled in power struggles between villagers who aspired to become national leaders.

Life on a united tribal reservation at the opening of the western Plains, the first such unification of the Shawnee people since the early seventeenth century, revealed the wide disagreements between tribal members. After removing to Indian Territory, Shawnee villagers became part of a nation that, for most Shawnees, resulted in a loss of autonomy. Curiously, the beneficiaries of the new, national discourse on the Shawnee reservation came from small, somewhat peripheral villages in both Ohio and Missouri. Spanning the region from modern-day Kansas City to Topeka, Kansas, the 1,600,000-acre reservation became an important site for the emergence of the modern Shawnee people.[5]

Christian missionaries created alternative communities based on denominational affiliation that further complicated relations between tribal members. As Baptist missionary Jotham Meeker put it, "the Shawanoes are more divided among themselves than any other tribe in this region. They are three bands [divisions] the Macochas, Piquas, and Chillicothes [Maykujay, Piqua, Chillicothe]—are again subdivided into Heathen and Christian parties—and still again into Meth. North Meth. South. Quaker and Baptists." Intensive proselytizing by Meeker and others like him began to rework the divisional and village ties that had structured Shawnee identity before 1830. Not surprisingly, anthropologists associate the Shawnees' transition from descent groups based on the divisions to bilateral, fictive name groups to the second and third decades of the nineteenth century. Jotham Meeker both promoted and witnessed this dramatic change in Shawnee social organization.[6]

Conflicts between the denominations and the Shawnees themselves were commonplace from the beginning of the missionary enterprise on the reservation. As the advanced guard of American expansion, missionaries did not simply arrive and dictate the terms of membership, cultural practices, and the possibilities for survival to a defeated people. The negotiation of power within these imported communities of faith was neither one-sided nor predictable. However, evangelical Christianity became an important part

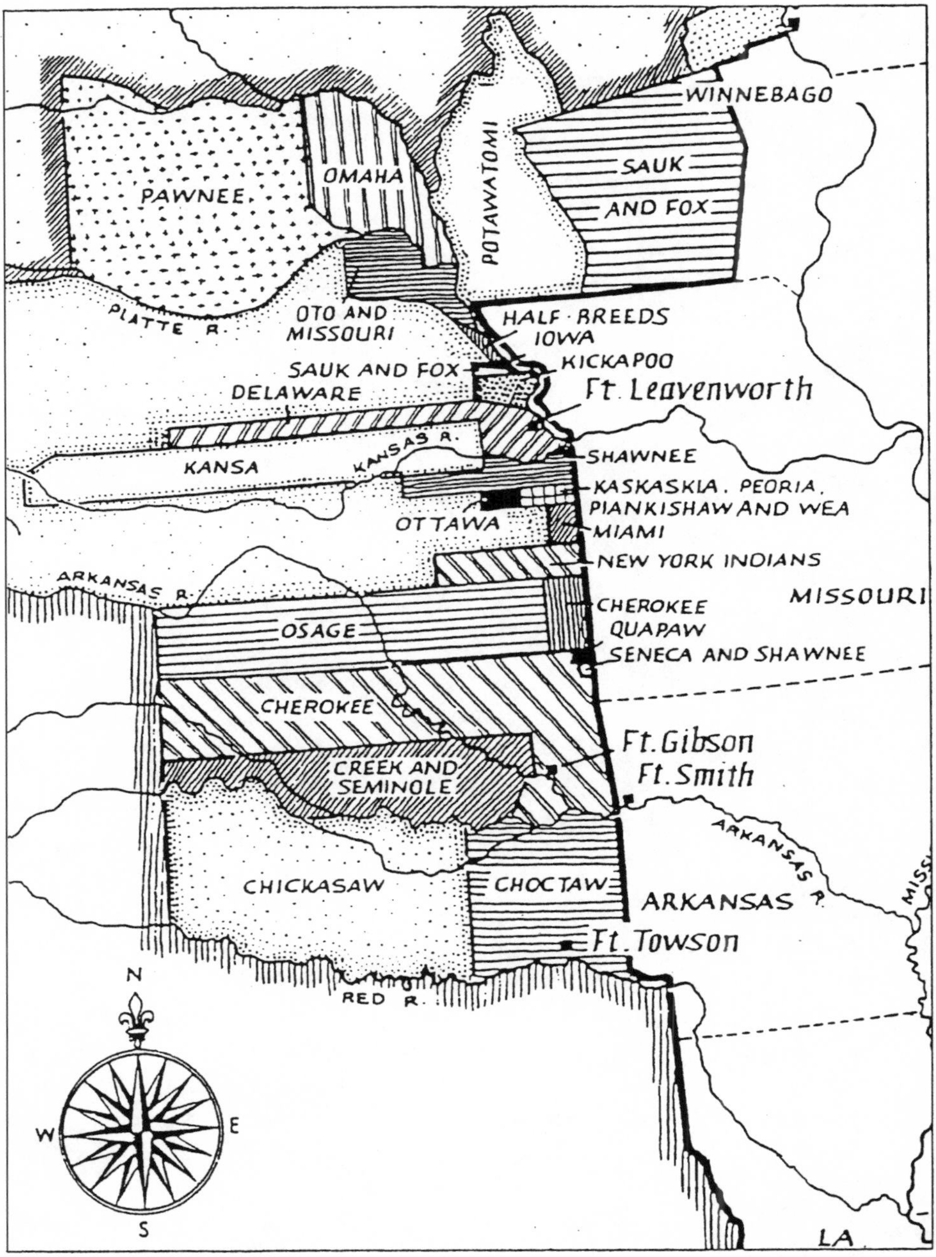

"The Permanent Indian Frontier in 1840." From Ralph K. Andrist, *The Long Death: The Last Days of the Plains Indians.*

of many Shawnee peoples' lives. New leaders emerged as they moved from prominence in evangelical communities of faith to secular positions within the new tribal government.

Baptist and Methodist missionaries created institutions and leadership roles that were unlike those developed by the Quaker missionaries who had defined Shawnee relations with Christianity between 1807 and 1830. Quakers believed that the war for Indian souls took place in the fields and behind the loom rather than in the emotion-filled benches of a camp meeting or the fiery rhetoric of a charismatic preacher behind the pulpit. Since baptism and conversion were not central to Quakerism, their missionaries did not separate believers from nonbelievers. Consequently, hereditary leadership based on village and divisional affiliation remained intact under the Quakers.[7]

In contrast, evangelicals proselytized among prominent men and their families. After achieving some notable converts, missionaries used the assistance of these Shawnees to expand their reach among tribal members. Some leaders assisted the missionaries by working as preachers, exhorters, assistants, and interpreters. Shawnees fluent in English were particularly useful, as they translated their religious messages verbally and in print form. Because so few Shawnees could read and write English in the third decade of the nineteenth century, this meant that some children of hereditary leaders, such as John and William Perry of Wapakoneta, Ohio, now shared power with the children of mixed marriages such as Lewis Rogers of Rogerstown. Children educated at boarding schools and by reservation missionaries came from families at the vanguard of acculturation. In this way, children raised on cultural compromise and collaboration with Americans became singularly attractive to government agents and missionaries as adults.

The consolidation of Shawnee villages on the reservation set up a competition between village chiefs whose roads to power varied tremendously. Some leaders established themselves through exploits in war while others achieved recognition through hereditary status based on their divisional affiliation. However, neither accomplishments in war nor heredity determined who should lead on the reservation. Shawnee chiefs were drawn from an elite class of intermediaries, men who had dual recognition in both American and Shawnee circles. Those without access to American resources were not able to maintain their privileged positions, regardless of their exploits prior to removal.[8]

Intermediary chiefs enhanced their status among both American bureaucrats and philanthropists, as well as other Shawnees, by hosting biweekly religious services. Belle Greene, daughter of the Shawnee Methodist missionary Jesse Greene, recalled that the Shawnees in attendance at these services "would arise in the congregation and testify." Another Methodist missionary believed that the Shawnees "were especially gifted in prayer and exhortation."[9] Christian Shawnees became central to missionary efforts. But their strengths and aptitudes were culturally defined, revealing the heavy hand played by Americans in shaping both political and religious affairs.

Missionaries to the Shawnees described a shared religious world. Perhaps unwittingly, Baptist and Methodist missionaries established channels of communication that provided the Shawnee people with a platform on which they could ask, answer, and argue about fundamental questions regarding the tribe's past, present, and future. At a time when most Shawnees were unfamiliar, even unknown, to the majority of their kinsmen after many years of separation, the institutions and rhetoric of Christianity provided a means for strangers to communicate. In exhorting kinsmen to join the faith at a camp meeting, in testifying to one's sinful existence, or even in translating an American preacher's message, Christian institutions initiated a national conversation.

The practice of Christianity provided the Shawnees with a chance to live their religion in new ways. As historian David Hall writes, religion "is shaped and experienced in the interplay among venues of everyday experience . . . in the necessary and mutually transforming exchanges between religious authorities and the broader communities of practitioners." Baptists and Methodists, in particular, made numerous concessions to their Native congregants between 1830 and 1870, building a faith reflective of the power struggles within Shawnee society even as they transformed the tribe's value system.[10]

Missionaries opened doors of communication previously closed to many Shawnees and their white neighbors, but they also did their best to marginalize those who refused to participate. Equipped with close ties to missionaries, new tribal leaders filled dual roles as both political and religious specialists. Charles Blue Jacket inherited the rights of a Piqua war chief through his father. Once on the reservation, Blue Jacket used his lineage and his family history to become a national leader. His father, George Blue Jacket, was born in 1781, the fourth child of a union between the famous trader and warrior Blue Jacket and an unnamed métis woman whose father was a French trader. Born in Michigan in 1817, Charles Blue Jacket was educated by missionaries near Fort Meigs (modern-day Toledo, Ohio) and then by the Quakers at Wapakoneta. He came to Kansas as a teenager and went on to become both a Methodist minister and head chief of the Shawnee nation. He often hosted young American missionaries in their initial weeks on the reservation. In this way, Blue Jacket's home became a focal point of both Shawnee and Methodist affairs.[11]

Another government chief of the Shawnees, Joseph Parks, used his knowledge of Shawnee life and his connections with American officials to become an important businessman, tribal leader, and member of the Methodist Church. Unlike Blue Jacket, Parks lacked a hereditary right to power. Some even doubted that he was Shawnee. Methodist missionary J. J. Lutz believed that Parks "was a half-breed, and a prominent character among the Shawnees." In contrast, the man who raised him for a time, none other than Lewis Cass, claimed that "he was a pure white man and had been captured by the Indians when very young. But among the Shawnees he claimed to be of Shawnee extraction, and the claim was universally acknowledged." His Shawnee contemporaries held that he had fought with the Americans in the Battle of the Thames, where Tecumseh died, in 1813. Regardless of these conflicting views on his identity, it is clear that Parks used his connections with the Cass family and the Shawnees to work as their tribal interpreter. He then became the Hog Creek Shawnees' removal agent and gradually gained enough status to work as both a trader and a chief until his death in 1859. Parks became quite wealthy in the process. He owned slaves, had a well-improved farm with an elegant, well-furnished brick house, and was married to a Wyandot woman.[12]

Methodist missionaries to the Shawnees contributed to the ascension of men such as Blue Jacket and Parks. Previously insignificant men, along with a handful of hereditary leaders, collaborated with missionaries and enhanced their long-standing reputations as intermediaries. Some Shawnees supported these new leaders because they had access to resources and individuals that became essential to survival as the tribe became increasingly dependent on the United States. Conversely, established and respected families that had dominated the last thirty years of Shawnee life on a national scale—the families of Black Hoof, Perry, and Tecumseh—witnessed the erosion of their influence.

Missionaries depended on these tribal leaders because they could deny the use of money from their school fund and pressure parents to withdraw their children from mission schools. Tribal leaders throughout Indian Territory expected would-be missionaries to consult with them prior to their arrival. Most missionaries did not risk establishing a mission until a formal request had been made. The first such request from the Shawnees came in July 1830, when the Rogerstown Shawnees asked their subagent, George Vashon, to write to "Jesse Greene, presiding elder of the Methodist Episcopal Church, asking that a missionary be sent to them." Later that summer, Thomas Johnson and Alexander McCallister met the Rogerstown villagers, who agreed to host a Methodist mission. Johnson and McCallister began the mission later that November.[13]

Lewis Rogers, "Thomas Johnson's great friend," was pleased to see Johnson and McCallister arrive. Family connections, and a long history of parallel migrations, contributed to their success. Both Johnson and McCallister migrated from Kentucky to Missouri, where they lived among other upland southerners, including Stephen Ruddell. The twenty-year-old Johnson arrived in Missouri at the apex of Shawnee displacement—part of the wave of settlers who forced the Shawnees from their Spanish land grant near Cape Girardeau. He became a Methodist minister in 1826, and started out as a circuit rider in the Arkansas and Missouri back country. Johnson's traveling ministry brought him into regular contact with the Shawnees, Delawares, Kickapoos, and their American neighbors until 1830, when he married another former Kentuckian, Sarah Davis. Like so many others, Sarah Davis's family migrated from Kentucky soon after the War of 1812. While in Kentucky, her mother's cousin, Stephen Ruddell, had been a captive of the Shawnees. After rejoining his family in 1795, he shared stories with Sarah Davis and other members of his family about his adoptive brothers, Tecumseh and Tenskwatawa.[14]

Daniel Morgan Boone, like his father, the famous frontiersman, also had extensive contact with the Shawnees and their Indian neighbors in Missouri. The younger Boone encouraged his brother-in-law, Alexander McCallister, "to get in their [*sic*] immediately and secure that fund," because the Shawnees "have a considerable sum of money set apart to support schools." Treaty stipulations, coupled with the annual congressional appropriation known as the Civilization Fund, devoted tribal monies toward schools run by missionaries. Johnson and McCallister arrived soon thereafter and gained control of the money devoted to Shawnee education. Both men owed their early successes to the curious nexus of ambition, kinship, and cultural ties between Indians and Americans on the frontier. On the trans-Mississippi frontier, both conquest and conversion were family affairs.[15]

Between Rogers's initial request in July 1830, and Johnson's arrival later that November, the Baptist missionary Isaac McCoy also met with Shawnee leaders. Like Johnson, McCoy spent the majority of his life living on the edges of white settlement. Born in 1784 in western Pennsylvania, McCoy and his family migrated to Kentucky in 1789 and homesteaded near Louisville, only to move across the Ohio River soon thereafter. After a brief and relatively unsuccessful period of proselytizing at Silver Creek in Indiana Territory, McCoy married sixteen-year-old Sarah Polke and inaugurated his career as a Baptist minister at the age of nineteen.[16]

In 1816, the thirty-two-year-old Baptist minister left several short-lived appointments at southern Indiana congregations to begin his work as a missionary. The Baptist Board of Missions assigned McCoy the task of establishing a mission among the tribes inhabiting northern Illinois, Indiana, and southern Michigan. More than a decade of mediocre results among the Potawatomi, Ottawa, and Miami tribes led McCoy to believe that "the contaminating influence of both the scum and the dregs" of frontier society had inhibited the Indians under his charge from progressing toward civilization. As McCoy saw it, the Indians of the Old Northwest occupied a declining economic and cultural position in which civilization was an impossibility and "indulging such habits of savage life as made it tolerable" was also denied them. This interpretation of the "Indian problem" led McCoy into an alliance with President Andrew Jackson and other advocates of removal in the 1820s. McCoy soon became a respected speaker on Indian reform. He dreamed of tying the tribes of the Old Northwest to a pan-Indian state. National Indian governments were a vital stepping-stone to this ultimate goal.[17] McCoy thus helped both to create and implement Jacksonian Indian policy, and he tested these reforms on the Algonquian tribes.

McCoy clearly favored the Missouri Shawnees, believing that "through them [the Rogerstown Shawnees] . . . access could be obtained to the main body of the nation."[18] But the agreement between Johnson and the Rogerstown Shawnees forced McCoy to shift his attention toward Perry, Cornstalk, Tenskwatawa, and the Ohio Shawnees who had arrived several years prior to the main contingent of their Ohio kinsmen. McCoy was distraught at the prospect of establishing a mission among Perry and Cornstalk's people, due in part to their association with the Shawnee Prophet. He believed that their people "felt little desire for schools, and still less to hear preaching." Lamenting his failure to win the favor of the Rogerstown Shawnees, McCoy confided in his autobiography that he "felt a disappointment which I could not remedy."[19]

With the help of Charles Blue Jacket and Joseph Parks, the Methodist missionaries soon became influential enough to cause problems for their rivals. John Campbell, the Shawnee subagent, was a Baptist with more than twenty years' experience as an Indian agent and disliked Johnson from the start. The Methodist missionary's obvious quest for power threatened Campbell's influence over the tribe. William Gordon, a disbursing agent for the Indian department in the West, had the relationship between Thomas Johnson and John Campbell in mind in a letter he composed to William Clark. He wrote that subagents were frequently hassled by missionaries and that when "they consist of different denominations the harmony and good feeling of the Indians have been very injuriously affected." In his defense, Campbell complained that the Rogerstown Shawnees were "entirely under the influence of Mr. Thomas Johnson."[20]

In May 1833, Campbell made the mistake of getting involved in the competition between the missionaries. Earlier that year, several Shawnee and Delaware families from Ohio approached the subagent for advice concerning the best mission school for their children. According to a letter of self-defense filed with Clark months later, Campbell recommended the Baptist school. He admitted that "if this is a crime, I am guilty."[21]

Such partisan recommendations were nothing new to the Indian department. Recognizing this, Johnson accused Campbell of drunkenness and of deliberately interfering with all philanthropic pursuits among the tribe. Campbell admitted to being a daily drinker, but claimed that he never allowed alcohol to interfere with his duties. Nevertheless, the charges caught the attention of Campbell's superior, Richard Cummins, who supervised the subagents of the Indian Territory from Fort Leavenworth, less than thirty miles from the Shawnee subagency. But Cummins was also a Methodist. This spelled trouble for the subagent, whom Cummins described as "an old man—very ineffective [and] not able to render much assistance." William Clark agreed with Cummins' assessment. By July 1833, Campbell had been dismissed.[22]

According to the Ohio Shawnees, Campbell's removal had little to do with either the subagent's drinking habits or the inefficiency of the Indian department. John Perry, the younger Black Hoof, and the Wapakoneta Shawnees believed that Johnson's charges against Campbell were part of a premeditated attempt to extend Methodist influence over the Ohio Shawnees. In a letter to Clark, Perry claimed that Johnson "don't want anybody to have schools but himself amongst all our brothers the redskins." Campbell's dismissal was a direct affront to the independence of the Wapakoneta Shawnees, who feared the interference of a Missouri Shawnee–Methodist coalition on the reservation. Perry reaffirmed the separate status of the Ohio and Missouri villages, writing that "We gave him [Johnson] leave to have a school for our friend Fish [a Rogerstown Shawnee], but we don't want him to meddle himself with our party."[23]

Missionaries thus became associated with either Ohio or Missouri Shawnees. Their presence often exacerbated the tension between Shawnee villages, particularly as religious affiliations determined access to scarce resources. The contest for power in the vacuum left by the elder Black Hoof's death became even more extreme after tribal consolidation in Indian Territory. Leaders who had guided their villages into alliances with other tribes and accommodation with Americans were growing old and losing influence to younger leaders more interested in tribal integrity and "national" decision-making. Chronic economic difficulties also taxed the Shawnees. Having sold their agricultural implements for next to nothing prior to removal, and often robbed of what remained, the Shawnees had little alternative but to wait for the promised federal funds to arrive. By 1834, tribesmen from Ohio and Missouri were losing their patience. The Wapakoneta Shawnees had waited three years for their annuity payments to begin. And the Rogerstown Shawnees wondered if they would ever see the benefits guaranteed them in their 1825 treaty.[24]

The tribe's situation was desperate. Without plows, oxen, and money for seed, most Shawnees hoped that Johnson and McCoy would help them through the hard times, yet neither missionary society possessed the capital necessary to meet the tribe's needs. During the winter of 1830–1831, the missionary society of the Methodist Episcopal Church provided just $600 to McCallister and Johnson for the expense of establishing a mission. In September 1832, the Missouri Methodist Conference delivered an additional $4,800 for the missions within the bounds of their conference. In contrast, the American Baptist Home Missionary Society in Boston refused to allocate funds for secular institutions and equipment, including boarding schools, model farms, plows, food, and clothing. Board members believed that McCoy's primary duty was conversion, not material assistance. While many Baptist missionaries eventually established small farms on the reservation, they remained subsistence farmers rather than large-scale producers capable of feeding hundreds of Indian children, as the Methodists under Thomas Johnson intended.[25]

In the early years of the reservation, Johnson, McCoy, and the Fort Leavenworth agent, Richard Cummins, alienated themselves from the vast majority of Shawnees. Most of the tribe was excluded from power by new leaders allied with Johnson, who often cut down reservation timber along the Kansas River without consulting those outside Methodist circles. Timber sales were often the only source of capital for destitute families in the lean years following removal. Moreover, Richard Cummins refused to honor the Shawnees' choice for a mill site in 1834. The Fort Leavenworth agent rejected their choice in spite of the tribe's "full confidence in their own judgement" and the knowledge that the Shawnees "will be very much displeased if their wishes are not complied with." Cummins's ability to enhance the prestige of Shawnee leaders and then to veto their decisions undermined the authority of the intermediary chiefs. Few Shawnees trusted them. For the first time in Shawnee history, it became difficult, if not impossible, for ordinary Shawnees to discern the line between the tribal leaders and their American benefactors.[26]

The outright neglect of treaty responsibilities further complicated the Americans' hunger for credibility. Since the 1790s, most Shawnees had supported themselves without government assistance. And those who did accept government funds received them from agents such as John Johnston and Quaker missionaries such as Thomas Harvey. Moreover, Quaker missionaries had often mediated disputes between the tribe and the federal government. Still more Shawnees traded with Frenchmen such as Pierre Menard and Louis Lorimier, often using them as tribal advocates. Both the French and the Quakers worked as cultural brokers and provided much-needed economic assistance. In Indian Territory, Americans attempted to fill the void left by their absence. Yet acrimony between men such as Johnson and McCoy and an unwillingness to meet the direct needs of the tribe nearly jeopardized the missionary stations between 1833 and 1834.[27]

Disputes between the Shawnees and the Americans revealed the extent to which allied evangelicals and government officials were able to arrive and dictate the terms of survival. The Shawnees' deep attachment to their language, for example, worked against the civilizing mission as Thomas Johnson understood it. He believed that English-language instruction should be used exclusively at the Methodist schools. The Baptists offered an alternative, and increased the pressure on Johnson when Baptist missionary Jotham Meeker arrived, carrying with him a printing press and an earnest desire to translate Native languages into script. Soon after his arrival, Meeker began distributing Shawnee-language publications, including a tribal newspaper, the *Shuwaunowe Kesauthwau (Shawnee Sun)*.[28]

Shawnees took advantage of the rivalry between the Methodists and Baptists to preserve cherished cultural traditions. Controversy surrounding Shawnee-language instruction became one flash point of the contest between the Shawnees and missionaries. Meeker's translation of Shawnee into script met with widespread approval, and tribal leaders worked hard to ensure that Shawnee-language instruction would take place at all of the mission schools. Baptist missionary Ira Blanchard recalled that the Shawnees told Johnson that "if the books were shut out from [the Indians'] society [the Methodists] were too." After the council's vote, Johnson reached an agreement with Meeker for the publication of Methodist hymns in the Shawnee language.[29]

Problems remained in spite of these adjustments, and the Methodists, Baptists, and Quakers gathered together later that summer with the goal of saving their missions from dissolution. Few adult Shawnees attended their religious services, and those who did regularly moved between denominations. Missionaries chastised Shawnees who refused to remain loyal to their church. However, the Methodists and Baptists, in particular, encouraged these shifts in church membership by proselytizing the others' members.[30] Mixed messages over church attendance also contributed to rising tensions.

The missionaries' tenuous alliance with Shawnee leaders became even more unsteady in October 1834, when non-Christian Shawnees, approximately 80 percent of the population, rebelled against Americans and called for their expulsion from tribal lands. Leaders of the independence movement demanded that the newly appointed subagent, Marston Clark, force "all the Indians [from other tribes] and missionaries settled on their land" from the reservation. The Shawnees hoped to liberate themselves from the interlopers among them. Independence-minded Shawnees also asked the federal government to unite the Shawnee people by consolidating the Absentee Shawnees and the Seneca Shawnees on the reservation. Once again, Shawnees struggled for self-government, free from the domination of men such as Isaac McCoy, Richard Cummins, Thomas Johnson, and Joseph Parks.[31]

The scope of Shawnee resistance to missionaries and the new tribal government will never be fully known. Few commentaries on the nature and meaning of discontent on the reservation survive in the documentary record, illustrating the extent to which the new power elite maintained their dominant positions by controlling the flow of information between the Shawnees and the Americans to the east. Marston Clark and Isaac McCoy used their authority as dictatorial intermediaries to downplay both the sincerity of the Shawnees' demands and the number of those involved. McCoy wrote to the commissioner of Indian affairs and explained that "excepting the party of the Shawanoe prophet, the dissatisfaction is limited to some six or eight persons, and even these I believe have been prompted by white men to say."[32] Shawnee intermediaries failed to identify the "dissatisfied" party's white coconspirators, revealing the oft-used tactic of blaming Indian dissent on the deleterious influence of morally suspect American settlers. McCoy and his allies thus used the incident to support their contention that the cultural quarantine between Indians and Americans was not strong enough. But at another level, their sweeping assertions reveal just how easily Americans swept aside the real concerns of their critics.

Americans dismissed the movement as the work of a few disaffected tribesmen. In this way, American philanthropists made sense of Shawnee behavior for eastern audiences that were both unwilling and unable to experience the Indian Territory firsthand. Missionaries to the Shawnees were acutely aware of their privileged viewpoint and used their "knowledge of geographically distant phenomena" to enhance their power. Evangelicals enhanced their own personal prestige as they moved from American settlements to places and people that were becoming increasingly strange and alien to Americans east of the Mississippi. McCoy and Johnson ensured that the Shawnees could not personally articulate their complaints to federal officials. In his "Address to Philanthropists," McCoy claimed that "these people cannot present themselves before you; I am here among them, in sight of their wants, and witnessing their readiness to avail themselves of offered assistance."[33]

McCoy's deft use of the Shawnee Prophet as the isolated author of Shawnee dissent on the reservation also made it easier for federal officials to ignore the tribe's demands. The Baptist missionary equated honoring the entreaties of Shawnee dissenters with conceding defeat to men like the Prophet—individuals long since subjugated in the War of 1812. Tenskwatawa's symbolic value as the representative of Indian resistance to American expansion and Christianity highlighted both the difficulty of the missionary enterprise and enhanced McCoy's own image as a missionary hero. For more than thirty years, Americans had described their interaction with the Prophet as a kind of morality play in which the pious Christian challenged the ignoble, degraded savage. J. A. Chute, a doctor sent to the Prophet by the Baptists in November 1836 described Tenskwatawa as a man "who hated civilization." Upon entering the Prophet's cabin, Chute discovered "a form emaciated in the extreme, but the broad proportions of which indicated that it had once been the seat of great strength."[34]

In 1832, the famous artist George Catlin completed a portrait of the Prophet that reinforced these literary assessments of the man as a militant opponent of American civilization. Catlin's painting reflects Tenskwatawa's role in the Battle of Tippecanoe rather than his more recent incarnation as Lewis Cass's ally and removal advocate. In the journal he kept of their meeting, Catlin wrote that Tenskwatawa was "quite equal in his medicine and mysteries, to what his brother was in arms; he was blind in his left eye, and in his right hand he was holding his '*medicine fire,*' and his '*sacred string of beans,*' in the other."[35] Both McCoy and Catlin utilized the historical memory of the Prophet's actions to spark interest in their work. More important, they emphasized the differences between themselves and the Prophet instead of their common interest in creating a new political culture on the Shawnee reservation. Catlin, McCoy, and other Americans searched for their Indian adversaries from an earlier time, even when these old rivals were out of favor with their own people. Interestingly, Catlin did not ask Lewis Rogers, Paschal Fish, the younger Blackhoof, John Perry, Charles Blue Jacket, or Joseph Parks to pose for him. Catlin painted the Shawnee Prophet and two leaders from Arkansas once affiliated with the Absentee Shawnees: Paithuckoosaw and Lailawsekah. Reservation chiefs did not interest him.[36]

Missionaries avoided expulsion from the Shawnee reservation, but the revolt forced Americans on tribal lands to adopt an even more flexible cultural and political stance toward the tribe. Both the Shawnees and the Americans lived in a parochial, somewhat isolated world. Local concerns and intertribal relations rather than national issues continued to drive Shawnee decisions. Travel was often limited by heavy rainfall or a severe cold spell. And it often took three to four weeks for communications to reach Washington, D.C., from the Indian Territory. Shawnee intermediaries used these realities to their advantage and often threatened to withhold Shawnee children and their parents from the missions if the Americans refused to listen to their demands. But the revolt's failure also demonstrated that the Shawnees' pursuit of autonomy from colonial powers would become increasingly difficult in the years ahead.

Following the 1834 revolt and the successful recruitment of new missionaries, McCoy assumed a more administrative presence on the reservation. A new crop of Baptist missionaries initiated a grassroots approach to converting the Shawnees. Jotham Meeker and Francis Barker spoke with Shawnees individually and met with their families in church services held at Shawnee homes. Their efforts among Shawnees from various social classes and geographic backgrounds won back the respect of many Shawnees after the initial years of turmoil and confusion.

Jotham Meeker was the first such missionary to adopt a more conciliatory stance toward tribal leaders. A native of Cincinnati, Meeker ran the Shawnee Baptist mission from 1833 to 1837. Unlike McCoy, Meeker measured his success in the smaller world of his immediate surroundings. His mission concerned him far more than federal policies or border politics. A child of one of the missionaries recalled that "when an Indian first commenced to plow, he would go with him and hold the plow, and show him how to manage it. He would often go and work with an Indian for hours." After a day of shared labor, Meeker "would sit down to rest, taking that opportunity to instruct the Indian in some matter of religion or morality." In nearly all of his activities, including the printing of Shawnee-language materials, Meeker worked with the Shawnees he hoped to convert. His diary and other accounts of his life describe a man who labored longer in the fields than in the pulpit. Meeker epitomized "the farmer-preacher;" a man who "earned his living as a farmer but who—in addition—took the lead in organizing a church and proclaiming a social gospel."[37]

Meeker inaugurated a new era of collaboration with the Shawnees. Beginning in the summer of 1834, Meeker preached to the Shawnees every one to three weeks. Ohio Shawnees such as William Barnett, Blackfeather, William Parks, Wawalapea, and Henry Blue Jacket hosted these Baptist religious services and a school associated with them. Most of the Shawnee Baptists were Piqua and Maykujay Shawnees who had migrated with John Perry and the Wapakoneta Shawnees in 1827. William Parks, Henry Blue Jacket, and many other members of this group were looked down upon by their well-known Ohio brothers who were generally allied with the Methodists. The fifteen to twenty-five Shawnees who usually attended Baptist religious meetings became the nucleus of Shawnee opposition to the increasingly formidable Methodist-Shawnee alliance on the reservation. Hosting Baptist services enhanced the prestige of opposition leaders and the men Meeker employed to interpret for the missionaries. Following these sermons, one of the tribal leaders, typically the Shawnee war chief Blackfeather, addressed the congregants in the Shawnee language. Meeker based the success of the religious services on the emotional engagement of those in attendance. After one service in December 1834, Meeker, always a master of understatement, noted that ". . . after I had spoken Blackfeather addressed the Inds. with warmth."[38]

Many Shawnees were grateful to Meeker for translating the Shawnee language into script and for publishing Shawnee-language resources, including the tribal newspaper. Printing Shawnee-language materials provided a service to both believers and nonbelievers who understood that the illiteracy of tribal leaders made them vulnerable to predatory traders and corrupt government agents. In 1838, the unnamed "Chiefs, Counsellors, Headmen" of the Shawnees admitted as much in a congressional deposition regarding one trader's bogus claim against the tribe. According to the Shawnee leaders, "We have borne many impositions because we are ignorant and illiterate. This and other difficulties would not have happened respecting our late treaty, if we had fairly understood everything."[39] Meeker's orthography answered an immediate need for most Shawnees who recognized the growing necessity of negotiation with anonymous government officials. The Baptists' Shawnee-language work also cultivated a new base of potential converts, a crucial move designed to increase numbers at the thinly supported Shawnee Baptist mission.

Translation and printing projects created a number of leadership roles for the Shawnees and enhanced the partnership between Meeker and his supporters. Joseph DeShane, an Ohio Shawnee, worked closely with Meeker, translating and writing hymns in the Shawnee language. DeShane also contributed regularly to the *Shawnee Sun*.[40] Within three years of his arrival, Meeker's efforts had translated, quite literally, into a core group of Shawnee supporters, led by Blackfeather and DeShane. Meeker's Shawnee advocates performed a host of religious and secular duties—helping the Baptists tailor both a palatable religious message and essential services for their kinsmen.

Blackfeather was the most important supporter of the Baptist mission on the Shawnee reservation. The self-proclaimed war chief and successor of Tecumseh hoped to parlay his hereditary powers into an esteemed position on the reservation. Meeker and Barker recognized Blackfeather's status in the tribe and attempted to lead the Piqua war chief to the anxious bench and conversion. Tireless evangelizers that they were, the missionaries chronicled their efforts for more than eleven years in the *American Baptist Magazine*. To their dismay, Blackfeather remained uninterested despite the fact that he had hosted religious meetings and spoke to his kinsmen regarding the virtues of Christianity since the early years of the mission. Baptist missionaries found some consolation in the fact that a highly regarded Shawnee had expressed interest in their message. Johnston Lykins, McCoy's son-in-law, noted that "attention to religious worship has greatly increased since the development of Capt. Blackfeather's views." By 1835, the Baptists could only boast a total of eight converts between a united Shawnee-Delaware church. Throughout the 1830s, the Shawnees and their neighbors continued to regard the evangelicals as more of a curiosity than a serious religious and cultural alternative to their own ways. Blackfeather's ambivalence regarding full membership in the Baptist church also indicates that many Shawnees did not regard tribal rituals and evangelical Christianity as mutually exclusive religious systems.[41]

Missionary societies were not the only means of obtaining status on the reservation. Like generations of men before them, some Shawnees continued warrior traditions by fighting with the Americans against their varied enemies. Between 1835 and 1842, federal troops attempted to remove by force a diverse agglomeration of Yuchis, Tallapoosas, and Spanish Indians from the Florida peninsula. The vast majority of these tribes refused to abide by the removal agreement, and the Second Seminole War resulted. But the Seminoles, who were expert at guerrilla tactics in the swamps, outmatched most American troops. Consequently, General Thomas Jesup asked the secretary of war to recruit one thousand "northern Indians," including the Shawnees, Delawares, and Kickapoos, to assist them. In response, Joseph Parks organized and led a combined detachment of eighty-four Hog Creek and Rogerstown Shawnees to Florida. Some Wapakoneta Shawnees traveled to Florida as well between 1837 and 1838. However, the vast majority of the men were from small, relatively insignificant preremoval villages. Internal rivalries between Shawnee villages clearly played a role in the decision either to remain at home or fight in Florida. Large numbers of Missouri Shawnees, as well as Tecumseh's former allies, refused to go to war against the Seminoles because of years of cooperation and kinship ties between them. Shawnees from New Madrid, Missouri, had established villages with the Seminoles' Muscogulge relatives in the 1820s. Close connections also existed between Tecumseh's family and tribesmen from Alabama, including Osceola, the best-known Seminole opponent of American designs in Florida.[42]

Throughout the 1830s, John Perry, Cornstalk, and the Ohio Shawnee migrants from 1827 pressed Shawnees in Texas and Oklahoma to leave the Red River country and join them on the reservation. Shawnee advocates of consolidation hoped that their southern relatives might counterbalance the strength of the Hog Creek and Rogerstown villagers. Tenskwatawa and Perry had sent diplomats to the Red River ever since their removal to the Indian Territory. Some Absentee Shawnees were close relatives of the Prophet and other survivors of the Battle of Tippecanoe. In a letter to William Clark, John Perry informed the St. Louis superintendent that ". . . so desirous are we to have all the Shawnee again re-united as one nation . . . that we would cheerfully relinquish to those who might join us, our present improvements, for a moderate remuneration, and settle ourselves, on other parts of the tract." Unwilling to reside on what they considered "refuse land," most Absentee Shawnees rejected their overtures.[43]

Shawnee participants in the Second Seminole War were clearly concerned about the prospect of competing for land and influence with a larger number of Shawnees from the south. Isaac McCoy reported that Captain Parks and his men complained about "mischievous Indians at the council who might take advantage" of their absence. Shawnees sent to fight in Florida worried about challenges to their authority, believing that "some unfriendly design exists in the south" among those Shawnees who planned on returning to the reservation. In August 1838, Shawnee combatants in the Second Seminole War pleaded with government officials for the money owed them when they returned to the reservation. They rightly feared that assets from an additional land sale to the Absentee Shawnees might diminish their own ability to redistribute resources to their supporters.[44]

Some Absentee Shawnees did ultimately concede to Perry and Cornstalk's diplomatic forays and returned to the reservation. In July 1838, thirty Shawnees led by Tecumseh's son arrived from the Arkansas River. However, the vast majority, estimated at between 400 and 1,000 people, remained in Texas and Oklahoma. Stephen F. Austin's diplomacy allowed for amicable relations between American settlers and the emigrant tribes since he had become an empresario in 1823. Yet this all changed after the election of Mirabeau Lamar as president of the Republic of Texas in December 1838. Lamar considered the Absentee Shawnees to be spies of the Mexican government and, as such, waged war against John Linney of the Shawnees and Bowles of the Cherokees between January and August 1839. War with Texas forced many Shawnees, including Lailawsekah, the aged chief formerly from Cape Girardeau, to concede that they would live on the Shawnee reservation "and expect to remain on it as long as our God will let us live." Most Absentee Shawnees understood that removal to the Shawnee reservation would result in their diminished status within the tribe and would force them to live as neighbors with men and women they no longer recognized as kin. Resettlement among the western Cherokees and their Delaware and Kickapoo neighbors seemed a better alternative for most of the Absentee Shawnees.[45]

Shawnee–missionary partnerships became outlets for those with and without power, and reflected stark differences between Shawnee villages. The vast majority of the Shawnees were not interested in the abandonment of their traditional religious practices. Nevertheless, Baptists and Methodists, in particular, came to represent dispossessed traditionalists. Non-Christian Shawnees remained a mystery to most Americans. Missionaries relied on Christian Shawnees to make sense of traditional Shawnee culture for them. As such, Christian accommodationists became spokespersons for those without power. Conversely, dispossessed traditionalists became wedded to the various missions even as they rejected the call for conversion. Visiting Shawnee orphans at the Quaker mission, plowing a field with kin associated with Meeker and the Baptists, and obtaining much-needed supplies at the Methodist mission brought these less well-known Shawnees into intermittent contact with missionaries. Both Americans and their tribal intermediaries controlled information and material necessities. As a result, contact with them was unavoidable. While villagers such as the Absentee Shawnees did not concede their souls to missionaries, they did recognize their importance to life on the reservation.

New communities of faith encouraged the redefinition of Shawnee villages. Shawnee Baptists had an important role in determining the eligibility of prospective members. It was clear that Baptist missionaries were content with their grassroots approach to conversion. Meeker often revealed the debates over membership between congregants and missionaries in his journal. In December 1841, Meeker wrote that "three Shawanoes present themselves for membership. Their cases were postponed." Meeker went on to say that he spent the evening "with the brethren in further examining them." Achieving membership in a church often undermined the boundaries associated with village and divisional identities. Robert Simerwell, an ally of McCoy and a fellow Baptist missionary, reported that two Shawnees interested in joining the church "will have an opportunity to talk with the brethren." These conversations stressed Christian principles as much as preremoval identities. As such, Shawnees and missionaries cocreated new religious communities on the reservation.[46]

The familiar, even informal atmosphere of Shawnee-language services attracted both the curious and those sincerely interested in conversion. Flexible admission standards and congregational polity did not markedly increase the number of Shawnee Baptists. In 1841, they boasted no more than twenty-six members. Blackfeather's case, and the more casual support offered by men like William Parks and Henry Blue Jacket, indicated that many Shawnees attended Baptist meetings inconsistently at best and were generally uninterested in baptism. Those interested in attending the Baptist gatherings did so both to socialize with their kinsmen and listen to the American preachers. Missionaries recognized these mixed motives for attending the meetings. In July 1841, Barker wrote that "at one meeting I was unable to arrive until sometime after the appointed hour. Coming near at length, I heard the sound of prayer and praise in the Indian tongue. On entering, I found the house filled with worshippers." Baptist missionaries could only guess at the meaning of the speeches and songs they heard at these religious meetings. Regardless of their motives, the Baptists had clearly fostered a Shawnee gathering that resembled tribal councils of old and gave many Shawnees an excuse for meeting with their kinsmen.

Acceptance into the Baptist church was predicated on the delivery of a successful testimonial before the church members. In the testimonial, potential converts were required to contrast "their new condition with their prior wretchedness as sinners." To the Shawnees, such public confessions were more than an account of the movement from sin to salvation. Prospective members had to assure the congregation that they had forsaken previously accepted practices such as the easy dissolution of marriage. Devout Shawnees also voted against those Shawnees interested in continued participation in tribal rituals such as the spring and fall Bread Dances. In 1842, Jotham Meeker recorded one example of the required sacrifices that had to be made. In March of that year, an Ottawa woman approached Meeker after engaging in prayer for three months. Meeker wrote that "Kwakubequa gives me her *Medicine Skin,* and wants me to burn it . . . I according consign it to the flames." More often, members were required to give up drunkenness, adultery, and assistance from Native shamans. Evidence of departure from the past—from "tradition" as it was defined by church members—was crucial to every testimonial.[47]

Baptist Congregationalism appealed to those Shawnees in search of local control and independence from nameless government officials. Shawnee, Ottawa, and Potawatomi congregants had an important voice in determining membership. Unlike the Methodists, Baptists were generally opposed to "strict ecclesiasticism." Most Baptists, particularly the Shawnees, were not interested in taking orders regarding membership from church leaders outside of the Indian Territory. According to historian Dickson Bruce, Jr., "every member of the congregation had a hand in administering the congregational discipline."[48]

While Shawnee men occupied leadership positions in the church, Indian women often led their families into relationships with Christian missionaries. Shawnees, like most Woodland tribes, continued to divide the world and its tasks by gender. Women were responsible for events within the community and in and around the village, while men occupied the forest and its attendant tasks, including diplomacy, hunting, and war. Barker and Meeker recognized the importance of female converts and focused much of their daily energies on Indian women. For example, in 1847, a Shawnee woman named Sophie Bigknife "manifested a desire to be baptised and received" as a member of the Shawnee congregation. Four members of the Bigknife family joined the church within three years of her baptism. The same held true for the Dougherty family. In 1847, Silas and Lewis Dougherty joined the church after their mother, Nancy, converted. Congregations typically expanded, or contracted, along family lines, and Shawnee women frequently led the way for their loved ones. Conversion was often a family affair.[49]

In contrast to the Baptists, Methodist missionaries favored a top-down approach that appealed primarily to men from the Hog Creek and Rogerstown villages. Shawnee men associated with the Methodists began to erode the Wapakoneta Shawnees' influence and achieve some recognition for themselves by working as interpreters, exhorters, translators, and blacksmiths for both the federal government and the Methodist mission. The Methodists' plan, which included a more structured church hierarchy and the education of Indian children at manual labor schools, differed greatly from the Baptist operation. By the mid-1830s, prominent men from Hog Creek, Ohio, including Joseph Parks, Charles Blue Jacket, and Tucker joined the Rogerstown Shawnees in embracing the Methodists. Members of this new alliance remained out of favor—Black Hoof, John Perry, and Wawalepea-Shawnees originally from Wapakoneta who now lived at "Perry's Town" on the reservation. Perry and his allies controlled tribal assets and called themselves national leaders for most of the 1830s. Federal treaty annuities were delivered annually to their cluster of cabins.[50]

The Hog Creek and Rogerstown Shawnees challenged the authority of the Wapakoneta Shawnees by expanding their influence on the national council. This shared goal fit nicely with Thomas Johnson's own quest for influence in the Indian Territory. Lewis Rogers had a low opinion of the Wapakoneta Shawnees and their continued ability to maintain power as the spokespersons for the tribe. According to Rogers, "they came rich and found me poor . . . I provided a home for them here [and have] waited to see if my brothers would ever think of me as I did them." As one of the Missouri Shawnee signers of the first removal treaty of 1825, Rogers believed that the Rogerstown Shawnees were the exclusive owners of the reservation. Johnson's aggressiveness, both in Campbell's removal and the expansion of the manual labor school, appealed to the Hog Creek and Rogerstown Shawnees.[51]

Frontier Methodism, with its emphasis on individual conversion and the camp meeting, also appealed to the Shawnee people. Participation in the faith involved a host of religious activities, giving those interested a more active role in Christianity. Camp meetings were extraordinarily egalitarian in terms of the diverse groups such assemblies brought together. The laity exercised significant control over the proceedings. The diversity of the crowds and the shared responsibility for the success of the camp meetings gave those who participated "something painfully lacking in normal social life, a sense of connection and belonging."[52]

In 1835, more than 100 Shawnees, Delawares, and Kickapoos returned to Arrow Rock, the site of the Shawnees' last stop on their journey westward during removal, to attend a religious meeting of the Missouri conference.[53] The Arrow Rock conference marked the inception of a new Shawnee-Methodist community after enduring many years of exclusion and genocide at the hands of their American neighbors. Conferences and camp meetings brought these former enemies into a Christian community that embraced both Indian and white.

On a personal level, missionaries to the Shawnees frequently related the benefits of working with Christian tribesmen. Methodist missionary Nathan Scarritt described working with his translators, including the Hog Creek Shawnees Charles Blue Jacket and Silas Armstrong. He noted their divergent styles and effectiveness, and was generally untroubled by his reliance upon them. The Bible guided Scarritt's understanding of his relationship with the Shawnee interpreters. Paraphrasing Proverbs 27:17, he wrote that "steel sharpens steel, a fire is kindled more easily from two fire-brands, when brought into contact, than from either, when used separately." Interpreters were far more than figures off to the side as a white preacher dominated the crowd. It was common for interpreters to "leave the pulpit and make [their] way through the congregation, scattering the holy fire as [they] went, until almost the entire congregation would be on its feet praising and glorifying God."[54] A synergy existed between interpreters and missionaries in translating the Christian message. Methodist and Baptist missionaries who were not literate in the Shawnee language had to depend on the emotional responses of the audience, and the reliability of their interpreters, to gauge the efficacy of this shared message.

Some Native people, the most famous of whom was Mackinaw Boachman, moved from esteemed positions as traders and trappers to recognized preachers of the Missouri Methodist conference. Accounts of his identity vary somewhat, but evidence suggests that Boachman was born in Mackinaw Island, Michigan, the son of a French fur trader and a Chippewa woman. His diverse ancestry is typical of most American Indian people of the Great Lakes during the early republic. Boachman's mother fled to the Potawatomis when he was a young boy, and he remained with the tribe for the rest of his childhood. He eventually worked as a hunter and trapper with the American Fur Company—a profession that pulled him out of the Great Lakes and into the trans-Mississippi West. Perhaps because of their connections with prominent fur traders, including the Chouteau family, Boachman fell in with the Rogerstown Shawnees. In 1825, he married Henry Rogers's daughter, Polly. Soon thereafter, Boachman converted to Christianity under the guidance of Thomas Johnson. Boachman's daughter, Julia Ann Stinson, later remembered that "after my parents were married my father stopped going with the American Fur Company and interpreted for Mr. Johnson and joined church. After the Pottawatomies came to Kansas the Methodist church sent him to them as an interpreter because he could speak the language."[55]

The Boachman-Rogers family thus became essential to the survival of the mission and ultimately helped the Methodists to expand their reach to neighboring tribes. The Boachman family lived less than a half-mile from the Shawnee Methodist Mission in present-day Wyandotte County, owned two slaves, and made a decent living through the sale of horses and mules to overland migrants. In 1837, when she was seventeen, Annie Boachman married the Reverend Nathan T. Shaler. According to Methodist missionary J. J. Lutz, Annie "had been brought up at the mission, where she cared for Mrs. Johnson's children."[56] Marriage into the Rogers family led Boachman to positions of authority among both the Shawnees and the Methodists.

Boachman stood apart from the majority of the Christian Indians in the Indian Territory because he was the first to become a preacher and missionary at a time when most Indians occupied less prestigious positions in the church hierarchy. As a licensed preacher, by 1843 Boachman held the same position as Nathan Scarritt. The Reverend Joab Spencer, a missionary to the Shawnees in the 1850s and 1860s, credited Boachman with "exhort[ing] his Shawnee friends to forsake paganism and become Christians." Boachman's multitribal upbringing made him particularly useful to the Methodists. His linguistic skills allowed him to preach in several Native languages. Before his death in 1848, Boachman worked as a missionary to the Potawatomis, Sacs, Chippewas, and Weas.[57]

Boachman's Shawnee relatives through marriage, including Lewis Rogers, Paschal Fish, and Henry Rogers, worked as exhorters, interpreters, leaders, and stewards in the late 1830s and 1840s. Men with Methodist ties dominated government posts as blacksmiths and interpreters as well. Some of these positions were lucrative. In 1838, Paschal Fish and his brother, Charles, earned $120 and $60, respectively, as assistant blacksmiths. In that year, unnamed "Shawnee chiefs" earned $310. Richard Cummins made this possible by favoring Johnson's supporters. The promise of steady employment and greater influence appealed to men such as Joseph Parks, whose wealth in land and status in the Old Northwest was well known. Cummins managed to justify hiring Parks as his interpreter to the emigrant Indians, despite the fact that Parks "does not understand much of the languages" common in the Indian Territory.[58]

Methodist ties to government officials helped them lure prominent Ohio Shawnees, including Wewellipu, the speaker for the Shawnee nation, to their church. Their success with top Shawnee leaders led to an increasing number of converts and guaranteed their dominance on the reservation. Thirty-three Shawnees were baptized in 1841 alone, more than three times the number recorded by the Baptists in that same year. Between 1841 and 1844, members of the Perry and Blackhoof families abandoned the Baptists and began to appear at Methodist functions, suggesting that the Wapakoneta Shawnees' long-standing prejudice against Methodism, dating back to the 1820s, had begun to subside. Thomas Johnson's son, Alec, recalled that "every Johnson child was adopted by the Indians and given a name." The Shawnee "baptism" took place during the Green Corn Dance. Alec Johnson was adopted and named Wapakumseka, or "Sun Shining on the Water," by Paschal Fish. The younger Blackhoof accompanied Fish and adopted another missionary's child, naming him Katawekasa.[59] Early success with the Rogerstown and Hog Creek Shawnees, disciplined expansion of their mission, and the ability to procure steady financial support translated into a marked increase of Ohio and Missouri Shawnees to the Methodist ranks. The Methodists secured partnerships with both Ohio and Missouri Shawnee leaders, thus ensuring the economic and diplomatic prowess of their mission. The Methodists were the first denomination to significantly break down the division between villagers from Ohio and Missouri, and unite them in a new, Christian community.

Shawnees affiliated with the Methodist mission also conveyed Methodism to American Indians beyond the reservation. Exhorters were particularly important to the success of the camp meeting, for their chief duty was to invite "sinners to enter the pen by reminding them of the prospects of hell and damnation awaiting those who failed to take the step." They were responsible for those who remained unconvinced of the need for Christian conversion. At an intertribal camp meeting in 1842, a Methodist missionary described the exhorter's role. Three Kansa Indians had continually frustrated Thomas Johnson's wife, Sarah, in her attempts to convince them of the need for conversion. However, as the camp meeting wore on, one of their number "fell from where he was sitting . . . trembling under all the horrors of deep and pungent conviction." At this point "brother Fish" of the Rogerstown Shawnees arrived and "pointed him to Christ." Soon thereafter, the Kansa woke from his confused state and remarked that "the good Lord loves me now." Fish had done his job by exhorting the unconverted among them into the church. These early successes allowed the Methodists to expand their operation from their base on the Shawnee reservation to neighboring tribes, including the Kansa.[60]

This core group of Shawnee supporters helped Johnson move the mission to a more accessible location and open a boarding school to neighboring tribes in 1839. The move was an immediate success. By 1843, more than five hundred acres were under cultivation, and the manual labor school served an average of twelve different tribes surrounding the Shawnee reservation. In addition, neighboring Missourians and African Americans attended the religious meetings held there. The genius of creating a multitribal manual labor school was that it drew financial support from a number of tribes, in addition to private and federal sources. This strategy also allowed the Methodists to make up for the shortfall caused by the general lack of support from the vast majority of the Shawnees. In 1838, three-fourths of all Shawnees continued to practice their "ancient religion" in spite of Methodist gains.[61]

The expansion and institutionalization of the Methodist operation led to an increasingly strict interpretation of the requirements for membership. By the early 1840s, for example, the Methodists demanded a renewal of marriage vows for those interested in conversion. Jerome Berryman and Learner B. Stateler, two missionaries in charge of the daily operations at the mission, recognized that many Shawnees "have been together as man and wife" for many years. Nevertheless, the two established a requirement that "all our friends who unite with the church" must be married in "the Christian manner." Marriage regulations were significant in that they forced Shawnee Methodists to concede to the authority of a church council led by the Missouri Methodist conference rather than the Shawnees themselves. What the Shawnees gained in terms of jobs and status was often lost in the hierarchical channels of the Methodist Church.[62]

Methodist and Baptist missionaries created new positions of authority and established new alliances that redefined the relationships between villagers on the reservation. Nevertheless, dissension within and between denominations made it impossible for either religious body to consolidate its authority. Moreover, the imagined cultural quarantine that the creators of the Indian Territory had hoped for never materialized. The boundary between American Indians and Americans was porous at best. Commerce between American Indians and white migrants continued unabated, alcohol remained easy to acquire, and missionary conflicts continued, reminding the Shawnees and their neighbors that all was not utopia in the West.[63]

By the late 1830s most Shawnees managed to produce enough corn, potatoes, wheat, and other staples to sell a surplus to neighboring Missourians. Shawnee families also raised livestock, including chickens, cattle, hogs, and horses. Wage work making rails and clapboards for expanding American settlements across the Missouri line was also available. Ohio Shawnee chiefs distributed income derived from land sales to the Wyandots and to the federal government for military roads as well.[64] Americans profited from Indians through trading posts and other informal bartering with tribal members in towns such as Westport, Missouri. But the tribe's proximity to American towns also meant a ready supply of alcohol, a sad reality that missionaries were powerless to stop. However, the sources of "sin," as defined by missionaries, were not confined to off-reservation sites. For years Jotham Meeker struggled to prevent the Ottawas from gambling on the Sac and Fox reservation.[65]

Missionaries, painfully aware of the need to act as pious role models, often failed to conceal their own shortcomings. In 1848, Delaware missionary J. D. Blanchard was caught in the biggest sex scandal of the Indian Territory. In September 1844, he wrote that "Indians . . . know emphatically nothing of family discipline. The father, perhaps, having a half dozen sets of children in different parts of the nation." Less than four years later, Blanchard was dismissed from the missionary service for fathering a child with one of the teachers at the Delaware mission. Francis Barker and Jotham Meeker were deeply troubled by Blanchard's mistakes and the harm he had caused to his own family, not to mention the Baptist enterprise, which had always been on tenuous ground with the Delawares. In a letter to the Baptist board, Barker wrote: "We deeply sympathize with Mrs. Blanchard and her little daughters, five in number."[66]

The Indian Territory was the scene of bitter conflicts as the denominational schisms of the 1840s filtered westward. Nationally, the Methodist and Baptist churches split over the certification of slave-owning members. But on the Shawnee reservation, Joseph Parks, Thomas Johnson, and the Boachman-Rogers families owned slaves. Among the Baptists, slavery mattered far more to northerners such as Francis Barker than to their Shawnee congregants.

Thus, the schisms of the 1840s as they were expressed in the Indian Territory reveal much more about local concerns than they do about the proliferation of slavery in the West. The Baptist schism, in particular, confirms historian Jon Butler's contention that in the denominational schisms "theological, social, ethnic, and abolitionist sentiments all played important roles in hardening denominational institutions into increasingly provincial ones."[67]

The Methodist schism of 1845 proceeded with little acrimony, in spite of the northern missionaries and teachers who worked for the mission. Indian churches quietly shifted their allegiance to the Methodist Episcopal Church, South. The Methodists' original mandate from the Missouri conference certainly eased the transition, but Johnson's guiding influence contributed to the ease of the shift. Johnson himself remained ambivalent about slavery until his death in 1865.[68]

The Baptists' case was quite different. The congregational structure of Baptist theology led to bitter feuding over church policies. Isaac McCoy had always disliked the democratic impulses of Baptist missionaries and congregants alike, and, as a result, he attempted to lure Blackfeather, DeShane, and a small coterie of his supporters into the newly formed Southern Baptist Convention (SBC). Allegiance with the southern Baptists made sense for McCoy. The SBC was "frankly denominational in spirit, designed by men who did not hesitate to speak of the Baptist 'church'." McCoy eventually became the corresponding secretary for the American Indian Missionary Association (AIMA), the missionary society of the SBC. Working for the Southern Baptists granted McCoy the authority he craved. Of course, Barker, Meeker, and the missionaries McCoy had recruited firmly opposed joining with the SBC and worked hard to maintain the tribe's commitment to the northern Baptists and the American Baptist Missionary Union (ABMU) in Boston.[69]

National religious schisms led to even greater divisions between Shawnees on the reservation. DeShane and Blackfeather sided with McCoy, while more recent members of the church from less highly regarded families supported Francis Barker and other northern Baptists associated with the ABMU. Evidence suggests that Shawnee advocates of the independence movement of 1834 later moved to support Barker and his allies in their struggle against McCoy. Their wish for an autonomous Shawnee church in which membership standards were determined by tribal members, rather than missionaries, suggests an affinity between the two movements. After the disappointing conclusion to the independence movement, some Shawnees kept fighting for autonomy in more limited forms, such as an independent church.[70]

From the Shawnees' perspective, the Baptist schism was a conflict over who controlled church membership. Early supporters of the Baptist operation, namely Joseph DeShane and Blackfeather, were angry with Barker over the baptism of ill-reputed Shawnees. They preferred stricter terms for membership. In addition, DeShane and Blackfeather believed that McCoy represented their best chance of gaining political leverage within the tribe. Like those Wapakoneta Shawnees who had migrated to the Indian Territory in 1827, they feared the emerging coalition between the Rogerstown Shawnees, including Lewis Rogers and Paschal Fish, and the Wapakoneta Shawnees who had held onto their lands in Ohio until 1832, including the younger Black Hoof. Blackfeather and DeShane particularly resented Barker's recruitment efforts among the objectionable members of the tribe because it left the Baptists open to the derision of the emerging Methodist elite.[71]

Barker's actions confirmed the Shawnee Methodists' belief that the Baptists were supported only by those Indians who had been unable to conform to Methodist standards for admission to the church. Angry Methodist missionaries railed against Barker and the Baptists. Their extensive proselytizing among Methodist converts, and the ease with which Barker baptized excluded Methodists, diminished the Baptists' ability to maintain stringent standards among their own converts. As the Methodists and Baptists worked with the Shawnees in the hope of converting the largest number of Shawnees, it became clear that the aforementioned coalition of Rogerstown, Hog Creek, and Wapakoneta Shawnees were in command of the reservation.

Those Shawnees allied with Barker, and out of favor with their Methodist kinsmen, were not from a specific Shawnee division or village. A common bond they shared was their former association with the Methodist mission. In one case, an unidentified Shawnee woman approached Barker seeking membership in the Baptist church, and to the consternation of McCoy, "Mr. Barker had her under the water" soon after the visit. The Methodist missionaries and their Shawnee converts were shocked at Barker's ready acceptance of their less devout members. In March 1842, the Methodists sent a formal letter to the Baptists, accusing Barker of "receiving and baptizing persons under censure of crime, such as drunkenness, lying, theft &c. As well as repeated attempts to alienate and render dissatisfied members of our church." The Methodists wanted the Baptists to reject those Shawnees who did not hold a certificate of good standing from their operation. The ascendent Shawnee Methodists agreed with the missionaries, but for a different reason. The Shawnees rightly feared that Barker led a rival group of independence-minded tribesmen.[72] Blackfeather, DeShane, and Johnston Lykins branded the Shawnees in favor of an independent church "the very worst men in the nation." Lykins's outworn rhetoric of "drunkenness and adultery" may have been applicable to the excluded Methodist Shawnees. Yet his accusations lack detail and suggest that more was involved.

Later that November, DeShane and Blackfeather met at McCoy's home in Westport, Missouri, to plan for the removal of Barker and his allies. J. S. Bacon, a representative of the ABMU sent to the Indian Territory to mediate the dispute, attended the meeting. In a subsequent letter to Meeker, Bacon revealed that McCoy waged an "open & frightful attack" on Barker and his missionary opponents, and did his best to incite the Shawnees to rebel against them. In the days that followed, DeShane and Blackfeather, along with fifteen to twenty supporters, brought the full extent of their power to bear upon Barker and his allies. DeShane traveled across the entire reservation with a petition calling for Barker's removal and claimed to speak for the majority of the nation. Barker confirmed that his coalition had been "ordered to leave the station on peril of their lives." In a letter to his father, David Lykins wrote that the conflict "almost [caused] a war among the Shawnees." Blackfeather's party hoped that McCoy and Lykins would cross the Missouri border and take over the Baptist mission after they had driven Barker and his defenders from the reservation.[73]

By October 1844, Blackfeather and DeShane's opponents had survived the conflict and were granted their wish to form an independent church. The Shawnees and their neighbors remained under the control of the ABMU. While Bacon and other mediators from the ABMU noted that they could not prevent McCoy and his colleagues from establishing a competing Baptist mission under AIMA and the SBC, it became clear that they did not have enough support on the reservation to establish an alternative church. And in a move that must have devastated McCoy, Blackfeather wrote to Barker and conceded that "we give ourselves back to the Mission of the Baptist Board."[74]

Unlike the Blackfeather party, Barker and the new Shawnee converts understood the Baptist message as a tribal, rather than a multiethnic, religious system. Prior to the split between the ABMU and AIMA, the Shawnees, Ottawas, Potawatomis, and Delawares shared a single congregation located on the Shawnee reservation. Meeker, Pratt, and the other Baptists ran subordinate stations among the individual tribes. According to Pratt, "the relation is but poorly understood by native members . . . the acts of one branch sometimes has the appearance of interfering with the rights and interest of the other." Barker and Meeker viewed the fragmentation of the congregation along tribal lines as a sign of the maturation of church membership. Moreover, the two supported the Shawnees' endeavor to establish an independent church because of the limited gains made by the Baptists in the Indian Territory. A joint Ottawa and Potawatomi congregation made sense given the close linguistic and cultural relationship between the two tribes. Finally, a Shawnee-run church was better than no church at all. Meeker wrote McCoy and his adherents, firmly stating that they "will not be permitted to disturb that union which exists among the Indian brethren." He also warned that he and his colleagues would "use all our influence to increase and perpetuate it."[75]

The connection between Barker's sponsorship of a Shawnee-run church with considerable autonomy, run by former Methodists, indicates that allegedly "sinful" Shawnees may have simply been unhappy with both the Methodist mission and the dictatorial attitude of many American missionaries. McCoy's clear disregard for ongoing tribal distinctiveness among the emigrant Indians contributed to their discontent. Indeed, the whole idea of an Indian Canaan stemmed from McCoy's belief in a pan-tribal government based upon the United States Constitution.[76]

The Shawnees—whether Methodist or Baptist, or even practitioners of the tribe's "ancient religion"—had all been moving away from the vast alliances and confederacies common during Tecumseh's time. Even the distinctive village identities that had been so common since the beginning of Shawnee contact with colonizers began to change as missionary societies and political necessity required an increasingly tribal focus. The Baptist schism and the Methodist response reflected the ongoing struggle for power between the preremoval Shawnee villages. But in the fifteen years prior to the Civil War, Shawnee Methodists with a national "Shawnee" ideology assumed control of the reservation. Dissenters continued to voice their opinions, but new Shawnee leaders controlled the debate and institutionalized their authority on the reservation.

Most Missouri Shawnees, and the Wapakoneta villagers who had removed with Perry and Cornstalk in 1827, were powerless to stop the erosion of their own influence in the years between the schisms of the 1840s and the Civil War. The political maneuvering between Shawnee village chiefs for access to national leadership positions, and the influence of missionaries on those jockeying for power, points to the dramatic redefinition of authority in Shawnee politics unleashed by the creation of tribal reservations in Indian Territory. Regardless of their status, all Shawnees seized upon both the strengths and failures of the Americans on their reservation in an attempt to rebuild their lives in the aftermath of removal.

5. The Parable of the Rich Man and Lazarus: Wealth, Nationalism, and Its Discontents, 1845–1860

The Shawnees faced numerous challenges inside and outside the reservation in the summer of 1845. In mid-June, flooding swept the emigrant Indians from their homes and destroyed crops along the Kansas River and its tributaries. Baptist missionary Francis Barker reported that "fences were swept away . . . newly planted crops destroyed, young orchards, &c., among the rest . . . hogs were drowned . . . [and] many persons barely escaped with their lives." More than 170 Shawnee families, close to two-thirds of those on the reservation, lost everything. Malaria and cholera followed the economic and physical destruction. Approximately one-seventh of the Kansas Ottawas died because of the floods. Emigrant Indian settlement patterns contributed to the problem. Most settled in or near the flood plains of the rivers and streams of eastern Kansas, drawn by irrigation and the plentiful timber so essential to survival on the edge of the plains. The floods were especially devastating for many families because most had just established new farms and a degree of independence from government annuities after the lean removal years.[1]

Flooding and disease certainly destabilized reservation life in 1845, but massive human migration challenged the Shawnees and their neighbors in painfully familiar ways. Yet the Indian Territory was unlike previous sites of conflict between Shawnees and settlers in Ohio, Missouri, Arkansas, and Texas. The Kansas Territory "was opened to settlement at a time . . . when there was not within it an acre of land that was available for sale." Legally barred from the Indian Territory prior to 1854, white settlers had to content themselves with lands along the eastern border of the removed tribes' reservations.[2] As Shawnees watched American settlements along the border grow in size, they could only speculate as to when the bureaucratic logjam would break and they would be driven from their homes once again.

The porous boundary line separating the Indian Territory from Missouri led to varied encounters between Shawnees and Americans in border towns such as Westport and along the trails westward. In fact, the Santa Fe Road, linking New Mexico and the greater Southwest to the Missouri frontier, cut through the reservation, bringing trappers, traders, and migrants through Shawnee settlements. Less than thirty miles northeast, at the "jumping-off place" of Independence, Missouri, another 350,000 migrants between 1841 and 1866 began their long journey westward on the Overland Trail.[3]

Some Shawnees profited from the traffic. Paschal Fish, a Shawnee from Rogerstown, Missouri, ran a ferry on the Kansas River, a blacksmith shop, and a hotel for migrants. Fish, and a handful of others like him, had farms large enough to sell surplus produce and livestock to the travelers. Fish learned early on how to walk the boundary between Shawnee and American worlds. As a young boy he was sent to Richard M. Johnson's Choctaw Academy in Kentucky. As an adult he not only became a Methodist missionary among the Shawnees and Kickapoos, but also an entrepreneur for all occasions. The roads westward provided so many opportunities for Fish that J. J. Lutz, one

This depiction of Charles Blue Jacket's residence in Johnson County, Kansas, captures the elite status of national council members, even after American settlers robbed most Shawnees of their wealth in land and property. Copied from Heisler and Smith's *Atlas of Johnson County,* 1874. Kansas State Historical Society, Topeka, Kansas.

of Fish's Methodist colleagues, remembered that "P. Fish . . . was particularly fond of the parable of the rich man and Lazarus."[4] Fish's interest in this parable about a sinful man who selfishly accumulates wealth reveals that he worried about the consequences of his role in forging a new economic and political order on the reservation.

For most Shawnees—particularly after the summer floods—economic gain along the trails remained more of a dream than a reality. Most held a bleaker view of the migration, recognizing that increased settlement foreshadowed a new round of dispossession and removal. In 1842, two Quaker missionaries, John Lang and Samuel Taylor, described the Shawnees' perspective. According to the pair, an "aged Shawnee chief" addressed Shawnee concerns, saying that "he was now old and lame . . . [and] wanted to die and be buried here. [He] wished to know if we had heard the men at Washington talk about removing them again." The chief asked Lang and Taylor to help them gain a title to their present lands in Kansas as a final defense against the settlers.[5]

Some missionaries were unhappy with the traffic as well. True to his faith, Francis Barker condemned the hard drinking that came with American activity in the Indian Territory. A virtual epidemic of drunkenness on the reservation began in the 1840s, caused, according to Barker, "by the influence of soldiers and wagoners connected with the Mexican War."[6]

Talk of removal renewed the tension between Shawnee villages and threatened the newly established communities of faith. Christian Shawnees formerly allied with villages in either Ohio or Missouri began to take a closer look at earlier removal treaties. Most were troubled by what they found. The Ohio Shawnees believed that the 1825 Treaty of St. Louis described the eastern Shawnees as guests of the Missouri Shawnees. Consequently, national leaders originally from Wapakoneta and Hog Creek, Ohio, scrambled for the power and influence necessary to overturn the old removal treaties and grant their people a share in reservation lands. They feared being divested of land—and federal responsibility for their villages—in the event of a second removal. Ironically, this struggle between villages over resources prior to the creation of the Kansas Territory led to the formation of the Shawnee national council. Between 1845 and 1860, Joseph Parks, Charles Blue Jacket, and their detractors, including Paschal Fish, began a protracted intratribal feud over Shawnee sovereignty and the ability of national leaders to protect against those who would encroach upon it. Forces ranging from states' rights advocates to American settlers undermined the Shawnee nation. Missionaries and government agents quickly chose sides in this struggle driven by the nationalist ambitions of a small clique of Shawnee elites.

Most Shawnees remained unheard as new leaders asserted their paternalistic visions for the tribe. Ohio Shawnees such as Joseph Parks, supported by a small cadre of Shawnee Methodists, rose to power as federal officials anticipated the dissolution of the Indian Territory and cultivated a centralized leadership among the Shawnees to achieve these ends. Mixed-bloods such as Parks were well aware of the profits such cooperation would bring. They also supported the individual ownership of small farms and Indian citizenship that might result from the allotment of the Shawnee reservation.

Advocates of a politically unified Shawnee nation gained control of the reservation in the 1840s and 1850s, and it is no coincidence that they rose to power immediately prior to the creation of the Kansas Territory and the allotment of the reservation. Parks and this largely mixed-blood elite within the tribe used government support to create new power structures cloaked in the language of sovereignty and merit-based leadership. But as this new crop of leaders moved deliberately to assert its plans for a politically unified Shawnee nation, disparate opponents questioned the moral and political grounds for nationalism among a people accustomed to village-based autonomy. Denominational schisms, sectional conflict, and the advent of white settlement in the West provided a host of venues for the expression of these differences between advocates of the concentration of power and those of local-level, hereditary leadership. Parks and his associates used terms such as sovereignty and nation to defend their interests amid the chaos that enveloped the reservation in the 1840s and 1850s. But these political concepts were alien to most Shawnees.

Members of the newly created Shawnee national council were not always the willing partners of federal officials and the policies they forced on the tribes. Most Indian agents and higher-level officials had neither the means nor the will to defend "national" Shawnee leaders and their goals for the tribe. The Shawnee national government soon became a battleground for competing interests as the broken promises of federal officials and the questionable actions of Shawnee leaders dominated tribal affairs. While the national council often criticized federal officials for interfering with the sovereignty of the Shawnee nation, a majority of the underrepresented Shawnee people replied that political consolidation was foreign—even unwanted. Most Shawnees yearned for the return of village-based autonomy and tribal leaders more responsive to their needs.

More than any other Shawnee leader of the time, Joseph Parks epitomized the growing divide between the Shawnee people and their leaders. Before removal in 1833, Parks had a tenuous grip on membership in the tribe and was formerly associated with a marginal Ohio Shawnee village. His situation changed dramatically in Indian Territory. Parks used his bicultural heritage to his advantage. He was as comfortable at a meeting of the Masonic Lodge in Westport, Missouri, as he was at a Shawnee council meeting on the reservation.[7] By 1845, his ascendancy to power illustrated the transition from hereditary leaders with status in one of the Shawnee divisions to national leaders who lacked the kinship ties necessary to lead Shawnee villages, let alone the Shawnee nation, prior to removal. Moreover, his success demonstrates the extent to which most Shawnees, Christian and non-Christian alike, lost access to leaders representing their needs in the territorial period.

Parks maintained an esteemed position among the Shawnees from removal to his death in 1859.[8] Prior to the Shawnees' departure from Ohio, he had considered giving up membership in the tribe and living as an American citizen on a 640-acre land grant in Michigan that he had gained with the help of Lewis Cass. Parks ultimately chose to depart with the Hog Creek, Ohio, band in 1833. Yet he did not leave Ohio as one of many tribesmen forcibly removed west. Unlike most eastern Shawnees, Parks retained a large amount of his wealth, and he used part of his savings to finance the removal of the Hog Creek Shawnees. He acted as the removal agent for his own band, receiving federal pay and an additional land grant for directing his people westward. Upon their arrival in the West, Parks acted as interpreter for the agent at Fort Leavenworth. Government employment provided Parks with unheard of financial stability among his kinsmen. He moved on to new endeavors, establishing a trading firm in 1836 in Westport, Missouri, where he became one of the primary traders to the Shawnees and other tribes.[9]

Parks's exploitation of the Shawnees' involvement in the Second Seminole War cemented his superior position in the tribe. He and his business associates, Charles Findlay and Pierre Chouteau, submitted a claim of $9,600 against the tribe soon after the Ohio Shawnees returned from Florida in 1838. In 1850, Findlay described the events surrounding the claim to a sympathetic member of the Committee on Indian Affairs, Senator John Bell of Tennessee. According to Findlay, an unnamed army officer forced Parks to "enlist them [eighty-four Ohio Shawnees] by the influence of our house." Parks succeeded in fulfilling the officer's wishes, but only after promising the enlisted warriors large sums of money for their services. When the government supplies failed to materialize, the Ohio Shawnees proceeded to Florida anyway, equipped with arms and supplies given to them by Parks's trading firm. And as their families suffered during their absence, Parks's trading house supplied them with the means to survive.[10]

Both Parks and Findlay placed responsibility for the sad chain of events squarely on the government, arguing that "as they were disappointed in receiving the amount of pay promised them for their services in Florida, they were of course left largely in debt to us after paying all they could." In order to relieve the debt, Findlay and Parks asked the commissioner to transfer the entire amount of the United States' treaty obligations owed the Ohio Shawnees to their trading firm. Under pressure from the superintendent of Indian affairs in St. Louis, Thomas H. Harvey, the commissioner refused their request, believing that transferring the Ohio Shawnees' annuity to Parks's trading house would force ordinary Shawnees to become hopeless wards of the federal government. Parks and his allies were insulted by Harvey's refusal to go along with their plans for the annuity. Members of the national council angrily replied that "[we] are representatives of a *nation,* not of children." Ironically, the greatest threat to the Shawnees' annuity before 1854 came from the self-proclaimed head-chief of the Shawnee nation.[11]

The dispute between Parks, Findlay, and the commissioner of Indian affairs involved much more than tribal assets. Both sides claimed to have the best interests of the Shawnee people in mind. For example, when the commissioner pointed out that their claim would effectively wipe out the tribe's annuity, Findlay responded by arguing that the Shawnees "are now an agricultural people having entirely abandoned the chase as a means of livelihood, [and] are as fully capable of managing their money affairs as any people within my knowledge." Parks echoed Findlay's sentiments and explained that the Shawnees understood that federal annuities held them in shackles, dependent on government resources. The commissioner replied that federal responsibility for the tribe should continue as the Shawnees walked the long road toward civilization.[12] National Shawnee leaders and federal officials alike confidently asserted that they were acting in the tribe's best interests, yet neither group asked Shawnees outside the national council to voice their opinions on the issue. The judgments of common Shawnees on the value of the nation and the fate of their annuity were ignored.

Disputes between Parks and his contemporaries did not often diminish the respect his opponents had for him. Quaker missionary Henry Harvey, the longtime advocate of the Shawnees in both Ohio and Kansas, marveled at Parks's wealth. "His house has been the resort of all classes," wrote Harvey, "the sums he has bestowed on his people . . . within the last thirty years, would amount to a fortune, and still he is very wealthy." Buoyed by his membership in the Methodist Church, Parks redistributed some of his wealth to tribal members in order to maintain his base of support. His rise to national prominence developed as the divisional leaders of both the Missouri and Ohio Shawnees granted Parks power of attorney over their affairs in Washington by 1844.[13]

Travelers and missionaries admired the large farm he operated with the help of a handful of slaves while managing his trading firm in Westport. Parks both embodied and initiated American visions of progress among the removed tribes. The historian Francis Parkman even memorialized him in *The Oregon Trail.* He wrote "their chief, Parks, a remarkably large and athletic man . . . has a large farm and a considerable number of slaves. Indeed the Shawanoes have made greater progress in agriculture than any other tribe on the Missouri frontier."[14]

Parkman's romantic identification of Parks with Shawnee progress sheds light on one of the many ways Parks's contemporaries promoted him as the archetypal southern planter and Shawnee leader. As plans for the dissolution of the Indian Territory developed in Washington, D.C., American writers, artists, and missionaries followed suit. They were no longer interested in describing for eastern audiences their conflicts with recalcitrant Indian tra-

Western Log Cabin. By Alfred Jacob Miller, 1837. American travel writers and artists consistently noted the cultural divide between the emigrant Indians and the tribes indigenous to Kansas. Miller wrote about this cabin owned by Joseph Parks, "we encamped here for about a week, purchasing mules and making our final preparations for a savage life." The Walters Art Museum, Baltimore.

ditionalists like the Prophet. Rather, they promoted the Indian Territory and its residents. In a letter to his brother, Asbury C. Farnham, a teacher at the Methodist school, wrote that "the greater part [of the Shawnees] are heathen, but kind and much better to live among than many societies of whites in western Missouri."[15] By the late 1840s, western settlement reached beyond the Indian Territory. It became less common for those engaged with American Indians to describe themselves as Christian martyrs vis-à-vis the emigrant Indians. Highly acculturated Indians like Parks soon became popular examples of Indian progress in the West. His chroniclers engaged in western boosterism, redefining the land as a realm of agricultural and commercial possibility rather than a region of probable ruin amid "savagery."

Joseph Parks's steady accumulation of wealth and status between removal and the creation of the Kansas Territory in 1854 closely mirrored the political centralization of the Shawnee tribe. At the time of removal, Shawnee villagers focused their loyalties on their preremoval village chiefs, who retained their loyalty through gifts and other forms of support. Once in Indian Territory, the Shawnees maintained a united council house, but villagers rarely convened national meetings. Moreover, government treaty annuities flowed into the hands of the village chiefs who had been a party to individual removal treaties. In practice, the United States continued to recognize preremoval village leaders in spite of the official policy of tribal consolidation pursued since Tecumseh's time. Into the late 1840s tribal members identified themselves with village chiefs who organized their people into the familiar divide between eastern and western Shawnees.[16]

Shawnee Methodists worked against the balkanized nature of Shawnee politics. Parks, Lewis Rogers, and Paschal Fish—men from both the Hog Creek and Rogerstown communities—achieved some measure of centralized authority by moving the national council house to the Methodist mission in 1840. The partnership between the Rogerstown and the Hog Creek Shawnees was fragile in the early years. Charles Fish, Paschal Fish's brother, recalled that "at first we had to gather close around it and keep it alive with our breath, but very soon it grew beyond our control."[17] According to Charles Fish, by the late 1830s the partnership between the Rogerstown and Hog Creek villagers had adversely affected his people. Fish charged that the Methodists regularly bribed Parks and his associates in exchange for their support. Consequently, by the mid-1840s, Parks no longer appeased Shawnees who rejected his vision of Shawnee nationalism. Outside observers confirmed the newfound hegemony of the Shawnee Methodists. According to Methodist minister and historian William H. Goode, "The influence of the large mission establishment at the manual-labor school was strong. There were few to counteract or explain," thus allowing a core group of Parks's supporters to "exert a powerful influence over the tribe."[18]

Like Parks, Thomas Johnson and the Methodists rose to power by establishing a strong institutional and economic presence on the reservation. In 1839, Johnson expanded the Methodist operation from a mission to the Shawnees to a central manual labor school designed for both the Shawnees and their Indian neighbors. The Methodists cobbled together large enrollments composed of small numbers of children from more than twelve different tribes, easily surpassing their missionary competitors.[19] Johnson soon controlled a number of tribal school funds without having to bear the expense of constructing tribal missions across the Indian Territory.

Visitors and workers at the Methodist manual labor school marveled at the institution and its leading missionary, Thomas Johnson. William Patton, a teacher at the school, reported that Indians traveled from miles around to use the mission's flour mill and gristmill. In addition, the Methodists maintained a sawmill used by most of the Indians to build and repair their cabins. The Shawnees traded timber to the missionaries in exchange for flour, sugar, coffee, and other dry goods. Most Shawnees had no choice but to do business with either Parks's trading establishment or the Methodist mission at one time or another. Only the most independent-minded tribesmen could have avoided availing themselves of the resources offered by them.[20]

Shawnee dissidents, upset with the obvious political and economic influence of the Methodists, struggled to counteract the Shawnee nationalists' steady accumulation of power. Members of the Black Bob band led the opposition to the modern Shawnee nation. The Black Bobs were members of the Chillicothe division and were acknowledged by the Prophet, the elder Black Hoof, and Thomas Wildcat Alford as the keepers of the sacred pack—the descent group traditionally responsible for supplying national leaders. Chief Black Fish, Daniel Boone's captor and adopted father, was the original leader of the Black Bob band. Closely allied with the Yuchis and Creeks in the Southeast, these Chillicothe Shawnees moved to Missouri with Peter Lorimier in the early 1790s. As discontent among the Missouri Shawnees rose after the War of 1812, members of the Black Bob band refused to make yet another move to Arkansas and Texas with those who became known as the Absentee Shawnees. The Black Bobs struggled on until 1828, when they moved from Missouri to the reservation in Indian Territory. On the reservation, Black Fish's heirs became known as culturally conservative opponents of accommodation-minded Shawnees. Their observance of traditional rituals, and commitment to village-based autonomy, undermined the efforts of the missionaries and nationalists alike. On a tour of western lands in 1868,

Lyman Draper noted their commitment to the Bread Dance, writing that "they have since maintained a secret society of the band, meeting twice a year, in the spring and fall."[21]

These Chillicothe Shawnees tried to stop evangelical missionaries intent upon eradicating Shawnee customs. But the Black Bob band was also upset with the government's failure to protect their financial interests. Lewis Rogers, one of the few Missouri Shawnees fluent in English, spoke for members of the Black Bob band in a letter to the commissioner of Indian affairs, T. Hartley Crawford. Rogers made clear that the Missouri Shawnees had received little, if any, of their promised treaty annuities over the last decade. He argued that "we are sure that we have something coming to us" under the 1825 treaty.[22]

John Perry and the Ohio Shawnees also filed complaints with federal officials. However, Perry's concerns derived from the peculiar language of the various Shawnee removal treaties, which seemed to grant the Missouri Shawnees exclusive control over reservation lands. Perry feared the power of his western rivals. He and other Ohio Shawnees believed that, as guests of the Missouri Shawnees, they might be evicted from the reservation unless the federal government intervened. At the very least, the Ohio Shawnees wanted to receive title to 100,000 acres of land on their current reservation. Frustrated with the language of the Wapakoneta treaty (1831), Perry believed that any subsequent removal treaties would deprive his kinsmen of land and a share in promised treaty annuities. According to the Ohio Shawnees, they had been "badly taken" by James B. Gardiner, the Wapakoneta Shawnee removal agent, because he guaranteed that the Shawnees' reservation was to be shared by both the Ohio and Missouri Shawnees. Finally, Perry explained that the money owed Parks should be granted to him, for "in consequence of our absence [during the Seminole War] we lost much of our crops, which compelled us to enlarge our credits."[23]

Bereft of their preremoval intermediaries, many Missouri and Ohio Shawnee village chiefs placed the fate of their kinsmen in Parks's hands. In 1844, he traveled to Washington, D.C., on their behalf. Parks was assigned the task of dismissing the fraudulent claims some traders had made against the various Shawnee villages. Armed with power of attorney, he carried the day for the Shawnees when a particularly egregious $20,000 claim was dismissed. But in a mysterious turn of events, Parks withdrew several other requests made by tribal members. His actions aroused suspicion. Parks responded by asking the commissioner to notify him immediately "if the propriety of my withdrawing the original papers should be questioned." Divisional Shawnee chiefs continued to place their trust in Parks in spite of these suspect actions. Between 1844 and 1857, Parks received legal power of attorney no less than five times to manage Shawnee affairs as he wished.[24]

Government chiefs were slowly pulling their kinsmen toward a political culture that many grudgingly participated in or ignored outright. Casting ballots for leaders in elections monitored by government officials became just one startling example of the transformation in Shawnee politics. Annuity payments made to chiefs reinforced the coercive powers of the new elite and illustrated their dependence on the United States. Richard Cummins, the Fort Leavenworth agent, delivered approximately $1,000 to chiefs every January as the annuity payment until the late 1840s, when some members of the tribe began to protest against the practice. Several tribesmen—including Joseph Parks's brother, William—wanted to end payments to chiefs because of the way it usurped power from traditional leaders. They preferred that the annuity be paid to individual members [per capita payments] rather than chiefs. In January 1849, William Parks forced the tribe to hold a vote in order to stop the payments to chiefs. According to Cummins, eighty-five of the individuals present voted to continue the payment to chiefs, while fifty-five voted against the practice. The Fort Leavenworth agent seemed happy with the outcome, although he recognized that the vote was less than democratic. Cummins noted that "many Indians present refused to vote on either side, and the women, some of them even heads of households, did not vote." In addition, poor weather and the refusal of still more to accept money from the United States contributed to the absenteeism.[25]

The "national" leaders of the Shawnee tribe were both Ohio Shawnees and members of the Shawnee Methodist Church. In 1850, the Shawnee Indian agent, Luke Lea, selected three Ohio Shawnee leaders, Joseph Parks, George Francis, and Joseph Barnett, "as delegates to Washington City for the purpose of transacting some business with the government." With both Thomas Johnson and Luke Lea behind them, Parks and his allies were able to advance their own personal and preremoval village interests. Membership on the national council resulted from the extent of an individual's movement toward acculturation and wealth rather than the democratic impulses of the Shawnees themselves.[26] Not surprisingly, the trip mixed tribal business with personal goals. Parks continued to lobby federal officials for resolution of his nearly $10,000 claim against the tribe. Other difficulties included one of Parks's escaped slaves, a man named Stephen, who had been liberated by a group of abolitionists in Illinois. In this and other cases, Parks argued that he deserved federal compensation as stipulated by the Trade and Intercourse Acts and the Fugitive Slave Law. The Shawnee chief believed that U.S. laws should extend to Indian Territory and that American Indians deserved protection equal to that guaranteed to citizens of the United States.[27]

Before progress could be made on the tribe's future in the region, Parks demanded that American officials revisit Shawnee removal to the Indian

Territory and the treaties that brought them there. As settlement along the border with the Indian Territory increased, and depredations against Shawnee livestock and agriculture became more common, the Ohio Shawnees favored a plan for the future that included United States citizenship and the allotment of the Shawnee reservation to competent adult members of the tribe.[28] National Shawnee leaders anticipated the Dawes Act that would remake Native American communities nearly forty years later. Parks asked the Commissioner of Indian Affairs, Orlando Brown, to allow the Ohio Shawnees to sell 100,000 acres of land on the reservation and to set up a trust fund from the proceeds of the sale for the exclusive benefit of the Ohio Shawnees. The Ohio Shawnees, who conceded that their right to reservation lands was tenuous, worked to receive a clear share in the division of the reservation. They even hired an attorney, R. W. Thompson, to prosecute their cause in Washington. Thompson explained that "the Ohio Shawnees, of course, have no title to these lands. The *grant* was made to the Missouri Shawnees who consented that the *Ohio* Shawnees might have the use of them merely, but without any share or title."[29] Land disputes between Shawnees east and west of the Mississippi River created a tangible divide between the villagers, rendering the fragile communities of faith a relic of the past.

American officials refused the Ohio Shawnees' request for an exclusive treaty. However, both sides compromised on a plan that involved the creation of a Shawnee national council, supported by a tribal constitution, in spite of growing discontent with their handpicked leaders. Abelard Guthrie, a Shawnee-Wyandot and an abolitionist who vehemently opposed the Shawnee national council, claimed that the Ohio Shawnees "had a small annuity which they used adroitly to ingratiate themselves with some of the head men of the Missouri tribe." Opponents of the national council believed that a conspiracy of interested individuals, primarily Maykujay Shawnees from Ohio, were behind the creation of the national council. Guthrie, and the village chiefs he defended, opposed the measures and demanded that the government "stop the pay which they [Parks and his associates] have been receiving" so that "their influence will be greatly abridged."[30]

T. H. Harvey, superintendent of Indian affairs at St. Louis, had a more charitable perspective. He overlooked the obvious political corruption behind the emergence of the Shawnee nation. Harvey happily observed that "the Shawnees as a people have been trying for several years to adopt some simple laws for their government."[31]

Shawnee dissidents, including John Wolf, William Parks, and George Blue Jacket, were typically allied with competing missionary societies. As early as 1846, John Wolf, John Johnston's former hunter and assistant in Ohio, wrote to Johnston, remarking that "I go and sit with our Quaker friends . . . and I pray to god in my heart to help me to be good." But the ongoing controversy within the tribe over annuity payments was interfering with his devotion. Wolf asked that Johnston help the Shawnee dissenters, suggesting to him that "we need a friend to speak to him & the great men about our annuity money for we all know something is wrong." Like the Quakers, the Baptists redoubled their efforts among "the less favored portions of the tribe." Both denominations had conceded to the Methodists and to their partnership with the Shawnee government chiefs, turning their attention to the majority of the tribe—those who had been left out of the ongoing political revolution.[32]

The majority of the tribe—estimated at between two-thirds and one-half of the approximately 950 Shawnees on the reservation—refused to participate in the tribal government and the missionary organizations affiliated with the competing factions. However, most dissenters adapted to the changing economy. But their engagement in the frontier economy belied a deeper distrust for the suggestions of missionaries and government officials. Christian worship, linked as it was to the intrigues of reservation politics, did not appeal to many Shawnees. As Chief Little Jim of the Absentee Shawnees explained, "We were driven . . . at the point of bayonets in the hands of white men. Why should we become like them? . . . when I remember Tecumseh, I cannot suddenly love the long-time enemies of my people, who have taken away so much and given back so little."[33]

In contrast, leaders of the new Shawnee nation pursued many of the changes advocated by the Americans and worked hard to establish relationships with influential figures in Washington. Parks developed ties with members of the Committee on Indian Affairs, as well as prominent businessmen, including the trader George W. Ewing. These ties benefited the advocates of the new political order in their struggle for control over Shawnee affairs. National leaders countered the efforts of Shawnee dissidents with their wealth and their contacts with Americans—assets greatly augmented by unsuspecting village chiefs in search of intermediaries between their people and government officials.[34]

Conflicts over resources increased as the creation of the Kansas Territory became imminent. Shawnee Methodists, Baptists, and Quakers worried that their older village memberships might be used against them by their opponents within the tribe. As a result, most Shawnees were unwilling to accept national political consolidation without some guarantee that their preremoval rights as members of distinct villages would be protected.

Most of the Missouri Shawnee Methodists finally broke with the Ohio Shawnee members of the national council in April 1850. Since the 1844 schism of the Methodist Church, the western Shawnees had been searching for an opportunity to illustrate their distinctive, preremoval identities. Rogerstown Shawnees, including Paschal Fish and William Rogers, broke with Joseph Parks, Charles Blue Jacket, and the Methodist missionary Thomas Johnson in an attempt to preserve their autonomy. A Northern Methodist Church allied with minister Thomas B. Markham offered an ideal outlet for challenging the authority of the new Shawnee elites. In the winter of 1849, a coalition of eighty-five Shawnees threw their support to Markham. As Charles Fish explained it, "we as an independent people chose to remain in the old church." Fish was quick to point out that the decision to establish a separate church had little to do with the abolitionist leanings of his people. In fact, some Rogerstown Shawnees owned slaves. The split within the church reflected their desire to free themselves from the authoritarian practices of their Ohio Shawnee neighbors who now claimed to be national leaders. Western Shawnee dissidents were convinced that Parks and Johnson aimed to carry the entire congregation into the newly created Methodist Episcopal Church South.[35]

Markham, a Methodist from Missouri who chose to ally himself with the Northern branch of the church after 1844, brought the conflict between the two groups out into the open. Parks bitterly contested Markham's claim to the separate congregation and held a national council meeting to force him from the reservation. The Ohio Shawnees also persuaded the commissioner of Indian affairs, Luke Lea, to join with them in opposing Markham's inroads on the reservation. In March 1850, Lea wrote a letter to Markham in which he asserted that the council members "requested me to inform you that it was contrary to their wishes that you should preach any more within their country believing . . . that your sermons and conversations with their people are better calculated to divide and distract their nation than of uniting them." Markham abandoned his mission soon after Parks and Lea united in opposing him. The Ohio Shawnees remained in control of the religious and political affairs of the reservation.[36]

Markham's expulsion from the reservation did not end the dispute between the Ohio and Missouri Shawnees. Paschal Fish and the Missouri Shawnees asked Commissioner Brown to intervene, arguing that the conflict deserved his attention because it involved the protection of religious liberty and the abuse of power on the reservation. Fish was particularly distressed by the way his opponents had used a government official for what he described as "their mad scheme of proscription and oppression." The collusion between Lea and the Ohio Shawnees dismayed the Missouri Shawnees. Markham's defenders believed that the Shawnee subagent should have "informed the chiefs that it was not within their province to choose or in any way interfere with the religious sentiments of their people." Fish argued that these corrupt practices contravened the basic rights guaranteed to Native Americans and American citizens alike. The Missouri Shawnees demanded concrete action from the commissioner, including the suspension of the Shawnee school fund. Fish, Rogers, and Johnson's former advocates among the Missouri Shawnees wondered if the commissioner would allow "we who live on free soil [to] enjoy less liberty than the citizens of a slave state."[37]

Like Parks, Fish and Rogers explained their perspective in terms of their rights as both village chiefs and Americans. Leaders on both sides of the dispute defined their struggle in terms of basic rights, religious liberty, and other political terms that were unmistakable to most Americans in the antebellum period. The Markham controversy reflected their desire to maintain a dual identity as Shawnees and Americans as the dissolution of the reservation became imminent.

As outspoken defenders of slavery, both Parks and Johnson became vulnerable to their northern opponents who used the slave question as a pretext for questioning their moral ability to lead Indians to civilization. Quaker missionaries, for one, were open abolitionists and condemned the slaveholders on the reservation. In 1847, Quaker missionary Richard Mendenhall submitted an editorial to *The National Era* of Washington, D.C., "for the purpose of bringing to public notice the violation of the Missouri Compromise in the Indian Territory." Mendenhall described the tasks performed by the slaves owned by Johnson and Parks, and questioned the morality of using slave labor under the guise of christianizing the Indians. The editorial was eventually run by *The Liberator,* ensuring that the Shawnee reservation would become one of many sites of violence between the sections in the years ahead.[38]

The Ohio Shawnees retaliated against Mendenhall by attempting to seize control of the Shawnees' orphan fund in order to pay off tribal debts. The commissioner of Indian affairs refused their request. If Brown had agreed, the move would have dealt a severe financial blow to the Quaker operation. Throughout their tenure on the reservation, the Quakers appealed to a small number of Ohio Shawnee adults. Consequently, revenue for the mission was generated mostly from treaty money dedicated to the care of an average of thirty to forty orphaned children. Parks was incensed at Brown's refusal to transfer the fund from the Quakers to the head chiefs, writing that ". . . you have, until this decision, received us as the 'accredited' '*representatives*' of our '*nation.*'" The chiefs lambasted the commissioner, calling Brown's decision a violation of Shawnee rights and tribal sovereignty.[39]

Richard Cummins shared Parks's animus for both the Quakers and Markham's Shawnee advocates, but for different reasons. In a letter to Superintendent Harvey, Cummins warned "let the Indians become tainted with abolition doctrines, commence harboring, or running off slaves belonging to citizens of our state [Missouri], & finally let the citizens of the State once become jealous & suspicious of Indians on the subject & the consequences . . . would be very easy to conjecture."[40] Cummins searched for a way to immunize the emigrant tribes from open sympathy with northern abolitionists. As a long-standing member of the Indian service in Kansas, Cummins did not believe that the Shawnees and their neighbors adequately understood issues of national importance. To his mind, American Indians remained primitive peoples, wards of the federal government. Cummins was somewhat surprised to learn that, however much they disagreed, both the Ohio and Missouri Shawnees linked tribal sovereignty, slavery, and religious freedom to national debates regarding the Constitution and the revolutionary principles on which it was based.

Francis Barker and Jotham Meeker were much more guarded in their critique of the national council and the Shawnee Methodist Mission. In fact, Jotham Meeker regularly enrolled Ottawa Indian children in the Methodist manual labor school. The Baptists remained politically innocuous as they continued to deal with the repercussions of their own denominational schism. Some of the missionaries formerly united with Barker and Meeker switched allegiances and supported the American Indian Missionary Association run by Isaac McCoy and the Southern Baptists. For this reason, Barker monitored recent missionary arrivals for any pretense of southern sympathies. In one instance, Barker assured Solomon Peck, a key member of the American Baptist Missionary Union in Boston, that the "sympathies" of a new missionary, James Cusick, "are with the North and in harmony with our operations."[41]

Blackfeather, the lone Shawnee Baptist admitted to the meetings of the Shawnee national council, remained Barker's most influential supporter among the Shawnees. In spring 1847, Barker happily reported that Blackfeather was "erecting a cabin upon his premises for the accommodation of the meeting, and seems desirous of spreading the interest to others not as yet opened to the glad news of salvation." Shawnee Baptists united with Blackfeather in asserting even greater control over the church. Unlike the increasingly hierarchical and institutionally minded Methodists, the Baptists preferred Shawnee-language services in private residences.[42]

Shawnee Methodists, who advocated for collaboration with government officials and incorporation into American settlements, remained in control of the reservation. And with federal officials and wealthy Shawnees behind them, the southern Methodists continued to receive most of the Shawnee school fund. The Ohio Shawnees understood how to negotiate with members of the Bureau of Indian Affairs in Washington, D.C., had ready access to important politicians, and knew how to navigate the channels of power there. Unlike their predecessors, they were not in need of intermediaries like the Quakers to help them arrange meetings and travel east to the nation's capital. Parks and the Ohio Shawnees achieved success by promoting their interests in language that American officials could understand.

Marginalized tribal members became the subjects of the overlapping paternalistic visions of American officials and Shawnee leaders. Both used the language of sovereignty to promote the American civilization program. In negotiations with Americans, government chiefs defined their quest for increased authority as a struggle between Christian morality and "heathenism," productive farming versus idleness. These basic dualisms underwrote the philosophy used to create a sovereign, national Shawnee government. Members of the national council described the coalition of Shawnees allied against them as "reckless & dissipated" opponents who desired to remain in misery. Government officials accepted these stereotyped depictions of culturally conservative Shawnees. Officials with the Bureau of Indian Affairs characterized those against the Shawnee nation as hopeless wards of the United States in search of a return to the misguided ways of the past. Government officials overlooked the corruption of Shawnee council members and approved the consolidation of tribal authority.[43]

But within Shawnee society, the struggle between Parks and his antagonists defied such easy categories. In fact, the dispute over the emerging national government pitted both Christians and more traditional Shawnees against the Shawnee Methodists. The people the Shawnee Methodists characterized as drunken and lazy traditionalists were, in fact, a diverse amalgam of Baptist, Quaker, and Black Bob Shawnees. They were concerned about the radical departure from the accepted model of Shawnee leadership in which hereditary chiefs traced their authority through one of five Shawnee divisions affiliated with a host of autonomous villages. Opponents of the council were raised amid the practical democracy of the preremoval village world—a political culture in which individuals and families voted with their feet and moved elsewhere when chiefs ignored their wishes. The reservation narrowed this kind of political mobility considerably, and the national council's control over tribal lands and the allocation of federal resources further hindered the average Shawnees' political choices.

The dispute between the Shawnees also involved complicated financial issues that were further confused by the inconsistent payment of treaty annuities to the Shawnees since removal. The Rogerstown Shawnees looked on as their Ohio Shawnee kinsmen received regular annuities from the Wapakoneta Treaty of 1831. The Missouri Shawnees, who rarely received the money owed them from the treaties of 1825 and 1831, vociferously opposed the sudden cash windfall designed for the exclusive benefit of the Ohio Shawnees. They asked for a share of the Ohio Shawnees' largesse, arguing that they were their guests. The Ohio Shawnees rejected any division of the money and insisted that the Missouri Shawnees were not entitled to the proceeds from the Wapakoneta removal treaty.

Opponents of the national council advocated the per capita distribution of annuity payments to counteract the increasing authority of chiefs. In a remarkable turn of events, the federal government agreed. A new round of government regulations for the Indian Territory contravened council members' goals for national government and personal aggrandizement by depriving Parks and his colleagues of the money needed to engineer widespread Shawnee support. In 1847, Congress passed a number of laws regarding the payment of annuities and associated problems with alcohol in the Indian Territory. For one, the new laws compelled Indian agents to pay annuities to heads of families rather than to chiefs. Second, the law protected these heads of families from signing their annuities away to alcohol traders in advance of the payment by declaring any contracts between Indians and whites null and void.[44]

Members of the national council responded immediately to the reforms, asking President Millard Fillmore to grant the Shawnees an exemption from the laws. Parks believed that the laws invalidated Shawnee sovereignty and made a mockery of the American civilization program. The law also threatened to invalidate the numerous contracts between Parks, his business partners in Westport, and his advocates in Washington, including R. W. Thompson. Parks asked the president to allow the chiefs to use the money for national purposes. According to Thompson, "per capita law destroys their authority and breaks down all their influence over national affairs." Government chiefs warned that the twin goals—individuality and independence—at the heart of the civilization program would be destroyed forever by the reforms.[45]

Thomas Moseley, the new Shawnee agent, explained the council's position to President Fillmore, writing that "they would prefer to see their annuities entirely abolished and the whole sum paid to them at once, that there might not be a single idler left in their nation." They even outlined a plan for the money to allay any fears of tribal corruption held by the president and the commissioner of Indian affairs. Parks described their plans for a new council house and mill to be built with the money. "The balance, if any," Thomas

Moseley declared, "will be distributed per capita." Nevertheless, the president refused to override the 1847 laws, citing evidence of collusion between the Shawnee agent and members of the council. In addition, Fillmore doubted that Parks had received power of attorney from a majority of the tribe.[46]

Moseley defended these ongoing interventions in tribal politics and reminded his superiors that the United States had a keen interest in assisting the growth of the Shawnee nation, given the impending dissolution of the reservation. But because of the latest round of government intervention in Shawnee affairs, Moseley believed that "it would be impossible now, under any circumstances, to get the Missouri or Chilcothe [*sic*] band to unite with the Ohio band." Beyond the controversy over the national council, Moseley also pointed out that disputes over treaty money eroded confidence in the Christian missions. The Shawnee agent echoed the sentiments of R. W. Cummins, who recognized that paying the money to chiefs is "the fruitful source of dissensions and quarrels." Government officials were clearly aware that annuity payments tended to affirm preremoval village identities and loyalties, thus creating a real obstacle to American plans for the Indian Territory on the eve of the Kansas-Nebraska Act.[47]

The Ohio Shawnees' attorney reacted to Fillmore's decision by challenging the logic behind Indian removal and subsequent American policies. Speaking on behalf of the national council, Thompson argued that the 1847 laws indicated that President Andrew Jackson and his advisers designed the reservations to house politically disparate but culturally similar kinsmen attached to independent villages. Put simply, the 1847 law affirmed the distinctiveness of Shawnee villages and slowed the progress of the American civilization program. These same officials used loftier goals, including the creation of national tribal governments, Indian civilization, and the eventual incorporation of American Indians into American society, as little more than rhetorical devices intended to rationalize their removal from the eastern United States. Parks, Eli Black Hoof, and their supporters accused "their great father" of encouraging "their young men and many of their old ones to act dishonestly."[48] For members of the national council, the 1847 laws made clear the Americans' disregard for tribal sovereignty and the ultimate viability of the Shawnee nation.

The Ohio Shawnees who dominated the national council continued to press the United States for a clear share in the reservation land originally granted to their Missouri Shawnee kinsmen. Accordingly, "Joseph Park, the Head Chief, elected for the said tribe of Indians, our true and lawful attorney," secured $63,000 for the Ohio Shawnees after Commissioner Lea refused to subdivide the reservation between the Ohio and Missouri Shawnees.[49] Parks worked with R. W. Thompson in Washington, D.C., to sway congressional opinion in their favor. Months later, a man employed by Parks in Washington, Samuel Huffacker, described how Parks and Thompson had succeeded in gaining the cash payout. Huffacker explained that he hired a friend "to keep the Senator [opposed to the settlement] away when the vote was taken." Huffacker confidently asserted that "I got the bill passed and got your money" by engineering the senator's absence. He now sought reimbursement from the tribe for money spent in the process.[50] The cash settlement with the United States was a triumph for the Ohio Shawnees, who had been fighting for an acknowledged share in the reservation for nearly ten years. The problem of distributing the money, however, threatened to invalidate the national council's success.

Distributing the cash settlement renewed the conflicts between village leaders and family members alike. Albert Cumming, the St. Louis superintendent of Indian affairs under Lea, again refused to override the 1847 law and grant the national council full control over the $63,000. But Lea sympathized with the Shawnee council and disliked per capita payments. Lea understood that the law contributed to "the slighting of chiefs" because "it was through the chiefs that the government carried on business with the tribes."[51] Nevertheless, Superintendent Cumming and the Shawnee agent, B. F. Robinson, remained committed to upholding the law. Thus the authority of the Shawnee nation was only partially realized soon after it had been established.

Most Shawnees were grateful to Cumming and Robinson for defending the per capita distribution of the Shawnee settlement. Blackfeather and his supporters hoped that "their agent may secure orders not to pay any part of the annuity to the chiefs & councillors for national purposes."[52] They were particularly concerned about rumored legal fees to R. W. Thompson and other questionable debts to traders, both of which they believed were Parks's responsibility. One of the traders, George Ewing, submitted a $20,000 claim against the Shawnee nation. Outraged opponents of the national council refused to acknowledge debts owed to Parks and his allies. To do so would result in greatly diminished treaty annuities to tribal members.

At the 1853 annuity payment, violence nearly erupted between Shawnees for and against per capita payments and alleged debts to tribal lawyers and traders. As a result, Cumming ordered a detachment of ten soldiers to the agency to ensure that Thompson, Ewing, and his cohorts did not try to force heads of households to hand over their per capita payment to the chiefs and creditors.[53] Parks later conceded that the supervision of the annuity payment had spoiled their plans. Thompson and Ewing set up a table just outside the annuity payment grounds in order to receive their money. But more than half of the tribe avoided surrendering their money to them, knowing that they were protected by the American soldiers. Parks, Black Hoof, and George McDougal were furious with Robinson over the presence of the soldiers and their own inability to pay their creditors. According to the council, the July payment represented "a violation of the treaty, and of our rights as a nation." They took their case to the commissioner, complaining that "it is impossible for the chiefs of the nation to do the business of that nation." Parks's letter to Lea must have troubled the commissioner, who sympathized with their position. Parks, an expert at framing the issues at stake, asked "who will you do the business of the nation with if your officers can come among us & degrade the chiefs & headmen?"[54] Members of the national council who had prided themselves on their leading economic and political position as reformers among the emigrant tribes wondered if "it is all idle talk about their civilization."[55]

The dispute over tribal sovereignty, per capita payments, and tribal debts illustrated some important truths regarding the relationship between the new tribal governments and the federal government. The United States remained unwilling to dissolve its financial obligations to the Shawnees given its need to manipulate tribal leaders into selling their land. Conversely, as the dissolution of the Indian Territory north of Oklahoma became imminent, tribal leaders who were dependent on federal dollars stood to benefit from American favoritism. They recognized the Americans' need for a centralized tribal leadership amenable to the designs of the United States. New Shawnee leaders had used their economic power to win support from tribal members since the 1840s. But their dominance over tribal affairs remained incomplete. Tribal members chafed under the authority of council members and American officials alike, and they constantly struggled against them both. Consequently, Shawnee leaders often resorted to extralegal means in order to subvert American plans for the tribe and to avoid open conflict with kinsmen yearning for a more complete democracy.

Parks, Eli Black Hoof, George McDougal, and Charles Blue Jacket worked harder to avoid future challenges to their own authority after the debacle at the 1853 annuity payment. On February 8, 1854, they convened a meeting of twelve men considered to be national leaders in order to "form a code of laws" for their people. The council took place only months before Kansas Territory would be opened to settlement on May 30. Parks began the discussion by accusing American officials of sending "me out without anything to work with. How can you expect me to do your work without anything to work with?" Council members joined with Parks in their common plea for increased authority in the enforcement of newly established tribal laws.[56]

The February meeting resulted in the first formally elected Shawnee national government. Prior to that time, the "national council" was little more than a creative fiction imposed on the Shawnee people by a shifting coalition of chiefs and government officials. After the February 1854 meeting, the Shawnee nation became a recognized institution. The first official national government consisted of a head chief, second chief, council clerk, and tribal sheriff. Each of these officials was elected to a one-year term. A tribal interpreter also participated in the new government, but the Shawnee agent appointed individuals to this position and made them paid employees of the U.S. Indian Service. Tribal chiefs included Joseph Parks, Charles Blue Jacket, Graham Rogers, and Paschal Fish. Most of these elected officials were mixed-race Shawnees. Others, such as the council clerk, Samuel Cornatzer, were Americans who had been adopted into the tribe.[57]

Abelard Guthrie questioned the authority of the national council. He claimed that they were little more than corrupt Ohio Shawnees who had used the cooperation of a handful of Missouri Shawnees to "overthrow the separate tribal organizations, and elect a council claiming to represent both tribes." Evidence supports Guthrie's conclusion. Of the nine delegates to the Shawnees' 1854 treaty, which opened the reservation to settlement, only two were Missouri Shawnees.[58]

The new national government further divided the Shawnee people and tore some families apart. George Blue Jacket, for one, objected to the new government. He argued that granting them such authority only exacerbated existing social ills on the reservation. Like his ally William Parks, Blue Jacket believed that the Shawnees had grown worse as a people since the large-scale incorporation of the habits and customs of white people. He attributed card playing, cheating, lying, and other vices to the creation of a tribal constitution among their neighbors, the Wyandots.[59] Opponents of the national council were uncertain about the new economic and political order, and questioned the benefits of assimilation.

While those for and against the adoption of a tribal constitution agreed on the basic social problems affecting the reservation, they disagreed sharply on possible solutions. Council members associated the small number of tribal laws with rampant alcoholism and adultery, while their opponents believed that tribal laws would only corrupt the Shawnees further. According to Richard Cummins, the controversy surrounding the national government "arrays brother against brother, friend against friend." Cummins believed that it mattered little if the dissenters were "actuated by proper motives for the good of his tribe" because Joseph Parks was now "using all his influence for the benefit of his class."[60]

The increasing definition of the Shawnee nation and concomitant authority of its chiefs enabled Parks, Eli Black Hoof, and George McDougal to assert their authority over their own people in unprecedented ways. For example, laws banning the sale and consumption of alcohol were passed. The national council forced habitual drinkers to give up their per capita annuity payment for one year. Women faced even stiffer penalties. In addition to the loss of treaty money, female alcoholics had their heads shaved for drinking on the reservation. Francis Barker, who constantly decried the effect of "the worm of the still" among the Shawnees, was pleased with these draconian temperance laws. He believed that they would "do much good if sufficient firmness . . . is sustained in the executing of laws." Endemic violence on the reservation offers a partial explanation of the harsh new penalties enforced by the national council. In 1852 alone, four Shawnees died in alcohol-related violence. Council members wanted to curb the bloodshed between tribal members by making an example of Shawnees convicted of murder. In 1856, the tribal sheriff demonstrated the national council's strength when he apprehended a Shawnee murder suspect. The accused, a man named David Daugherty, was found guilty by the national council and later hanged for his crime. Daugherty's punishment served notice to all Shawnees that national council members meant to assert their authority over domestic affairs.[61]

But their primary goal remained treaty negotiations with the United States. Christian missionaries and national leaders had similar motivations. Barker explained that "a majority of the council men are professors of religion." He added that their religious leanings provided the men "with an energy desirable in the transaction of business."[62] In the 1850s, business deals involving reservation lands were the paramount concern of council members and American officials alike.

Robinson's refusal to respect the wishes of the national council at the annuity payment of 1853 convinced the members of the Shawnee council, who desired complete autonomy over tribal affairs, that the federal government would continue to intervene in tribal politics in the years ahead. As the subagent for Delawares, Wyandots, and Shawnees, Robinson admitted that "the government of the United States, by its policy, has pretty much subverted the authority of the chiefs." In May 1854, when Congress created Kansas Territory, it became clear that the revolutionary changes initiated by the elected members of the national council would remain incomplete and contested. Federal officials and tribal opponents challenged their ability to control treaty annuities and make unilateral decisions on behalf of their people.[63]

Between 1854 and 1855, 10,679 emigrant Indians from nine different tribes ceded land to the United States in this context. Ranging from the Otoe and

Missouria tribes, whose ancestral homelands included Missouri and Iowa, to the Wyandots and Shawnees of Ohio, the tribes ceded 72 percent of their lands. Their reservations, which stretched westward from the Missouri border, originally encompassed 42,645,200 acres of land. After 1855, only 15,230,430 acres remained. The emigrant tribes, most of whom were Algonquian speakers originally from the midwestern United States, faced an insecure future. The Shawnees and their neighbors had reason to fear life in the newly created territory. Most of the tribes lived in small villages clustered along the border with Missouri, where access to trading posts, plentiful timber, and irrigation offered the best locations for settlements. More than 100,000 settlers crowded into the lands along the Kansas-Missouri border for similar reasons between 1854 and 1860. Indian survival became even more complicated when Congress opened the Kansas Territory to settlement before the treaties had been ratified and the boundaries between public and Indian lands had been clearly surveyed.[64] Consequently, settlers challenged the Shawnees and their neighbors in a protracted series of legal, and sometimes physical, struggles over land that drained tribesmen of precious resources and morale. Settlers contributed to the diminished sovereignty of the tribes precisely when those tribes worked to create tribal governments modeled after the United States.

In the years between the creation of the Kansas Territory and the Shawnees' ultimate removal from the state in 1871, federal subagents had the power to determine land sales, tribal membership, and the ability of tribal leaders to travel to Washington. The 1854 Shawnee treaty eroded the tribe's sovereignty by creating the legal justification for federal officials to intervene in tribal affairs.[65] Shawnee subagents, who were originally charged with protecting Indians from whites and delivering federal money to tribes, saw their responsibilities increase. The 1854 treaty granted their agent final approval of the choice of allotments, as well as determining the value of improvements on tribal land. In addition, the Shawnee agent interviewed tribal delegates interested in traveling to Washington and determined whether individual tribal members were fit to sell their land to prospective buyers.

The original Shawnee reservation spanned from modern-day Kansas City, Kansas, to Topeka, Kansas, and encompassed 1,600,000 acres of land. Following the 1854 treaty, the Shawnees were left with approximately 200,000 acres parceled out into three distinct clusters within thirty miles of the Missouri border. The majority of the tribe, nearly 690 Shawnees, accepted 200-acre allotments. Approximately 140,000 acres of land went to the individual heads of households. More than 160 Shawnees refused to accept individual allotments and joined with their leader, Black Bob, on 33,000 acres of communally owned land just across the Missouri line. Another group of Shawnees under Longtail also refused allotments and held their land in common. Finally, the tribe reserved 24,000 acres of land for those Absentee Shawnees who had refused to move north onto the now-defunct reservation in Kansas. Shawnee delegates to the 1854 treaty outraged their detractors in the tribe when they worked in a number of special provisions to the final settlement with the United States. Parks received more than 1,280 acres of land for his "faithful service to the nation." Black Hoof was granted an additional 640 acres of land. Finally, Thomas Johnson and the Methodists received 1,908 acres of land, while the Quakers and the Baptists were left with only 320 and 160 acres, respectively.[66]

Francis Barker and the Shawnee Baptists were furious over the additional land deals and the obvious favoritism shown for the Southern Methodists. Barker collaborated with a Shawnee named Daugherty later that June in drafting a remonstrance against the 1854 treaty, which they forwarded to the Office of Indian Affairs in Washington. They accused Parks of conspiring with the numerous Shawnee agents over the years in keeping the Shawnee settlements close to the Missouri state line, across the border from his trading house in Westport, Missouri. Barker and Daugherty also claimed that Parks accepted what amounted to "an annual bribe" by working for the United States as an interpreter and clerk while acting as head chief of the Shawnee nation.[67] Even Barker's soft-spoken colleague, Jotham Meeker, risked his friendship with Johnson and sided with Barker in the dispute, arguing that "the Shawanoe agent and the Shawanoe principal chief . . . have joined with him [Johnson] in his deadly hatred to our brother Barker."[68]

Baptist and Shawnee dissidents were no match for the powerful coalition of Shawnee elites, tribal missionaries, and government officials. Parks, Johnson, and Robinson joined forces to have Barker removed from the reservation, and by May 1855 they had achieved their goal. Barker was evicted from the 160-acre allotment for the Baptist mission, and the land was opened for sale. Hereafter, Shawnee Baptists met exclusively in private homes.[69]

The Barker controversy illustrates the paradoxical relationship between Shawnee agents and tribal leaders after the creation of the national council. Robinson played an essential role in defending the interests of the national council against their opponents within the tribe. When Parks and Johnson joined with Robinson against the Baptist missionary and his Shawnee supporters, they formed an insurmountable nexus of interests allied to ensure the national leadership's survival. The commissioner of Indian affairs, George Manypenny, disliked Johnson.[70] However, he was unwilling to go against the tribe's wishes with Robinson behind them. Robinson's role in the national council's victory over their opponents underscores the limited sovereignty of tribal governments in the mid- to late nineteenth century. Robinson championed the council's wishes for the tribe following the treaty, providing head chiefs with crucial legitimacy as they negotiated with government officials. Yet just one year earlier Robinson had blocked the national council's plans for the tribal annuity, revealing the extent of Shawnee dependence on the United States.

Officially sanctioned meddling in Shawnee affairs produced mixed results. For those Shawnees excluded from the national council, the tribe's subagent often acted as an important safeguard against abuse by more powerful kinsmen. But American intervention in Shawnee affairs was intermittent, unpredictable, and usually motivated by a desire to serve American interests rather than Shawnee dissidents. Ultimately, American settlers became a far more implacable foe of Shawnee political, economic, and cultural sovereignty between 1854 and the tribe's removal from Kansas seventeen years later.

With the creation of Kansas Territory, federal subagents became singularly preoccupied with the task of protecting emigrant Indians from settlers. Agent Robinson's job was further complicated by the U.S. troops stationed at Fort Leavenworth who sympathized with American squatters, and who often worked with them to defraud the tribes of the land they retained. Robinson warned Manypenny that if he did not intervene and discipline the soldiers at Fort Leavenworth, "the Indians will be wholly disregarded, and the Spring immigration will seize upon the Shawnee and every other valuable reserve similarly situated in the teritory [*sic*]."[71] But federal officials in Washington did not act. The Americans' "failure of institutional nerve" allowed squatter abuses of the tribes to go unchecked and contributed to flagrant corruption in the region.[72]

The situation worsened for the Shawnees following Robinson's departure from the Indian service in 1855. His replacement, William Gay, filed several complaints regarding the destruction of timber on Shawnee lands by unrepentant Americans. Gay's outspoken defense of Shawnee sovereignty proved fatal. In June 1856, he was shot to death and his son severely wounded by an armed band of squatters who were upset with him for opposing newly constructed settlements.[73] The general unwillingness of Presidents Franklin Pierce and James Buchanan to discipline the troops stationed at Fort Leavenworth, remove squatters from Indian land, and defend Shawnee allotments against frivolous lawsuits placed the Shawnees and their neighbors in a desperate position. Violence against Indians in the Kansas Territory was socially sanctioned, and federal unwillingness to intervene revealed that popular demands were more important than treaty promises.[74]

Most Shawnees put aside internal political differences and came together to protest the government's inability to control settlers in the Kansas Territory. Tribal unity on the issue of squatter depredations was caused, in part, by the indifference of settlers who did not discriminate between Shawnee elites and rank-and-file tribal members. Joseph Parks and other council members were victimized by whites as much as their less well-known kinsmen.

Samuel Cornatzer, the council clerk for the Shawnee nation, cited the weakness of tribal subagents and their failure to issue titles to the Shawnees as the primary reasons for the Shawnees' suffering. "The agents we have had for the last 18 years are or have been better judges of Brandy than their duty," complained Cornatzer in a letter to the secretary of the interior, James Thompson. The Shawnees willingly defended their land and property from squatters and timber thieves. But without title to their land, both the Shawnees and the settlers understood that it would be impossible for the tribe to receive justice. Cornatzer lamented that "some of them [squatters] laugh [at] the idea of an Indian suing him and making him pay for trespassing."[75]

By the summer of 1858, the plight of those Shawnees remaining in Kansas worsened as the white advance on their lands continued. In June, a prominent Shawnee named Tooly, who had once been part of a Shawnee delegation to Washington, was killed by white trespassers as he attempted to defend his family's timber. The Shawnee agent, Ben Newsom, recounted the Shawnees' response to Tooly's murder. "The young men of the Shawnees turned out upon learning the facts," he said, "and in the night burned down the houses and drove off all white settlers upon lands assigned to Indians in that vicinity." The Shawnees' own brand of vigilante justice "put an end to all such intrusions in that quarter."[76]

By 1860 the limited sovereignty of the Shawnee national council had become a bittersweet reality for the Shawnees. Council members benefited from federal support in the sale of Shawnee lands to Americans, but they rankled at their agent's disregard for their authority when determining tribal membership and other issues of importance. Shawnee opponents of the national council pleaded with federal officials to assist them in turning back the clock and protecting their rights as members of distinctive villages. George Blue Jacket, Black Wolf, and a host of then-unknown Shawnees claimed that "a majority of their nation are with them & would rejoice at an order from their Great Father putting an end to the present Government of their nation and restoring their old form of Government."[77] But the economic influence of the council members, and the federal government's need to diminish Shawnee landholdings in Kansas, ensured the survival of the national council.

By 1860, Christian missionaries were no longer a significant force in tribal politics and in the survival of the national council. In 1858, when Joseph Parks was the head chief, the Shawnee national council voted to dissolve financial ties with the Methodist Church by withdrawing the Shawnee school fund. Johnson's affiliation with southern interests made the tribe's association with the mission particularly dangerous during the 1850s. Moreover, Parks and his supporters had achieved enough influence in secular channels to forgo their dependence on missionaries as intermediaries in tribal affairs. Ironically, Shawnee Baptists remained the most active churchgoers in the years after Barker's forced removal from the reservation.

Methodist and Baptist communities of faith had been vital to the establishment of the national council. But the drastic reduction of Shawnee lands by the 1854 treaty forced most Shawnees onto individual allotments besieged by land-hungry whites. Indeed, most Shawnees feared coming together as a community after the creation of the territory. The multiracial camp meetings of the late 1830s and 1840s became a thing of the past in the Kansas Territory. Christian Shawnees were not welcome in the newly established Baptist and Methodist churches of eastern Kansas. After 1854, interracial unity advocated by Christian missionaries became ideals of an earlier time. The racist and often lawless environment of "Bleeding Kansas" placed severe limits on Shawnee sovereignty and made Christianity an individual, rather than a community, affair.

6. Dissent and Removal: Competing Sovereigns in the Civil War Era

On May 21, 1856, a group of border ruffians rode into the town of Lawrence, less than fifteen miles from the Shawnee reservation, and terrorized the town. Aptly named for their use of guerrilla warfare in defense of slavery, the group included such prominent citizens as A. G. Boone, Senator David Atchison, and the Potawatomi Indian agent George Clarke. During their raid, they burned the most potent symbol of free soil in Kansas—the Free State Hotel. Important members of the Indian service either supported or participated in the attack. Men such as Clarke owed their positions to Senator Atchison. Others, such as the Fort Leavenworth agent Richard Cummins, hailed from Missouri and had long defended slavery in Kansas. The connections between the Shawnee national council and the proslavery bloc were even more pronounced than was typical among most tribes. Joseph Parks sold his trading house in Westport to A. G. Boone, and a number of former teachers at the Shawnee Methodist Mission lived in the community. Methodist missionary Thomas Johnson, another friend of Parks, was elected the first president of the proslavery territorial council, which initially met at the Shawnee Methodist Mission.[1] Taken together, they formed an eminent clique of leaders who were determined to open Kansas to settlement and introduce it to the Union as a slave state.

In retaliation for the attack on Lawrence, the abolitionist John Brown and a handful of his relatives attacked a proslavery settlement south of Lawrence, at Osawatomie Creek, on what had been the Peoria and Kaskaskia reservation. Using sabers, Brown and his sons forced three men and two boys from their cabins and murdered them. Some Shawnees sympathized with the people of Lawrence and understood Brown's massacre as a defensive action. Paschal

Fish, for one, operated a ferry and a hotel for settlers moving to Lawrence. Like Johnson, Parks, and Boone, Fish profited from the settlers who came with the opening of the Kansas Territory. At the same time, Fish became a valuable intermediary for the Black Bob band and other Shawnee dissenters. They founded separate Shawnee villages near modern-day Olathe and Eudora, Kansas. Both sites became known as free-soil towns, and the border ruffians targeted their communities for destruction as a result.[2]

In April 1859, three years after the violence at Lawrence and Osawatomie Creek, Joseph Parks died. Paschal Fish, Abelard Guthrie, and the Black Bob Shawnees they represented had long opposed Parks and the national council. But Parks's death and the sectional violence provided his opponents with new political opportunities. "Bleeding Kansas" had a democratizing effect on Shawnee politics. In the 1850s and 1860s, the Black Bob Shawnees took advantage of the vacuum of power that resulted from the turmoil, as free-soilers and proslavery men searched for Indian allies and gave voice to their supporters. Even those Shawnees determined to remain in Kansas, such as the Black Bobs, had to ally themselves with Paschal Fish and other intermediaries to promote their cause. Such collaboration was a devil's bargain for all Shawnees. Both proslavery and free-soil men promoted settlement. No one was above the fray.

Opponents of the Shawnee national council clamored for alternative forms of government in the waning years of the reservation. Government officials further assisted in the disintegration of Shawnee sovereignty by regularly intervening in tribal affairs. Dissenters within the tribe and paternalistic government officials ensured that the national council would not achieve the control over tribal affairs it sought. Both Shawnee nationalists and representatives of the U.S. government watched their prestige erode as immigration to and sectionalism in Kansas revealed the impotence of their governments.

In the 1854 treaty, members of the Shawnee national council contributed to their weakened position by agreeing to dissolve their reservation. Thereafter, approximately 720 tribal members became known as severalty Shawnees because they had accepted individual allotments of approximately 200 acres upon the creation of the Kansas Territory. Their Shawnee opponents argued that the severalty Shawnees had become citizens of the United States. They had forsaken tribal membership by dividing commonly owned tribal lands.[3]

In practice, tribal leaders interpreted severalty according to their own self-interests. Shawnees whose wealth reached beyond the tribe looked forward to American citizenship.[4] Like many Shawnees before them, they saw no end to removal. Forced relocation was an ongoing reality, a cruel affirmation of their Indian identity. In this context, it is easy to imagine the lure of individual land ownership and citizenship. In theory, allotments offered them and their descendants a reprieve from American land hunger. Moreover, citizenship carried with it a final accounting for the treaty responsibilities that the United States was obligated to fulfill. Tribal members could look forward to a cash payout that would terminate American obligations to the Shawnee people. Accordingly, many severalty Shawnees asked for patents to their land and for permanent residence in the state of Kansas as American citizens.

Yet most severalty Shawnees, including members of the national council, accepted allotments with the understanding that their tribal status would not be jeopardized. They believed that tribal membership was not contingent on the existence of a tribal reservation. In their view, severalty Shawnees lived on islands of tribal sovereignty amid the increasing authority of the state of Kansas. Federal law confirmed their understanding: the United States held the allotted lands in trust for the Shawnee tribe. Their land could not be sold directly to settlers or taxed by the state.[5] The trust relationship between the Shawnees and the United States affirmed tribalism in Kansas.

Yet the promotion of settlement took precedence over the protection of Indian rights. The 1862 Homestead Act, for example, transferred land to settlers that had been recently ceded by the tribes. In this way, American policy-makers eased the way for settlers by opening the reservations of eastern Kansas to settlement. Subsequent violence between Indians and American settlers thus undermined policies designed to assimilate the tribes. In response to the violence, both the severalty Shawnees and the Black Bob band abandoned their individual allotments and concentrated their settlements after the Kansas-Nebraska Act. They created mutual-aid societies across what remained of their lands. Many pressed for another treaty that might reverse allotment. The severalty Shawnees in particular longed for a smaller tract of communally owned land in Indian Territory. According to the Shawnee agent James B. Abbott, the severalty Shawnees dreamed of "a new home, where they can reunite all the bands belonging to their tribe, settle in a more compact body . . . and . . . place themselves beyond the reach of the influence of bad white men." In this way, violence along the Missouri-Kansas border perpetuated tribal identities and reversed decades of religious, economic, and educational exchange between Shawnees and ordinary Americans.[6]

Unlike the Black Bob Shawnees, who hoped to retain their communal lands near Olathe after the war, the severalty Shawnees believed that life in Kansas had become untenable. Between 1862 and 1867, the national council agreed to four treaties with the United States, all of which were rejected by Congress. Viewed as impediments to progress by Americans who dreamed of making a "garden in the grasslands," Shawnees found themselves increasingly segregated from whites. In fact, American preachers and teachers blocked Shawnees from participating in their services and their schools. The Shawnees responded by conducting church services in their homes, where most preached to their kinsmen in the Shawnee language. However, the Shawnees were unable to provide a substitute for the American schools during the war years. According to James Abbott, the author of the unratified 1862 treaty, the Shawnees had become "demoralized by various temptations" brought by American settlement and wished to move south, where they might "extend to each other council and guardianship which is necessary for their safety and protection." They asked for 88,160 acres of land in Indian Territory. These Maykujay Shawnees, formerly from Ohio, also wanted the total amount of U.S. treaty money ($89,000) paid to them because of "the almost total failure of the crops." Finally, they claimed that the Black Bob Shawnees, "being unwilling to adopt the habits of the white man, desire also to remove."[7] The Shawnee national council, which represented the interests of the severalty Shawnees, claimed to speak for all Shawnees.

Endemic violence, racism, and declining contact with ordinary Americans certainly took their toll on the Kansas Shawnees. But an increasingly institutionalized racism forced the Shawnees from their homes more effectively than the border ruffians. County and state officials used taxation and the law against those Shawnees determined to remain on their lands. Between 1859 and 1866, the commissioners of Johnson County, who administered land carved out of the Shawnee and Wyandot reservations, began taxing their allotments. North of the Kansas River, the Leavenworth County commissioners also taxed Delaware allotments. The Kansas Supreme Court defended its right to tax Shawnee lands, arguing that communal land ownership was essential to their status as domestic nations as outlined in both the commerce clause of the Constitution and the Marshall Trilogy.[8] State and local governments in Kansas worked diligently to undermine tribal governments, which they viewed as competing sovereigns. Missionaries such as Thomas Johnson and Indian agents such as James Abbott assisted county governments and the state by hosting the territorial legislature and opening Shawnee lands for settlement. Ordinary Shawnees thus fell victim to their former American benefactors and the Shawnee leaders allied with them.[9]

The U.S. Supreme Court finally intervened in 1865 with the landmark reversal of the state Supreme Court in *Blue Jacket v. Commissioners of Johnson County.* Named for one of the founders of the national council, Charles Blue Jacket, the decision divorced tribal sovereignty from communal land ownership. In effect, the justices ruled that tribes can exist without owning land. Nevertheless, Johnson County's seven years of taxation had irreparably harmed the severalty Shawnees. By 1862, just three years after taxation began, James Abbott estimated that the severalty Shawnees owed roughly $15,000 to Johnson County.[10] The Wyandot-Shawnee Abelard Guthrie claimed that by 1868, one-half of the tribe had lost its land.[11]

Shawnee dissidents joined with the commissioners of Johnson County in rejecting the severalty Shawnees' claim to power. Approximately 130 Black Bobs asserted that they were the true representatives of the Shawnee nation. Unlike the severalty Shawnees, hereditary chiefs remained in control of Chillicothe affairs. Moreover, female elders remained in charge of the spring Bread Dance. In effect, the Black Bob Shawnees worked the land together, under the direction of male and female leaders who inherited their positions of authority. Like the Johnson County commissioners and the Supreme Court of Kansas, the Black Bob band argued that citizenship in both the Shawnee nation and the United States was mutually exclusive. In their opinion, the acceptance of individual allotments carried with it the forfeiture of their rights as tribal members. Yet in spite of vocal opponents in the Shawnee Tribe, Johnson County, and the state of Kansas more generally, federal officials continued to recognize members of the Shawnee national council as the legitimate representatives of the Shawnee people.

Undeterred by these setbacks, in February 1861, Black Bob, along with Charles and Paschal Fish, asked the president and the secretary of interior to ignore anyone in Washington, D.C., who claimed to represent the Shawnee nation. The Chillicothe Shawnees expected federal officials to "rebuke those, who seek to devour us." The Black Bob band continued to reside on 33,000 acres of communally owned land, and they had also been instrumental in setting aside 24,000 acres of land for the Absentee Shawnees who had been in Texas and Oklahoma when Kansas Territory was opened for settlement. They dreamed of uniting with their southern kin, creating a powerful alliance against the severalty Shawnees. Formerly associated with the Missouri villages, Shawnee dissenters made Eudora, Kansas, their new capital. Black Bob and his allies clearly separated themselves from the accepted national council because they had learned that the Maykujay Shawnees wanted to sign a removal treaty.[12]

By challenging the severalty Shawnees' right to lead the nation, Black Bob made clear an inherent contradiction in American policy. Officials ranging from the commissioner of Indian affairs William P. Dole to the Shawnee agent James B. Abbott sustained the authority of the original Shawnee council and the severalty Shawnees they represented. In effect, Dole and Abbott defended the interests of Shawnee national leaders, some of whom owned slaves and sympathized with the Confederacy. As the Civil War progressed, American officials repeatedly warned representatives of the severalty Shawnees to avoid doing business with anyone known to be disloyal. Yet many Shawnees and Americans remained unconvinced of their trustworthiness. Abelard Guthrie blasted Dole for continuing to acknowledge the national council as the legitimate representatives of the Shawnee people. Guthrie was "astonished" that Dole had not done more to limit the power of those Shawnees associated with "that nursery of secessionism," the Shawnee Methodist Mission. In January 1863, Abbott acknowledged Guthrie's complaints and forced every member of the national council to take a loyalty oath. Not surprisingly, doubts about their commitment to the United States remained.[13]

Thomas Johnson, the upland southerner who ran the Shawnee Methodist Mission, promoted a version of American civilization that resembled the values of the plantation South more than the ideals of hardscrabble yeoman farmers such as Baptist missionary Jotham Meeker. Joseph Parks, Charles Blue Jacket, and Graham Rogers owned slaves, developed fruit orchards, and sold livestock to western migrants as they promoted the Christian gospel. Blue Jacket and Rogers lived near the Shawnee mission, and in both their

The Shawnee Methodist Mission became an important commercial and political center in Eastern Kansas. Copied from Heisler and Smith's *Atlas of Johnson County,* 1874. Kansas State Historical Society, Topeka, Kansas.

homes and in their work as public officials, national council members demonstrated their wealth and their status atop the class hierarchy of Kansas.[14]

The Black Bob and Absentee Shawnees were marginalized by the alliances crafted between the Shawnee national council and American elites along the border between Kansas and Missouri. Ironically, federal officials assisted in the dispossession of those Shawnees willing to fight for the United States. Both Abbott and the Shawnee national council collaborated to block members of the Black Bob-Absentee alliance from returning to the older mode of government. In fact, Black Bob charged that "some one, either the agent or some of the counsel, without his knowledge or consent" had signed his name to a petition requesting a new treaty. The treaty was anathema for Black Bob. Eighty-eight Shawnee men joined him in protesting abuses perpetrated by the national council. Black Bob claimed that "he has reason to believe . . . that there is a formal conspiracy to disturb him and his associates in the enjoyment of their property." He was incensed with the Shawnee agent and amazed that the United States intended to remove his people once again. In a pointed letter to the commissioner of Indian affairs, he asked how the United States could force a new treaty on his people when "everything in the way of energy and power" is required "to put down this unwholy [*sic*] revolution."[15]

National council members intended to limit the power of the Black Bob band by selling Absentee Shawnee lands and preventing their allies from joining with them. Severalty Shawnees with heavy tax debts to Johnson County looked forward to the sale of land set aside for the Absentees. The 1854 treaty stipulated that Absentees' land was to be held for five years, after which the Kansas Shawnees could sell off any unclaimed land on the 24,000-acre tract. Members of the national council wanted "the Land to be appraised and sold to the highest bidder at public sale" now that the five-year waiting period had passed. By 1859, depredations and liens on Shawnee property were immense, and many Shawnees planned on using revenue from the sale of Absentee lands to offset their losses.[16]

Severalty Shawnees hoping to conclude a new treaty placed harsh restrictions on tribal membership. Shawnees had moved on and off the reservation for decades, as trade, hunting, and warfare drew tribal members toward new opportunities. The Civil War accelerated this movement and prolonged years of separation between relatives. But as the dissolution of the reservation became imminent, many Shawnees returned to Kansas to claim a share of their birthright. These returning Shawnees soon became subjects of intense debate and scrutiny. Economics drove the investigation into their lives. Placing strict limits on tribal membership increased the individual share of money derived from a potential treaty. "Absent Shawnees," particularly those now living in Texas and Indian Territory, raised important questions about Shawnee identity. The national council argued that "being Shawnee" required long-term residence on the Kansas reservation.[17] The Black Bob band favored a different approach. In their view, kinship—membership in one of the five Shawnee divisions—was essential to tribal membership. Second, a willingness to work the land communally and to participate in the rituals that defined Shawnee culture was imperative. The Absentee Shawnees continued these time-honored practices. The Chillicothe Shawnees also regarded their southern kin as crucial supporters in their fight against removal and the often heavy-handed tactics of the national council. As such, the Black Bob Shawnees had an affinity for the Absentees that had long since decayed for the severalty Shawnees.

Severalty Shawnees played an essential gatekeeping role in the acceptance and rejection of Shawnees returning to Kansas in the hopes of being reinstated as tribal members. They also determined the competency of those wishing to sell their land. The resulting disputes over tribal membership illustrated the divergent perspectives of the Shawnee people and the important role played by government officials in determining tribal membership. Applicants for membership in the tribe unwittingly contributed to these larger struggles over sovereignty and tribal identity.

Returning Shawnees whose family histories conflicted with those of the members of the national council were also scrutinized. In February 1860, a man named George Ironsides, a mixed-blood Shawnee and a physician who had resided in Canada, journeyed to Kansas and applied for Shawnee tribal membership. Both the national council and the commissioner of Indian affairs, Charles Mix, rejected Ironsides's claim. Ironsides's family history doubtless contributed to their trepidation. His father was a British trader who had worked closely with Tecumseh and Tenskwatawa in the War of 1812. Ironsides's father moved to Canada when the United States asserted its sovereignty over the Great Lakes. Ohio Shawnees whose ancestors had fought with the Americans against Tecumseh and his allies were loath to admit a man with his history onto the tribal roll. They argued that his long residence outside of the United States, apart from fellow tribesmen, nullified his right to membership in the tribe. The Black Bob band protested, arguing that the Absentee tract was designed for people like Ironsides, whose "birth away from the present residence of the tribe" should not be used against them.[18]

National council members also joined with the Shawnee agent in denying applicants whose protracted economic and military adventures pulled them from the reservation. In March 1863, a man named Matthew Brown applied for Shawnee membership. He had traveled widely and had fought with the U.S. military over the years. The Mexican war brought him deep into Mexico, where he fought at Chapultepec and Cerro Gordo. After the war, Brown tried his hand at prospecting for gold in California, only to be drawn back east by the possibility of combat in the Civil War. He fought in the Battle of Cane Hill "and was lately shot through the shoulder and breast while charging on the rebel battery." Writing from his hospital bed, Brown petitioned to join his Shawnee mother on the reservation. The national council rejected his application as well as similar claims from other people of Shawnee descent who wished to settle on the Absentee tract. The Shawnee agent supported the council's decision.[19]

Federal officials sometimes overrode the national council, which consistently sought to exclude individuals from the tribal roll. In the case of John Owen, a white widower of a Shawnee woman, the Shawnee agent overruled the council's wishes and granted him land and membership in the tribe. Being Shawnee was not always based on the decisions of the Shawnee national council. The United States could sometimes force the Shawnees to accept unwanted individuals as tribal members. It seems that the Black Bob Shawnees were the only community of interest that was consistently ignored in these disputes regarding tribal membership.[20]

Yet, in spite of the conspiracy of interested parties allied against them, the Civil War inadvertently contributed to parity between the Shawnee rivals. Between fall 1862 and winter 1863, so many Absentee Shawnees fled their settlements between the forks of the Canadian River for Kansas that the Black Bob band claimed to represent a majority of the nation. By summer 1863, other reports placed them at between 480 and 541 persons—well short of a majority. Nevertheless, new Civil War refugees inadvertently increased pressure for reform. They mounted a successful campaign to close the Methodist mission, alleging that the institution was a haven for Confederate sympathizers and that Shawnee children received poor treatment from those in charge.[21]

For a brief period between 1862 and 1866, the Absentee–Black Bob allies had the numbers to challenge the authority of their rivals within the tribe. By 1863, approximately 170 of their southern kin had fled the Indian Territory and joined with the Chillicothe Shawnees.[22] According to Thomas Wildcat Alford, who migrated with his family from Indian Territory to Kansas when he was three years old, "though the two bands had been separated for more than fifty years . . . they took up their life together with no jar or discord and again they were an undivided people." Now united, the two bands merged and held their first independent election in January 1863. By 1866, the Absentee and Black Bob band achieved parity with their opponents, with both sides numbering approximately 770 supporters.[23]

Invigorated by the Shawnee refugees from the south, Shawnee dissenters also criticized American policy-makers, such as Abraham Lincoln, for failing to protect the rights of dissenters within the tribe. In a January 1863 letter to the president, Black Bob pointedly requested "a decision from you and the Indian Bureau [concerning] which [group] shall Govern[,] the majority or the minority."[24] The Chillicothe leader wanted the Shawnees to return "back to the old Indian custom of perpetual chief[s]." Like members of the national council before them, Shawnee dissidents asked American officials to uphold basic principles of human rights and tribal sovereignty. They continued to test the Americans' commitment to the values they purported to hold dear.[25]

Federal officials ranging from Abraham Lincoln to the Shawnee subagent James Abbott refused to acknowledge the Chillicothe Shawnees as legitimate opponents of the national council. In a curious allusion to the Civil War, Abbott remarked that they had "rebelled" against the council because of the actions of a few designing white men who had manipulated the more traditional members of the Chillicothe division. Abbott also cast doubt on Black Bob's claim to be the rightful heir to national leadership, based on his direct descent from "the old Shawnee chiefs." Not surprisingly, the national council agreed with Abbott's assessment. They implicated Paschal Fish and Abelard Guthrie, both of whom were determined enemies of James Abbott and Thomas Johnson. Black Bob rejected these accusations by distancing his people from the assistance of literate Shawnee entrepreneurs and tribal intermediaries. Theirs was a grassroots protest movement.[26]

The Black Bob Shawnees' outspoken criticism of the national council and the Shawnee Methodist Mission in the early years of the war contributed to their reputation as Union sympathizers. In September 1862, William Quantrill led over 200 men across the Missouri line in an attack on the Black Bob's communal settlement. They rode in on horseback and overwhelmed the outnumbered and poorly armed Shawnees. Quantrill and his men killed one Shawnee man dressed in a Union uniform and sexually assaulted some of the Shawnee women. James Abbott, the Shawnee subagent during the war, explained that Quantrill "threatened to kill every Shawnee that was found wearing a U.S. uniform." According to the survivors of Quantrill's raid, the bushwhackers robbed the Shawnees of bedding, blankets, clothing, and other goods necessary for survival as winter approached.[27] The Chillicothes spent the remainder of the war as refugees on the western boundary of the reservation, far removed from their land and improvements. "Believing their lives immediately in danger," Abbott reported, the Black Bobs decided to live "as best they can upon the charities of their friends."[28]

Quantrill's raid drove the Black Bobs west, to Belmont, Kansas, where they became allied with approximately 7,000 refugees from Indian Territory, including the Delawares, Kickapoos, Caddos, Wichitas, Absentee Shawnees, Seminoles, and Creeks. These tribes abandoned Indian Territory in a final attempt to remain neutral in the Civil War. Confederate sympathizers within their tribes had made life untenable, and the refugees chose to flee northward rather than endure violence within and without their own communities. In the winter of 1861–1862, two detachments left the Indian Territory. A band of Absentees led by Bob Deer and Jo Ellis abandoned their villages along with Opothleyahola's Creeks. They had been attacked on Christmas Day, 1861, by Creek warriors allied with the Confederacy. A second detachment under the Delaware chief, Black Beaver, left their homes near modern-day Anadarko, Oklahoma, for Kansas. Formerly associated with the Wichita Agency, these allied tribes were forced out of the agency by the government agent, Matthew Leeper, as well as those tribes who sided with the Confederacy. Once in Kansas, many of the refugees combined forces and joined the Union Indian Brigade.[29]

The allied refugees soon exacted their revenge on both the agent and the tribes who had driven them from their homes. In September 1862, ninety-six Delaware and Shawnee warriors departed on a 500-mile trek back to the Wichita Agency. After stopping for a short time on the Neosho River, where they rested with their Seneca-Shawnee relatives, they traveled for another seventeen days. On October 23, not long after their arrival, a gunfight began. Shawnee and Delaware warriors killed Agent Leeper and three other government agents in the melee that followed. The Tonkawas, an Apachean-speaking tribe allied with the Confederate Indian agents, fled the agency. The Delawares and Shawnees hunted them down, killing all but fifty of an estimated one hundred fifty to three hundred men, women, and children. So ended the biggest Shawnee military engagement of the Civil War.[30]

Shawnee and Delaware motives for killing their former agent and massacring the Tonkawas vary. Some claimed that Shawnee warriors sought revenge on the Tonkawas for "having killed and eaten some Shawnees" during their stay at the Wichita Agency. Others claimed that age-old tensions between tribes indigenous to West Texas, such as the Comanches, Tonkawas, and Lipan Apaches, and Indian newcomers, such as the Shawnees, Delawares, and Caddos, motivated the attack. The Tonkawas' alliance with the Confederacy provided these newcomers with an excuse for destroying them.[31]

Whatever the ultimate rationale behind the attack, Union forces were clearly pleased with the outcome. The Shawnees and Delawares captured a number of documents from the agency, including copies of treaties executed by Albert Pike on behalf of the Confederate States of America with numerous tribes in the Indian Territory. As a result, the Union gained a clearer picture of its Indian enemies and the means by which the Confederacy drew them into their alliance. Finally, the Shawnee and Delaware raid cost the Union nothing, for the Shawnees and Delawares initiated the attack on their own terms.[32]

Such lopsided victories led some American officials to lobby for the full-scale recruitment of the emigrant tribes into the Union army. Rules for the enlistment of Indians varied. During the early years of the war, many eastern states enforced strict rules against the use of Indian troops. In the West, pragmatism seemed to mitigate American race prejudice. Most federal troops abandoned their western posts during the war, leaving their Indian charges with little protection against American settlers. Given the absence of Union troops, and their desire to prove their commitment and value to the United States, the Black Bob Shawnees favored the enlistment of Indians. According to Black Bob, they were "ready to take up arms" in defense of the United States at any time. Following centuries-old patterns established by their ancestors, the Black Bobs hoped to ally themselves with a powerful colonizer and to secure their land base in the process. Farther south, in the Indian Territory, the absence of federal troops forced the tribes to sign treaties with the Confederacy in order to receive a modicum of protection from their armies. In exchange, the Confederacy restricted Indian combatants to fighting in Indian Territory.[33]

Shawnee troops fought in a limited number of engagements in and around their home territories in both the Indian Territory and Kansas. The Civil War burdened both women and men, but the violence and poverty of the war fell upon Shawnees loyal to the United States to a far greater extent than those who sympathized with the Confederacy. Bordered by Missouri to the east and Indian Territory to the south, both Indians and Americans lived in a largely southern context. Moreover, open partisans of the Union did not receive promised treaty annuities from their opponents on the national council. This combination of physical and economic violence debilitated the refugee communities that refused to recognize the Shawnee national council.

The severalty Shawnees served in the Union army in spite of their close ties with white southerners and Indian tribes sympathetic to the Confederacy. Similarly, Quantrill's efforts were not enough to sway Shawnee dissidents from joining in the fight. Like their predecessors in Ohio, who generally fought on behalf of the United States in the War of 1812, the Shawnees moved from neutrality to support for the Union by 1863. However, most saw action toward the end of the conflict, as Union generals became desperate for men. Civilians between the ages of eighteen and sixty were pressed into service by Samuel Curtis, the general in charge of the Department of Kansas. Curtis established martial law and the enlistment of able-bodied men. Indian agents soon notified their charges of Curtis's demands. In October 1864, seventy-three Shawnee men responded to Curtis's call the day after he issued the order.[34]

The Missouri Confederate leader, Sterling Price, led approximately 10,000 soldiers north from Arkansas to Missouri in a final effort to shift the balance of the war toward the Confederate States of America. Price believed that a series of Confederate victories—and a long reign of destruction—from Arkansas to Kansas might deter Union General William Tecumseh Sherman, who was then engaged in his own "march to the sea." On October 23, 1864, Price's campaign to break the will of the Union army to fight in the West began to fail at the decisive Battle of Westport. Some 20,000 federal troops met 9,000 Confederate soldiers just across from Kansas City, Kansas, on what was left of Shawnee land. The Confederate army retreated into Kansas as they headed south toward Indian Territory. On October 25, Confederate and Union forces met again below the Marais des Cygnes River. It was the first engagement between regular armies in Kansas since the war began.[35]

The Shawnees and their neighbors—both Americans and American Indians—experienced a Civil War conducted by irregular forces. Kansans followed Price's movements and anticipated the conflict at Westport. But for ten years prior to the Battle of Westport, sudden, unpredictable bursts of violence fell upon the civilian and Indian populations. Noncombatants suffered mightily from abuse heaped on them by partisan neighbors on either side of the conflict. Elizabeth Walton's experience in the Civil War provides some insight into the impact of the conflict on ordinary Shawnees. She spent most of the war without her husband and supported herself and her three children on wages earned as a seamstress, a trade she probably learned from one of the mission schools. Then, in the winter of 1864, tragedy struck. A smallpox epidemic swept across eastern Kansas, nearly blinding Elizabeth and two of her children before it had run its course. Then she received news that her husband, an enlistee in the Union army, had been arrested for desertion and jailed. Destitute, and without assistance from the tribe, Elizabeth asked the national council to acknowledge her competency. She planned on selling forty acres of her allotment to the highest bidder. Four years later, Graham Rogers, then head chief of the Shawnee nation, wrote that Walton had married a white man and that she wished "to dissolve her connection with the tribe on their removal." As the Civil War progressed and removal became imminent, members of the national council increasingly reported on, and contributed to, the dispossession of their own people by assessing the competency of tribal members wishing to sell their lands.[36]

As Elizabeth Walton and an unknown number of Shawnees chose citizenship over yet another removal, the Shawnee national council continued its attempts to secure a new home in Indian Territory. Their first choice remained the Seneca-Shawnee reservation, which had been established in 1832. They hoped to continue their dream of consolidating the Shawnee people on a united, albeit diminished, reservation. In August 1864, the national council voted to "send a delegation . . . into the Indian country . . . to select and make some arrangements for a new home." Not surprisingly, the Black Bob band protested the national council's plan to make an early exit from Kansas. In a letter to the commissioner of Indian affairs, William P. Dole, they argued that "we . . . still claim that we have a chief and council, and will have nothing to do with elections that are called by the other council." Both the Absentee and Black Bob bands continued to live on the western edge of the reservation. Denied support from their agent, Shawnee refugees subsisted by hunting buffalo.[37]

The power struggle between the Shawnee national council and the Black Bob Shawnees manifested itself in a variety of ways between the creation of the Kansas Territory and the conclusion of the Civil War. The conflict between the various Shawnee villages was, in many ways, a by-product of American policy. The United States' misguided attempt at consolidating disparate villages onto tribal reservations made clear the distinctions between them. The American Civil War thus became an inner civil war between the Shawnees and revealed the Janus-faced nature of Shawnee politics. The Black Bobs argued for a return to hereditary chiefs whose authority derived from their divisional affiliation and the villages they represented. Centuries of political fragmentation and cultural evolution made the political consolidation of the Shawnee people as a nation an impossibility. The "republican" form of government, which became the theoretical basis for the creation of the Shawnee national council, was simply too authoritarian and unrepresentative to unite the Shawnee people.

Nevertheless, members of the Shawnee national council maintained their right to speak for all Shawnees, from Kansas to Texas. In their view, the Shawnees were originally one people, united as a political and cultural entity. As such, the government they created represented their best attempt at turning away from their long history of village-based autonomy. They hoped to reconstitute the Shawnee people as the nation they believed they had been before colonization. But the newly created Shawnee nation was challenged, and ultimately destroyed, by the crisis of the sectional conflict. The Civil War in Indian country illustrates the failure of national Shawnee leaders to eliminate historical identities that had become even stronger than pre-Columbian memories of tribal unity. Ultimately, Shawnee villagers whose cultural and political identities had been shaped in conversation with colonizers and their Indian neighbors preferred shared, multiethnic histories over tribal memories. Localism and village-based autonomy prevailed.

The tension between tribal consolidation and village-based autonomy remained unresolved as the Shawnees' tenure in Kansas came to a close. Both the Black Bob and the Absentee Shawnees insisted that they had always conducted themselves as a separate government from their counterparts on the national council. According to Black Bob, Paschal Fish, and their supporters, they maintained their separate status until "the year 1852, when the Ohio Shawnees, relying on their superior numbers and shrewdness insisted on abolishing the old organization and establishing . . . a council elected by the two tribes." The political revolution they engineered would not have been possible without the support of the various government agents who had always conspired with the Ohio Shawnees in an effort to consolidate tribal authority.[38]

Not surprisingly, the severalty Shawnees offered a competing memory of the early years on the reservation and the birth of the Shawnee nation. They recalled a tradition of tribal unity rather than the Black Bob-Absentee belief in village-based autonomy. Supporters of the national council, who had formerly been known as Ohio and Rogerstown Shawnees, celebrated the reservation. They described it as the site which made "the council fires complete after centuries of separation." In their opinion, the reservation fulfilled the long-sought reunification of the Shawnee people. Council members explained that "we were one people with customs alike or the same though separated for long years." Shawnee unification was complete in 1852, "when civilization with its teachings overthrew the old order of things and our hereditary leaders bowed to the will of the people [and] abdicated their seats from their hereditary chairs."[39]

Conflicting memories of the Shawnee national council, and the reservation that fostered its birth, had important consequences for both sides. The Black Bob Shawnees sought both political independence and geographic separation from the Shawnee national council. Conversely, the Shawnee national council continued to promote the national unity of the Shawnee people, even as they faced overwhelming restrictions on the amount of land and sovereignty that the United States was willing to grant the Shawnees in Indian Territory. For the various divisions of the Shawnee people, history and memory merged into an important defense of their unique perspectives on what it meant to be Shawnee.

Their long-standing debate, focused as it was on whether the Shawnees were a tribe or a series of villages united by language and cultural practices, has a long history. Years earlier Tenskwatawa and Black Hoof had focused their interviews on these same questions. Two distinct interpretations of Shawnee political identity, first articulated in the 1820s, remained unresolved as the Black Bob, Absentee, and severalty Shawnees were forced from Kansas. Neither side agreed on the traditional identity of the Shawnee people. Village-based autonomy and tribal unity remained irreconcilable political options for both in spite of U.S. domination of Shawnee politics between 1830 and 1870.

Between 1864 and 1871, the Kansas Shawnees began the slow process of removal to what remained of Indian Territory. Unlike earlier removals, which swept tribes like the Shawnees from their homes through a determined set of treaties and organized removals, settlement in Oklahoma proceeded in a piecemeal fashion. In 1867, the Shawnees signed a treaty with the United States that provided for the creation of a new reservation in Indian Territory. Shawnees such as Elizabeth Walton, who wished to remain in Kansas, were given the option of citizenship. But 770 severalty Shawnees, along with an equal number of Absentee and Black Bob Shawnees, soundly rejected citizenship and moved south.[40]

The architects of the Shawnee nation lost their bid to live alongside their Seneca-Shawnee relatives in northeastern Indian Territory. In June 1869, the United States forced the Cherokees, some of whom had fought on behalf of the Confederacy, to accept both the severalty Shawnees and the Kansas Delawares into their tribe and their reservation. As a punishment for joining the Confederacy, the United States compelled the Cherokees to accept the Shawnees and Delawares "on equal terms in every respect, and with all the privileges and immunities of native citizens of said Cherokee nation." "The late Chiefs of the Shawnee tribe of Indians," including Graham Rogers and Charles Tucker, became known as the Cherokee Shawnees. Their dream of national unity and sovereignty was shattered. As satellite nations within the Cherokee nation, the Shawnees and Delawares were now dependent on both the United States and the Cherokee tribal government. Although both the Shawnees and Delawares received voting rights and tribal benefits, it remained difficult for both to carve out an independent space for themselves.[41]

Nevertheless, generations of Cherokee Shawnees kept the dream of Shawnee sovereignty alive. Between 1980 and 2000, the Cherokee Shawnees lobbied both the United States and the Cherokee Nation for the right to reestablish their sovereignty as an independent tribe. Finally, on December 28, 2000, the Cherokee Shawnees achieved independence from the Cherokees and federal recognition from the United States. Now known as the Shawnee Tribe, approximately 1,300 Shawnees have transferred their tribal membership from the Cherokee Nation. Tribal officials estimate that another 6,000 Shawnees—most of whom can trace their descent through the Shawnees, Cherokees, and other tribes—have chosen to remain part of the Cherokee Nation.[42]

The Shawnee Tribe's long, and ultimately victorious, struggle for federal recognition has been bittersweet. Their essential problem stems from their geographic consolidation within the boundaries of the Cherokee Nation in the 1860s and 1870s. While the Shawnee Tribe has achieved federal recognition, they have not been granted trust land for their exclusive benefit on the former Cherokee reservation. The Cherokee Nation continues to own the trust land that had been set aside for the Shawnees and Delawares in what is now Craig County. Shawnee tribal leaders acknowledge that sovereignty is incomplete without land. In a sense, landless tribes operate at the sufferance of the landowners. The legacy of the Civil War, and the removal treaties that closely followed the war, continues to shape the contemporary struggles of the Shawnees and their neighbors.[43]

The Absentee Shawnees have faced similar conflicts with both the United States and neighboring tribes that have grown out of the Civil War and subsequent treaties. For example, the Shawnees' 1867 treaty was not ratified by Congress. Had it been approved, the Black Bobs and Absentees would have been compelled to join with the severalty and Eastern Shawnees on the Cherokee reservation. While some Black Bobs selected land in what is now Craig County, Oklahoma, the vast majority (approximately 80 percent of the band), joined the Absentee Shawnees. Together, the Black Bob and Absentee Shawnees who had lived as refugees in Kansas returned to lands recently purchased from the Oklahoma Seminoles, between the forks of the Canadian River, in present-day Cleveland and Pottawatomie County, Oklahoma. They rejoined several hundred Absentee Shawnees who had managed to remain on their lands in Indian Territory since 1839, when they were driven from Texas by Governor Mirabeau Lamar in a wave of Indian-hating that followed Texas's independence from Mexico. Nevertheless, the United States refused to recognize the Absentee Shawnees' unbroken history between the forks of the Canadian River. Regarded as squatters on their former homelands between 1864 and 1872, the United States pressured both the Absentees and the Black Bobs to join the Cherokee Shawnees in northeastern Oklahoma. In 1872, the United States conceded defeat and recognized their sovereignty as an autonomous tribe.[44]

The Absentees now hold approximately 11,300 acres of trust land, 358 acres of which is owned by the tribe as a whole. They are unique among the three federally recognized Shawnee tribes for basing tribal membership on one-quarter blood quantum rather than lineal descent from one of several nineteenth and early-twentieth century tribal rolls. With 2,947 members as of December 31, 2002, the Absentee Shawnees have continued a long population recovery. They have also persevered in their quest for self-determination. In September 1990, the Absentee Shawnee Tribe became a self-governing nation, reversing centuries of U.S. paternalism. Tribal members now receive health care, educational funds, and a host of other social services from tribally operated programs. In fact, the Absentee Shawnees were among the first seven tribes in the nation to become a self-governing tribe.[45]

Yet challenges to tribal sovereignty remain. For one, the Absentee Shawnees live on land that was sold by the Seminoles to the United States and then promised to the Citizen Band Potawatomis. According to the Shawnee historian Thomas Wildcat Alford, "the land that had been taken by the Absentee Shawnees was promised to them [Citizen Band Potawatomi], because there was no record showing it to be occupied."[46] Put another way, the United States' attempt to consolidate the Shawnee tribes into one nation, and their related refusal to acknowledge the independence of the Absentee and Black Bob Shawnees, meant that these Shawnee dissidents became a people without a country. The United States removed the Citizen Band Potawatomis from Kansas to land held by the Absentee Shawnees in the early 1870s, and subsequent conflicts between the two tribes nearly resulted in open warfare in the last decades of the nineteenth century. The Bureau of Indian Affairs, the Indian Claims Commission, and the U.S. federal court has consistently sided with the Citizen Band Potawatomis. They have argued that the Absentee Shawnee Tribe does not "share a common 'former reservation'" with the Citizen Band. While the Absentee Shawnee Tribe has maintained its political independence from the Citizen Band, they must obtain the consent of both the United States and the Citizen Band before placing additional land into trust status. These rulings have significantly hindered several economic-development projects conceived by the Absentee Shawnee Tribe that are contingent on the acquisition of trust land. Ongoing conflicts between the Absentee Shawnee Tribe of Oklahoma and Citizen Band Potawatomis stem from the haphazard removals and land policies of the United States during the removal period of the 1860s and 1870s.[47]

The Black Bob, Absentee, and Shawnee Tribes' long search for cultural autonomy and political sovereignty—from both the United States and competing branches of the same tribe—illustrates the complexity of tribal identities and the diversity of Shawnee responses to American colonization. For centuries, the various branches of the Shawnee tribe have struggled to achieve a measure of independence. Tribal histories typically conclude with military defeat, insinuating that as armed resistance failed, long years of loss, dependence, and accepting the unacceptable followed. The Shawnees' long nineteenth century seems to prove as much. Yet a closer look at the three federally recognized Shawnee tribes today reveals a longstanding commitment to both tribal sovereignty and cultural autonomy. The Shawnees continue to fight for greater control over their lives, and the result of their efforts reveals deep continuities in the Shawnee commitment to independence and their response to various colonizers over time.

Notes

Introduction

1. Author interview with Cultural Advisory Council, Absentee Shawnee Tribe, Shawnee, Oklahoma, 23 June 2002.

2. Raymond J. DeMallie, "'These Have No Ears': Narrative and the Ethnohistorical Method," *Ethnohistory* 40 (Fall 1993): 516, 525; Peter Nabokov, *A Forest of Time: American Indian Ways of History* (New York: Cambridge University Press, 2002), 2.

3. From the transcript of interview M6, pp. 1–2, conducted on 15 April 1968 in Little Axe, Oklahoma, for the Doris Duke Oral History Project, Western History Collections, University of Oklahoma; Julie Cruikshank, *Life Lived Like a Story: Life Stories of Three Yukon Native Elders* (Lincoln: University of Nebraska Press, 1990), 14.

4. For more on Tecumseh and the myths that have been created about him since his death on the Thames River, see John Sugden, *Tecumseh: A Life* (New York: Henry Holt and Company, 1997), 383–401. See also R. David Edmunds, *Tecumseh and the Quest for Indian Leadership* (Boston: Little, Brown, 1984), 213–25.

5. Thomas Wildcat Alford, *Civilization and the Story of the Absentee Shawnees* (Norman: University of Oklahoma Press, 1979); *Twenty-Two Years Work of the Hampton Normal and Agricultural Institute at Hampton, Virginia: Records of Negro and Indian Graduates and Ex-Students* (Hampton, Va.: Normal School Press, 1893).

6. Author interview with Lamont Laird (Eastern Shawnee), Miami, Oklahoma, 21 June 2002. Fieldwork notes, Attendance at Absentee Shawnee War Dance, 10 August 2002. For an extensive description of the Shawnee War Dance, see James H. Howard, *Shawnee! The Ceremonialism of a Native American Tribe and Its Cultural Background* (Athens: Ohio University Press, 1981), 273–85.

7. Nabokov, *Forest of Time,* 43.

8. Donald L. Fixico, "Ethics and Responsibilities in Writing American Indian History," in *Natives and Academics: Researching and Writing about American Indians,* ed. Devon A. Mihesuah (Lincoln: University of Nebraska Press, 1998), 94. Two dissertations on the

Shawnees provide extensive data on the range of Shawnee villages, primarily during the colonial period. See Noel W. Schutz, Jr., "The Study of Shawnee Myth in an Ethnographic and Ethnohistorical Perspective" (Ph.D. diss., Indiana University, 1975), and Jerry E. Clark, "Shawnee Indian Migration" (Ph.D. diss., University of Kentucky, 1977).

9. For more on Andrew Jackson and the intricacies of the Indian Removal Act, see Ronald N. Satz, *American Indian Policy in the Jacksonian Era* (Lincoln: University of Nebraska Press, 1975), 97–125. See also Reginald Horsman, *Race and Manifest Destiny: The Origins of American Racial Anglo-Saxonism* (Cambridge, Mass.: Harvard University Press, 1981).

10. Morris W. Foster, *Being Comanche: A Social History of an American Indian Community* (Tucson: University of Arizona Press, 1991).

11. The lack of research about and interest in the Shawnee Indians after 1815 is particularly ironic given the central role they played in both the Ohio Valley and the Great Lakes region as a whole in the eighteenth century. For a description of the Shawnees and the "shared world" in which they participated, see Richard White, *The Middle Ground: Indians, Empires, and Republics in the Great Lakes Region, 1650–1815* (New York: Cambridge University Press, 1991). Nevertheless, scholarly attention is shifting slowly toward Native American politics after removal. For examples of recent work, see Rebecca Kugel, *To Be the Main Leaders of Our People: A History of Minnesota Ojibwe Politics, 1825–1898* (East Lansing: Michigan State University Press, 1998), and Bradley J. Birzer, "Entangling Empires, Fracturing Frontiers: Jean Baptiste Richardville and the Quest for Miami Autonomy" (Ph.D. diss., Indiana University, 1998).

12. Harvey Carter, *The Life and Times of Little Turtle: First Sagamore of the Wabash* (Champaign: University of Illinois Press, 1986).

13. See Elizabeth A. Perkins, *Border Life: Experience and Memory in the Revolutionary Ohio Valley* (Chapel Hill: University of North Carolina Press, 1998), 8. Two recent dissertations explore the postremoval experience of American Indians from the Great Lakes: see Kevin J. Abing, "A Fall from Grace: Thomas Johnson and the Shawnee Indian Manual Labor School, 1839–1862" (Ph.D. diss., Marquette University, 1995), and Birzer, "Entangling Empires, Fracturing Frontiers." Several articles exist on Tecumseh's survivors between 1815 and 1830. For examples, see John Mack Faragher, "'More Motley than Mackinaw': From Ethnic Mixing to Ethnic Cleansing on the Frontier of the Lower Missouri, 1783–1833," in *Contact Points: American Frontiers from the Mohawk Valley to the Mississippi, 1750–1830*, ed. Andrew R. L. Cayton and Fredrika J. Teute (Chapel Hill: University of North Carolina Press, 1998), 304–26; Donald L. Huber, "White, Red, and Black: The Wyandot Mission at Upper Sandusky," *Timeline* 13 (May-June 1996): 2–17; Ronald Miriani, "Against the Wind: The Shawnee at Wapakoneta," *Queen City Heritage* 48 (Spring 1990): 33–47.

14. Francis Parkman, *The Oregon Trail* (1846; New York: Penguin Books, 1978).

15. Faragher's *Daniel Boone* and Richard White's *The Middle Ground* trace the cultural, demographic, and economic free fall of Indians following the "closing" of the frontier. John Mack Faragher, *Daniel Boone: The Life and Legend of an American Pioneer* (New York: Henry Holt and Company, 1992).

16. David Thelen's thought-provoking analysis of the way in which historians have been consumed with the creation of national histories and the quote from George Bancroft can be found in Thelen, "Making History and Making the United States," *Journal of*

American Studies 32 (1998): 382. Frederick Hoxie adds that "because most contemporary scholarship does not explore the detailed history of Indian societies, and because historians working the field have been reluctant to engage central interpretive themes, the duality that Parkman outlines—lives on." See Hoxie, "The Problems of Indian History," *Social Science Journal* 25 (1988): 389–99.

17. For a detailed analysis of the opposing concepts of savagism and civilization, see Roy Harvey Pearce, *Savagism and Civilization: A Study of the Indian and the American Mind* (Baltimore: Johns Hopkins University Press, 1967).

Chapter 1

1. Tenskwatawa was referred to as the Shawnee Prophet after the vision he experienced along the White River in Indiana Territory during the winter of 1805. Tenskwatawa discarded his previous name, Lalawathika, at this point in his life. The name Tenskwatawa has been interpreted to mean "The Open Door." For more on his life, see R. David Edmunds, *The Shawnee Prophet* (Lincoln: University of Nebraska Press, 1983). For more information on Charles C. Trowbridge, see James V. Campbell, "Biographical Sketch of Charles Christopher Trowbridge," *Pioneer Collections: Report of the Pioneer Society of the State of Michigan* 6 (1907): 478–91.

2. Multilingual Ottawa speakers lived in and around Detroit, the site of this foray into Shawnee history. For more on Ottawa as the language of the fur trade, see Susan Sleeper-Smith, *Indian Women and French Men: Rethinking Cultural Encounter in the Western Great Lakes* (Amherst: University of Massachusetts Press, 2001).

3. Reports of the Prophet's inability to speak English are numerous. For example, see Richard McNemar, *The Kentucky Revival, or a Short History of the Extraordinary Outpouring of the Spirit of God in the Western States of America* (Albany: E. and E. Hosford, 1808), 112. See also Emma Helen Blair, *The Indian Tribes of the Upper Mississippi Valley and the Region of the Great Lakes* (2 vols.; Lincoln: University of Nebraska Press, 1996), 2:274; Edmunds, *Shawnee Prophet*, 163–64, 167–68.

4. R. David Edmunds, "'A Watchful Safeguard to Our Habitations': Black Hoof and the Loyal Shawnees," in *Native Americans and the Early Republic*, ed. Frederick E. Hoxie, Ronald Hoffman, and Peter J. Albert (Charlottesville: University Press of Virginia, 1999), 167.

5. Vernon Kinietz and Erminie Wheeler-Voegelin, eds., *Shawnese Traditions: C. C. Trowbridge's Account*, Occasional Contributions from the Museum of Anthropology of the University of Michigan, no. 9 (Ann Arbor: University of Michigan Press, 1939); Campbell, "Biographical Sketch," 487.

6. Two book-length studies of Indian allies of the United States in the Great Lakes region exist: Bradley J. Birzer, "Entangling Empires, Fracturing Frontiers: Jean Baptiste Richardville and the Quest for Miami Autonomy" (Ph.D. diss., Indiana University, 1998), and Harvey Carter, *The Life and Times of Little Turtle: First Sagamore of the Wabash* (Champaign: University of Illinois Press, 1986). In contrast, recent studies of militant resisters, including John Sugden, *Tecumseh: A Life* (New York: Henry Holt, 1997), point to their continuing popularity.

7. Kinietz and Wheeler-Voegelin, *Shawnese Traditions*, 17.

8. *Ibid.*, 3–4, 5.

9. *Ibid.*, 7–8.

10. *Ibid.*, 62. Erminie Wheeler-Voegelin has speculated that Black Hoof was a member of the Thawegila division. This probably is not the case, given this statement in the Trowbridge interview and the historical reality that the Thawegila voluntarily removed west of the Mississippi. The Maykujay were the last division to leave Ohio. In addition, members of this division were the majority at Wapakoneta. Given the Shawnee tradition of drawing chiefs from the largest divisional population of a village, it seems that Black Hoof was a member of the Maykujay division. Historians R. David Edmunds and John Sugden agree that Black Hoof was a Maykujay. See Sugden, *Tecumseh,* 129, and Edmunds, "'Watchful Safeguard,'" 167.

11. Jedidiah Morse, *A Report to the Secretary of War of the U.S. on Indian Affairs* (1822; New York: Augustus M. Kelley Publishers, 1970), 362, 66.

12. For evidence on Tenskwatawa and Tecumseh's parents, see Edmunds, *Shawnee Prophet,* 29n2. Considerable controversy surrounds the cultural identities and the movements of the Shawnee brothers' parents. For an alternative view of Methoataske as a Shawnee woman, see Sugden, *Tecumseh,* 13n1.

13. Tecumseh Papers, Lyman C. Draper Manuscripts, 4yy 21-1, State Historical Society of Wisconsin, Madison, Wis.; Helen Hornbeck Tanner, ed., *Atlas of Great Lakes Indian History* (Norman: University of Oklahoma Press, 1987), 122.

14. Anthony F. C. Wallace, *The Death and Rebirth of the Seneca* (New York: Vintage Books, 1969), 217; Reginald Horsman, *Expansion and American Indian Policy, 1783–1812* (Norman: University of Oklahoma Press, 1967), 48, 148; Thomas Jefferson to William Henry Harrison, *Messages and Letters of William Henry Harrison, 1800–1811,* ed. Logan Esaray (20 vols.; Indianapolis: Indiana Historical Society, 1922), 7:271.

15. For recent studies on the multiethnic texture of Native American communities in the colonial period and their impact on life in the Old Northwest, see Gregory C. Dowd, *A Spirited Resistance: The North American Indian Struggle for Unity, 1745–1815* (Baltimore: Johns Hopkins University Press, 1992). Historian Michael McConnell uses the term "Ohio Indians" to avoid the problems associated with categorizing these villagers as members of single tribes. See Michael N. McConnell, *A Country Between: The Upper Ohio Valley and Its Peoples, 1724–1774* (Norman: University of Oklahoma Press, 1992), 31–33; Richard White, *The Middle Ground: Indians, Empires, and Republics in the Great Lakes Region, 1650–1815* (New York: Cambridge University Press, 1991).

16. Charles Callender, "Shawnee," in *Handbook of North American Indians: Northeast,* vol. 15, ed. Bruce Trigger (Washington, D.C.: Smithsonian Institution, 1978), 623.

17. Kinietz and Wheeler-Voegelin, *Shawnese Traditions,* 9; Tanner, *Atlas of Great Lakes Indian History,* 159; John Johnston to Lewis Cass, 26 June 1817, Shawnee File, Great Lakes-Ohio Valley Indian Archives, Glenn A. Black Laboratory of Archaeology, Indiana University, Bloomington (hereafter cited as GBLA).

18. Lucy Eldersveld Murphy writes that creole communities "developed a culture that was neither purely European nor Native American but had elements of both in a creative mix." For a definitive explanation of creole communities in the Great Lakes, see Murphy, *A Gathering of Rivers: Indians, Métis, and Mining in the Western Great Lakes, 1737–1832* (Lincoln: University of Nebraska Press, 2000), 47–49.

19. Henry Dearborn to William Henry Harrison, 21 February 1803, Shawnee File, GBLA.

20. James Bruff to James Wilkinson, 12 March 1805, in *The Territorial Papers of the United States: Louisiana-Missouri Territory,* vol. 13, *1803–1806,* ed. Clarence E. Carter (27 vols.; Washington, D.C.: Government Printing Office, 1934–), 101–103; Francis Paul Prucha, *The Great Father: The United States Government and the American Indians* (2 vols.; Lincoln: University of Nebraska Press, 1984), 1:73.

21. Henry Dearborn to William Henry Harrison, 23 February 1802, Shawnee File, GBLA.

22. Dearborn to Harrison, 23 February 1802, Shawnee File, GBLA; Henry Dearborn to William Henry Harrison, 3 July 1802, Shawnee File, GBLA; Harrison to Secretary of War, 25 March 1802, in Esaray, *Messages and Letters of Harrison,* 1:47; Jefferson to Harrison, 27 February 1803, in Esaray, *Messages and Letters of Harrison,* 1:71.

23. Report of George Ellicott and Gerard T. Hopkins to Baltimore Yearly Meeting Committee on Indian Affairs, 15 October 1804, Shawnee File, GBLA; Edmunds, "'Watchful Safeguard,'" 169. For more on the efforts and impressions of the Quakers among the tribes of the Old Northwest, see Daniel K. Richter, "'Believing that Many of the Red People Suffer Much for the Want of Food': Hunting, Agriculture, and a Quaker Construction of Indianness in the Early Republic," *Journal of the Early Republic* 19 (Winter 1999): 601–28.

24. John Sugden, *Blue Jacket: Warrior of the Shawnees* (Lincoln: University of Nebraska Press, 2000), 282n4.

25. Black Beard to Thomas Jefferson, 1806, Shawnees File, GBLA.

26. *Ibid.;* Edmunds, "'Watchful Safeguard,'" 167.

27. For more on American policy and the increased authority of chiefs, see Wallace, *Death and Rebirth of the Seneca,* esp. 192.

28. Black Beard and Black Hoof were particularly annoyed with Blue Jacket, then a supporter of the Prophet, for whom he acted as a spokesperson with neighboring Americans and government officials. See Thomas Jefferson to the Chiefs of the Shawnee Nation, 19 February 1807, in *The Writings of Thomas Jefferson,* ed. A. A. Lipscomb (20 vols.; Washington, D.C.: A. E. Dergh, 1904), 16:421–25.

29. Jefferson ultimately believed that once centralized tribal leaders had been established, "the Indians . . . will in time either incorporate with us as citizens of the United States or remove beyond the Mississippi." Jefferson to Harrison, 27 February 1803, in Esaray, *Messages and Letters of Harrison,* 2:71; William Wells to Secretary of War, 31 December 1807, in Carter, *Territorial Papers: Indiana Territory,* 7:510.

30. For a history of Old Northwest tribes that relocated to what is now Missouri, see Louis Houck, *History of Missouri* (Chicago: R. R. Donnelley, 1908); see also Gilbert C. Din and Abraham Nasatir, *The Imperial Osages* (Norman: University of Oklahoma Press, 1983); Edmunds, *Shawnee Prophet,* 28–32; Forsyth to Clark, 23 December 1812, in *The Indian Tribes of the Upper Mississippi Valley and Region of the Great Lakes,* Emma Helen Blair, ed. (2 vols.; Lincoln: University of Nebraska Press, 1996), 2:274.

31. For the best description of the continuity among nineteenth-century Indian revitalization movements, see Dowd, *Spirited Resistance;* Edward Deming Andrews, ed., "The Shaker Mission to the Shawnee Indians," *Winterthur Portfolio* 7 (1972): 122.

32. For an excellent description of intratribal warfare resulting from the conflicting responses to American expansion, see Joel Martin, *Sacred Revolt: The Muskogee's Struggle for a New World* (Boston: Beacon Press, 1991).

33. Leonard U. Hill, *John Johnston and the Indians in the Land of the Three Miamis* (Columbus, Ohio: Stoneman Press, 1957), 52.

34. Edmunds, *Shawnee Prophet,* 28–32; John Mack Faragher, *Sugar Creek: Life on the Illinois Prairie* (New Haven, Conn.: Yale University Press, 1986), 29.

35. Richard McNemar, *The Kentucky Revival* (1808; New York: Edward O. Jenkins, 1846), 112, 114; Sugden, *Blue Jacket,* 240. See also Tanner, *Atlas of Great Lakes Indian History,* 103; Prophet to Harrison, 1 August 1808, in Esaray, *Messages and Letters of Harrison,* 1:299.

36. Moravian missionaries quoted in Alfred A. Cave, "The Failure of the Shawnee Prophet's Witch-Hunt" *Ethnohistory* 42 (Summer 1995): 457. Anthropologist Raymond J. DeMallie's assessment of Native American revitalization movements writes that "within the context of nondoctrinal religion, there can be no heretics, only believers and nonbelievers." Raymond J. DeMallie, "The Lakota Ghost Dance: An Ethnohistorical Account," *Pacific Historical Review* 51 (November 1982): 387–88.

37. Hendrick Apaumat to William Wells, 26 February 1808, Shawnee File, GBLA. For more on the political and religious dimensions of the Prophet's witch hunt, see Jay Miller, "The 1806 Purge among the Indiana Delaware: Sorcery, Gender, Boundaries, and Legitimacy," *Ethnohistory* 41 (Spring 1994): 257–58; White, *Middle Ground,* 506; Dowd, *Spirited Resistance,* 136–37.

38. McNemar, *Kentucky Revival,* 115; Prophet to Harrison, 1 August 1808, in Esaray, *Messages and Letters of Harrison,* 1:300.

39. Governor Browne to Secretary of War, 6 January 1807 in Carter, *Territorial Papers: Louisiana-Missouri Territory,* 14:72–73; Henry Dearborn to William Henry Harrison, 20 June 1805, Records of the Secretary of War Relating to Indian Affairs, Letters Sent, RG75, M15, roll 2.

40. Tanner, *Atlas of Great Lakes Indian History,* 139.

41. At the turn of the century, James Mooney flatly declared that after 1806, "there were no more doubters" among Tenskwatawa's followers in James Mooney, "The Ghost Dance Religion and the Sioux Outbreak of 1890" *Bureau of American Ethnology: Fourteenth Annual Report* (Washington, D.C.: Government Printing Office, 1896). Subsequent historians interested in the links between tribes in the Old Northwest often hide the equally powerful strain against foregoing tribal loyalties. For example, Gregory Evans Dowd privileges the shared traits that united members of the resistance movement over the local concerns of small family groups that existed within the pan-Indian movements of the Old Northwest. Dowd claims that "Tecumseh, did not, however, differ significantly from his followers in culture or in vision, nor was it tribalism that blocked his success." Dowd, *Spirited Resistance,* 143.

42. See Edmunds, "'Watchful Safeguard,'" for a description of the timely arrival of William Kirk at Wapakoneta given the increasing popularity of the revitalization movement at Prophetstown; "A letter expressing thanks . . . from Mother's Children in Ohio," 10 July 1809, "Western Letters, Manuscript III," Number 248, Microfilm Reel 18 (Library of Congress, Washington, D.C.); Andrews, "Shaker Mission to the Shawnee Indians," 118.

43. Andrews, "Shaker Mission to the Shawnee Indians," 126, 119; J. P. MacLean, *Shak-*

ers of Ohio: Fugitive Papers Concerning the Papers of Ohio, with Unpublished Manuscripts (Columbus, Ohio: F. J. Heer, 1907), 271.

44. Sydney E. Ahlstrom, *A Religious History of the American People* (New Haven, Conn.: Yale University Press, 1972), 494.

45. For the best discussion of the violence between women and men in Great Lakes Indian communities, see Sleeper-Smith, *Indian Women and French Men*, 23–24, and Blair, *Indian Tribes of the Upper Mississippi Valley*, 2:277.

46. Andrews, "Shaker Mission to the Shawnee Indians," 119.

47. "To Lalluatseekah the Shawnees Prophet & Brothers," 1 September 1807, A67, Reel 24, Western Reserve Historical Society, Cleveland.

48. Benjamin Youngs et al., to Lalluetsekah, 1 September 1807, A67, Reel 24, Western Reserve Historical Society, Cleveland.

49. Emil Schlup, "Tarhe—The Crane," *Ohio Archaeological and Historical Publications* 14 (June 1905), 132; Anthony F. C. Wallace, *Jefferson and the Indians: The Tragic Fate of the First Americans* (Cambridge, Mass.: Harvard University Press, 1999), 308.

50. Claus to Selby, 3 May 1808, in Esaray, *Messages and Letters of Harrison*, 2:290.

51. Indian Council at Amherstburg, 5 June 1805, in *Collections of the Michigan Pioneer and Historical Society* (40 vols.; Lansing: Thorp and Godfrey, 1874–1929), 23:41; Charles E. Cleland, *Rites of Conquest: The History and Culture of Michigan's Native Americans* (Ann Arbor: University of Michigan Press, 1992), 172; R. David Edmunds, *Tecumseh and the Quest for Indian Leadership* (Boston: Little, Brown, 1984), 109.

52. See Wilcomb E. Washburn, *The Indian in America* (New York: Harper & Row, 1975); Alameda McCullough, *Battle of Tippecanoe: Conflict of Cultures* (Lafayette, Ind.: Tippecanoe County Historical Association, 1973); William Clark to the secretary of war, 5 April 1809, in Carter, *Territorial Papers: Louisiana-Missouri Territory*, 14:260.

53. Clark to the secretary of war, 5 April 1809, in Carter, *Territorial Papers: Louisiana-Missouri Territory*, 14:260; William Wells to the secretary of war, 2 April 1808, in Carter, *Territorial Papers: Indiana Territory*, 7:541; R. David Edmunds, "Main Poc, Potawatomi Wabeno," *American Indian Quarterly* 9 (Summer 1985), 262–63.

54. John Conner, Statement before William Wells, 18 June 1808, Shawnee File, GBLA.

55. *Ibid.*

56. Harrison to the secretary of war, 19 May 1808, in Esaray, *Messages and Letters of Harrison*, 7:291.

57. William Wells to the secretary of war, 20 April 1808, in Carter, *Territorial Papers: Indiana Territory*, 7:555–59; Carter, *Life and Times of Little Turtle*, 83–84; Edmunds, *Shawnee Prophet*, 74–76.

58. The Prophet to Harrison, 24 June 1808, in Esaray, *Messages and Letters of Harrison*, 7:292; Diary of William Claus, May-August 1808, *Michigan Historical Collections*, 23:53–55. For other accounts of the Prophet and his emissaries' dealings with Harrison during the summer of 1808, see Sugden, *Tecumseh*, 170. See also Edmunds, *Tecumseh and the Quest*, 117–18.

59. Matthew Elliott to Major Hunter, 19 May 1809, Shawnee File, GBLA; William Hull to William Eustis, 16 June 1809, Ottawa File, GBLA; Diary of William Claus, *Michigan Historical Collections* 23:56; Richard White, *The Middle Ground: Indians, Empires, and Republics in the Great Lakes Region, 1650–1815* (New York: Cambridge University Press,

1991), 509–13; Cleland, *Rites of Conquest,* 138–39; R. David Edmunds, *The Potawatomis: Keepers of the Fire* (Norman: University of Oklahoma Press, 1978), 3.

60. White, *The Middle Ground,* 508, 513, 513n73; Matthew Elliott to Major Hunter, 19 May 1809, Shawnee File, GBLA.

61. Walter B. Miller, "Two Concepts of Authority," *American Anthropologist* 57 (1955): 271–89; William Hull to William Eustis, 16 June 1809, Ottawa File, GBLA; Edmunds, *Shawnee Prophet,* 76–77.

62. Dowd, *Spirited Resistance,* 131; William Hull to William Eustis, 16 June 1809, Ottawa File, GBLA; Michael Paul Rogin, *Fathers and Children: Andrew Jackson and the Subjugation of the American Indian* (New York: Alfred A. Knopf, 1975).

63. Harrison to the secretary of war, 25 April 1810, in Esaray, *Messages and Letters of Harrison,* 7:417.

64. "A Correct Statement of the Number of Indians that Attended the Treaty of Fort Wayne," William Wells to the secretary of war, 5 December 1809, Records of the Secretary of War Relating to Indian Affairs, Letters Received, RG75, Roll 53, M221; Governor Harrison to Secretary of War, 29 August 1809, in Esaray, *Messages and Letters of Harrison,* 1:345; Harrison to Secretary of War, 26 June 1810, in Esaray, *Messages and Letters of Harrison,* 1:417; Edmunds, *Shawnee Prophet,* 80–81; McCullough, *Battle of Tippecanoe,* 5.

65. Edmunds, *Potawatomis,* 153; Speeches of Gomo and Little Chief, 16 August 1811, in *History of Illinois from 1778 to 1833,* Ninian W. Edwards (Springfield: Illinois State Journal, 1870), 47–51.

66. Harrison to the secretary of war, 25 June 1810, in Esaray, *Messages and Letters of Harrison,* 1:452; *Western Sun,* June 23, 1810, p. 3.

67. A. M. Gibson, *The Kickapoos: Lords of the Middle Border* (Norman: University of Oklahoma Press, 1963), 62–63; Harrison to the secretary of war, 26 June 1810, in Esaray, *Messages and Letters of Harrison,* 1:433; Harrison to Secretary of War, 14 June 1810, in Esaray, *Messages and Letters of Harrison,* 1:423–24; Sugden, *Tecumseh,* 209; "The Indian in Ohio," *Ohio Archaeology and Historical Society Publications* 27 (December 1919): 432–33. For more on Leather Lips's execution and the historical debate on the motives of his executioners, see Sugden, *Tecumseh,* 437n13.

68. Harrison to the secretary of war, 14 June 1810, in Esaray, *Messages and Letters of Harrison,* 1:424.

69. C. A. Weslager, *The Delaware Indians: A History* (New Brunswick, N.J.: Rutgers University Press, 1972), 339.

70. Dowd, *Spirited Resistance,* 131; Edmunds, "'Watchful Safeguard,'" 164.

71. John Johnston to William Eustis, 25 July 1810, Shawnee File, GBLA.

72. Burnett quoted in Sleeper-Smith, *Indian Women and French Men,* 92, see also 31–32; Harrison to the secretary of war, 15 May 1810, in Esaray, *Messages and Letters of Harrison,* 1:420–21; *Western Sun,* June 23,1810, p. 3. For Great Lakes population figures, see Tanner, *Atlas of Great Lakes Indian History,* 96.

73. Edmunds, "'Watchful Safeguard,'" 174–81.

74. Edwards, *History of Illinois,* 1–3; Draper Manuscripts, 26S90, 91, Kickapoo File, GBLA.

75. Speech of Techkumthai to William Claus, 15 November 1810, A. B. Farney Papers, Fort Malden Historic Park, Amherstburg, Ontario; William Hull to William Eustis, 12 July

1810, in Carter, *Territorial Papers: Michigan Territory,* 10:314–16; Harrison to the secretary of war, 25 April 1810, in Esaray, *Messages and Letters of Harrison,* 1:417–18; Johnston to the secretary of war, 25 July 1810, Shawnee File, GBLA; Harrison to the secretary of war, 14 June 1810, in Esaray, *Messages and Letters of Harrison,* 1:425.

76. Snelling to Harrison, 20 November 1811, in Esaray, *Messages and Letters of Harrison,* 1:643–44; McCullough, *Battle of Tippecanoe,* 4; Edmunds, *Shawnee Prophet,* 108–9; J. W. Whickar, "Shabonee's Account of the Battle of Tippecanoe," *Indiana Magazine of History* 17 (December 1921): 356; Harrison to the secretary of war, 18 November 1811, in Esaray, *Messages and Letters of Harrison,* 1:618–30.

77. Daniel K. Richter, *Facing East from Indian Country: A Native History of Early America* (Cambridge, Mass.: Harvard University Press, 2001), 230–31; Adam Walker, "A Journal of Two Campaigns of the Fourth Regiment of U.S. Infantry in the Michigan and Indiana Territories under the Command of Col. John P. Boyd, and Lt. Col. James Miller during the Year 1811, & 12," (Keene, N.H.: Adam Walker, 1816), 701–4; McCullough, *Battle of Tippecanoe,* 5–7; Andrew Cayton, *Frontier Indiana* (Bloomington: Indiana University Press, 1996), 223. For a thorough description of the Battle of Tippecanoe, see Sugden, *Tecumseh,* 226–36.

78. For the best description of women and the power of menstrual blood, see Dowd, *Spirited Resistance,* 6–7; Elliott to Brock, 12 January 1812, in Esaray, *Messages and Letters of Harrison,* 1:617; Harrison to the secretary of war, 18 November 1811, in Esaray, *Messages and Letters of Harrison,* 1:618–30; unpublished manuscripts, Tippecanoe County Historical Society, Wars: Battle of Tippecanoe—Military Units, Eyewitness Accounts, Tippecanoe County Historical Society, Lafayette, Ind.; Edmunds, *Shawnee Prophet,* 113–15.

79. Wars: Battle of Tippecanoe—Military Units, Eyewitness Accounts.

80. *Ibid.*

81. *Ibid.*

82. William Brigham quoted in Walker, "Journal of Two Campaigns," 705–8.

83. *Ibid.;* Edmunds, *The Shawnee Prophet,* 115–16.

Chapter 2

1. "Journal of the Ensign William Schillinger: A Soldier of the War of 1812," *Ohio Archaeological and Historical Quarterly* 41 (January 1932): 80, 82.

2. John Mack Faragher, *Women and Men on the Overland Trail* (New Haven, Conn.: Yale University Press, 1979), 50.

3. John Johnston to Benjamin Drake, 30 March 1833, *The Papers of John Johnston, Indian Agent,* transcribed from the Draper Collection, vol. 11YY, ed. Richard C. Knopf, Ohio Historical Society, Columbus.

4. Johnston quoted in R. Douglas Hurt, *The Ohio Frontier: Crucible of the Old Northwest, 1720–1830* (Bloomington: Indiana University Press, 1996), 342.

5. "Journal of Ensign William Schillinger," 83.

6. For more on the differences between frontier inhabitants after the Treaty of Ghent, see Andrew Cayton, *Frontier Indiana* (Bloomington: Indiana University Press, 1996), 262; *Niles Weekly Register,* 23 September 1815, p. 64. For the "perceived racial differences between native and newcomer," see Elizabeth A. Perkins, "Distinctions and Partitions among Us:

Identity and Interaction in the Revolutionary Ohio Valley," in *Contact Points: American Frontiers from the Mohawk Valley to the Mississippi, 1750–1830,* ed. Andrew R. L. Cayton and Fredrika J. Teute (Chapel Hill: University of North Carolina Press, 1998), 234.

7. "John and William Perry," *Niles Weekly Register,* 7 September 1816, p. 32.

8. Lucien Beckner, "Eskippakithiki: The Last Indian Town in Kentucky," *Filson Club Historical Quarterly* 6 (October 1932): 379; R. David Edmunds, "'A Watchful Safeguard to Our Habitations': Black Hoof and the Loyal Shawnees," in *Native Americans and the Early Republic,* ed. Frederick E. Hoxie, Ronald Hoffman, and Peter J. Albert (Charlottesville: University Press of Virginia, 1999), 186–87.

9. "John and William Perry," *Niles Weekly Register,* September 7, 1816, p. 32.

10. George W. Knepper, *Ohio and Its People* (Kent, Ohio: Kent State University Press, 1997), 115–16.

11. "Report of Mr. Benton, Committee on Indian Affairs," 18th Cong. 1st Sess., 14 May 1824, 79; Hurt, *Ohio Frontier,* 375; Cayton, *Frontier Indiana,* 264; Samuel R. Brown, "From *The Western Gazetteer;* or Emigrant's Directory," in *Indiana as Seen by Early Travelers,* ed. Harlow Lindley (56 vols.; Indianapolis: Indiana Historical Collections, 1916) 3:148.

12. Timothy D. Willig, "Prophetstown on the Wabash: The Native Spiritual Defense of the Old Northwest," *Michigan Historical Review* 23 (Fall 1997): 115–58; Ronald Miriani, "Against the Wind: The Shawnee at Wapakoneta," *Queen City Heritage* 48 (Spring 1990): 33–47; Black Hoof quoted in letter from John Johnston to J. C. Calhoun, 20 January 1819, Shawnee File, Great Lakes-Ohio Valley Indian Archives, Glenn A. Black Laboratory of Archaeology, Indiana University, Bloomington (hereafter cited as GBLA).

13. Benjamin Stickney to William H. Crawford, 12 November 1815, Shawnee File, GBLA; Michael McConnell, *A Country Between: The Upper Ohio Valley and Its Peoples, 1724–1774* (Lincoln: University of Nebraska Press, 1992).

14. John Johnston to Secretary of War, 26 November 1816, Shawnee File, GBLA; Shawnee Chiefs to Secretary of War, 29 December 1815, Shawnee file, GBLA.

15. Shawnee Chiefs to Secretary of War, 29 December 1815, Shawnee file, GBLA. For more on government policies and the creation of modern tribal identities, see Alexandra Harmon, *Indians in the Making: Ethnic Relations and Indian Identities around Puget Sound* (Berkeley: University of California Press, 1998), esp. 103.

16. John Johnston to W. H. Crawford, 3 January 1816, Shawnee file, GBLA; Robert B. McAfee, *History of the Late War in the Western Country* (Bowling Green, 1816; reprint, Ann Arbor: University Microfilms, 1966); John Johnston to Thomas L. McKenney, 7 May 1816, Shawnee file, GBLA.

17. James Ellicott and Philip E. Thomas, "Report on the feasability of introducing farming and other activities among the Indians at Waupaghkonnetta and Lewis Town by the Society of Friends," 1 August 1816, Shawnee File, GBLA; Leonard U. Hill, *John Johnston and the Indians in the Land of the Three Miamis* (Columbus, Ohio: Stoneman Press, 1957), 95.

18. Knepper, *Ohio and Its People,* 130; James H. Howard, *Shawnee! The Ceremonialism of a Native American Tribe and Its Cultural Background* (Athens: Ohio University Press, 1981), 49–52; Ellicott and Thomas, "Report," 1 August 1816, GBLA.

19. Secretary of War Henry Dearborn first coined the metaphor of the "gold chain" of friendship at a meeting with the aged chief in 1802. See Henry Harvey, *History of the*

Shawnee Indians, From the Year 1681 to 1854, Inclusive (Cincinnati: E. Morgan and Sons, 1855), 131; Shawnee Chiefs to Secretary of War, 29 December 1815, Shawnee File, GBLA; Ellicott and Thomas, "Report on the feasability of farming," 1 August 1816.

20. John Mack Faragher, *Daniel Boone: The Life and Legend of an American Pioneer* (New York: Henry Holt, 1992); Gregory C. Dowd, *A Spirited Resistance: The North American Indian Struggle for Unity, 1745–1815* (Baltimore: Johns Hopkins University Press, 1992), 6.

21. Vernon Kinietz and Erminie Wheeler-Voegelin, eds., *Shawnese Traditions: C. C. Trowbridge's Account,* Occasional Contributions from the Museum of Anthropology of the University of Michigan, no. 9 (Ann Arbor: University of Michigan Press, 1939), 65, 61.

22. Charles Callender, "Shawnee," in *Handbook of North American Indians: Northeast,* ed. Bruce Trigger (20 vols.; Washington, D.C.: Smithsonian Institution, 1978), 15:624–26; Erminie Wheeler-Voegelin, "The Place of Agriculture in the Subsistence Economy of the Shawnee," *Papers of the Michigan Academy of Science, Arts and Letters* 26 (1940): 518; Alford quoted in Noel Willi Schutz, "The Study of Shawnee Myth in an Ethnographic and Ethnohistorical Perspective," (Ph.D. diss., Indiana University, 1975), 269.

23. Howard, *Shawnee!,* 44.

24. Wheeler-Voegelin, " Place of Agriculture," 516.

25. C. F. and E. W. Voegelin, "Shawnee Name Groups," *American Anthropologist* 37 (1935): 618–19.

26. For more on the Quaker model, see A. F. C. Wallace, *The Death and Rebirth of the Seneca* (New York: Vintage Books, 1972), 272–77. The best single source on the Quaker missions to the Shawnees is Harvey, *History of the Shawnee Indians.*

27. Benjamin Hallowell, "Memorial of the Religious Society of Friends, in the States of Ohio, Indiana, and Illinois, Praying for the Adoption of Measures for the Civilization and Improvement of the Indians," 23 December 1818, Ohio Historical Society, Columbus; Benj'n Hallowell, "Memorial of the Society of Friends in Regard to the Indians," n.d., Ohio Historical Society, Columbus. For information on the Society of Friends and the impact of their missions, see Joy Bilharz, "First Among Equals: The Changing Status of Seneca Women," in *Women and Power in Native North America,* ed. Laura F. Klein and Lillian A. Ackerman (Norman: University of Oklahoma Press, 1995); see also Thomas D. Hamm, *The Transformation of American Quakerism, Orthodox Friends, 1800–1907* (Bloomington: Indiana University Press, 1988), 22.

28. Joseph Rhodes, "Diary of Joseph and Martha Rhodes' Mission to the Shawnee Indians, 1817: Part of the Story," Ohio Historical Society, Columbus.

29. *Ibid.*

30. John Johnston to Charles Cist, 14 May 1846, *The Papers of John Johnston,* Ohio Historical Society, Columbus; John Wolf to John Johnston, 20 July 1846, Mss. 42, Roll 3a, Cincinnati Historical Society, Cincinnati, Ohio.

31. Ellicott and Thomas, "Report on the feasability of introducing farming," 1 August 1816; John Johnston to William H. Crawford, 22 October 1816, Shawnee File, GBLA; The Chiefs and headmen of the Shawanoes Tribe of Indians to the President of the United States, 20 April 1809, in *Letter Book of the Indian Agency at Fort Wayne, 1809–1815,* ed. Gayle Thornbrough (56 vols.; Indianapolis: Indiana Historical Collections, 1961), 22:45.

32. William G. McLoughlin, *The Cherokees and Christianity, 1794–1870: Essays on Acculturation and Cultural Persistence* (Athens: University of Georgia Press, 1994), 114; Johnston to Drake, 30 March 1833, in *The Papers of John Johnston,* Ohio Historical Society, Columbus.

33. Johnston to Drake, 30 March 1833, in *The Papers of John Johnston,* Ohio Historical Society, Columbus.

34. Hill, *John Johnston and the Indians,* 97.

35. *Ibid.*

36. John Johnston to Secretary of War, 4 May 1818, Shawnee File, GBLA; Benjamin F. Stickney to William H. Crawford, 12 November 1815, Shawnee file, GBLA; Harvey, *History of the Shawnee Indians,* 165; R. David Edmunds, *The Shawnee Prophet* (Lincoln: University of Nebraska Press, 1983), 159–66.

37. Rhodes, "Diary of Joseph and Martha Rhodes' Mission," Ohio Historical Society, Columbus.

38. John Johnston to Lewis Cass, 13 June 1817, Shawnee file, GBLA.

39. Harvey, *History of the Shawnee Indians,* 164–66; "Treaty with the Wyandots. etc., 1817" in Kappler, *Indian Affairs,* 2:235.

40. Cass quoted in Francis Paul Prucha, *The Great Father: The United States Government and the American Indians* (2 vols.; Lincoln: University of Nebraska Press, 1984), 2:263. The ascension of Oshkosh as "Grand Chief" of the Menominee Nation is also described in Patricia K. Ourada, *The Menominee Indians: A History* (Norman: University of Oklahoma Press, 1979), 79, and Helen Hornbeck Tanner, ed., *Atlas of Great Lakes Indian History* (Norman: University of Oklahoma Press, 1987), 184.

41. Lewis Cass to McArthur, 24 May 1818, RG 75, M1, Roll 3, Michigan Superintendency of Indian Affairs, National Archives, Washington, D.C.: Duncan McArthur to John Johnston, 26 July 1818, Johnston Papers, Mss. Number 42, Roll 3a, Cincinnati Historical Society, Cincinnati, Ohio; Lewis Cass to William Crawford, 24 April 1816, Shawnee file, GBLA.

42. Treaty annuity payments were annual disbursements of either cash or goods for a specific period of time or in perpetuity.

43. John Johnston to George Graham, 6 January 1817, Shawnee file, GBLA; "Treaty with the Wyandots. etc., 1817," in Kappler, *Indian Affairs,* 2:145; Prucha, *Great Father,* 1:154.

44. Harvey, *History of the Shawnee Indians,* 226.

45. Duncan McArthur to John Johnston, 26 July 1818, Johnston Papers, Mss. 42, Roll 3a, Cincinnati Historical Society, Cincinnati, Ohio; "Treaty with the Wyandots, etc., 1818," in Kappler, *Indian Affairs,* 2:162–63.

46. Lewis Cass to Duncan McArthur, 18 September 1818, *American State Papers: Indian Affairs, Public Lands, Finance, Miscellaneous* (38 vols.; Washington, D.C.: Gales & Seaton, 1832–1861), 2:177; C. Vandeventer to Lewis Cass, 29 June 1818, *American State Papers,* 2:175–76; Morris Birkbeck, "Notes on a Journey in America from the Coast of Virginia to the Territory of Illinois," in *Indiana as Seen by Early Travelers: A Collection of Reprints from Books of Travel, Letters, and Diaries Prior to 1850,* ed. Harlow Lindley (56 vols.; Indianapolis: Indiana Historical Collections, 1916), 3:181.

47. Wallace, *Death and Rebirth of the Seneca,* 184; Duncan McCarthur to William H. Crawford, 6 April 1816, *American State Papers,* 2:135–36.

48. For more on the massacre, see Brian M. Doerr, "The Massacre at Deer Lick Creek,

Madison County, Indiana, 1824," *Indiana Magazine of History* 43 (March 1997): 19–47; see also R. David Edmunds, "Justice on a Changing Frontier: Deer Lick Creek, 1824–1825," *Indiana Magazine of History* 43 (March 1997): 48–52. Andrew Jackson quoted in Ronald N. Satz, *American Indian Policy in the Jacksonian Era* (Lincoln: University of Nebraska Press, 1975), 45.

49. John Johnston to J. C. Calhoun, 20 January 1819, Shawnee file, GBLA.

50. Hurt, *Ohio Frontier,* 175; John Mack Faragher, *Sugar Creek: Life on the Illinois Prairie* (New Haven, Conn.: Yale University Press, 1986), 71.

51. "Mount-Pleasant," *Niles Weekly Register,* 12 December 1818, p. 268; Faragher, *Sugar Creek,* 66, 71; John Shaw to Lewis Cass, 11 November 1820, Shawnee file, GBLA. For more on white homesteads in the Midwest, see Knepper, *Ohio and Its Peoples,* 117; Cayton, *Frontier Indiana,* 179.

52. Indiana Yearly Meeting of Friends, *Minutes of the Indiana Yearly Meeting of Friends Held at Richmond, Indiana* (Richmond, Ind.: Ballinger Press, 1821–1822), 8. For more information on Isaac McCoy and his vision for the Indian Territory, see George C. Schultz, *An Indian Canaan: Isaac McCoy and the Vision of an Indian State* (Norman: University of Oklahoma Press, 1972).

53. Historian R. Douglas Hurt argues that "the frontier did not serve as a land of equal opportunity when matters of race determined relationships." See Hurt, *Ohio Frontier,* 386–87, sp. 388.

54. John Johnston to J. C. Calhoun, 20 January 1819, Shawnee file, GBLA; John Johnston to Lewis Cass, 9 May 1820, RG75, M1, Roll 7.

55. Edmunds, *Shawnee Prophet,* 166–67; "Treaty with the Wyandots, etc., 1818," in Kappler, *Indian Affairs,* 2:162–63; Hill, *John Johnston and the Indians,* 106; John Johnston to Lewis Cass, 9 May 1820, Shawnee file, GBLA.

56. Philip E. Thomas to J. C. Calhoun, 11 April 1820, Shawnee File, GBLA; John Calhoun to John Johnston, 21 April 1821, RG75, M1, Roll 8; Charles F. Wilkinson, "Indian Tribes and the American Constitution," in *Indians in American History,* ed. Frederick E. Hoxie and Peter Iverson (Wheeling, Ill.: Harlan Davidson, 1998), 109–10.

57. Will Oliver to Ethan Allen Brown, 3 February 1824, Folder 4, Box 3, Roll 4, Ethan Allen Brown Papers, Ohio Historical Society, Columbus; Oliver to Brown, 23 February 1824, *ibid.*

58. "Indians," *Niles Weekly Register,* July 28, 1827, pp. 559–60.

59. John Johnston to Ethan A. Brown, 31 July 1821 Folder 9, Box 2, Roll 3, Ethan Allen Brown Papers, Ohio Historical Society, Columbus; John Johnston to E. A. Brown, 27 January 1824, Folder 4, Box 3, Roll 4, *ibid.*

60. "Committee on Indian Concerns," Indiana Yearly Meeting of Friends, *Minutes,* 1823, 1824.

61. John C. Calhoun to John Johnston, 10 April 1821, RG75, M1, Roll 8.

62. Edmunds, *Shawnee Prophet,* 173–74.

63. "Wapaghkonetta," *The Piqua Gazette,* 9 July 1825, p. 14.

64. *Ibid.;* Donald L. Huber, "White, Red, and Black: The Wyandot Mission at Upper Sandusky," *Timeline* (May/June 1996): 14, 17.

65. Citizens of Bellafontaine to Allen Trimble, 3 April 1829, Folder 10, Box 1, Roll 1, Allen Trimble Papers, Ohio Historical Society, Columbus.

66. For a groundbreaking new description of Indian efforts to hide their identities and avoid Indian removal in the Midwest, see Susan Sleeper-Smith, *Indian Women and French Men: Rethinking Cultural Encounter in the Western Great Lakes* (Amherst: University of Massachusetts Press, 2001), 155–58.

67. "Memorial of the Ladies of Steubenville, Ohio: Against the forcible removal of the Indians without the limits of the United States," 15 February 1830, [Rep. No. 209], 21st Cong., 1st Sess., Ohio Historical Society, Columbus.

68. Harvey, *History of the Shawnee Indians,* 185–89.

69. *Ibid.,* 193–94.

70. Harvey, *History of the Shawnee Indians,* 197–98. For examples of scholars who place the blame for removal on American Indians, see Reginald Horsman, *Expansion and American Indian Policy, 1783–1812* (East Lansing: Michigan State University Press, 1967), 170. See also Hurt, *Ohio Frontier,* 4, and Robert V. Remini, *Andrew Jackson and His Indian Wars* (New York: Viking, 2001).

Chapter 3

1. Noel W. Schutz, Jr., "The Study of Shawnee Myth in an Ethnographic and Ethnohistorical Perspective," (Ph.D. diss., Indiana University, 1975), 390–91; Lawrence Kinniard, ed., *Spain in the Mississippi Valley,1755–1794,* Part 3, *Problems of Frontier Defense, 1792–1794* (Washington, D.C.: Annual Report of the American Historical Association, 1946), 231–32; Thomas Wildcat Alford, *Civilization and the Story of the Absentee Shawnees* (Norman: University of Oklahoma Press, 1936; reprint, University of Oklahoma Press, 1979), 200–203.

2. William Albert Galloway, *Old Chillicothe: Shawnee and Pioneer History: Conflicts and Romances in the Northwest Territory* (Xenia, Ohio: Buckeye Press, 1934); R. David Edmunds, *Tecumseh and the Quest for Indian Leadership* (Boston: Little, Brown, 1984), 217–18.

3. Schutz, "Study of Shawnee Myth," 308–13; Alford, *Civilization,* 93–103. See David LaVere, *Contrary Neighbors: Southern Plains and Removed Indians in Indian Territory* (Norman: University of Oklahoma Press, 2000).

4. Alford, *Civilization,* 201.

5. For more on the Shawnees and the period between the Battle of Fallen Timbers and the Indian Removal Act, see John Sugden, *Blue Jacket: Warrior of the Shawnees* (Lincoln: University of Nebraska Press, 2000). See also John Sugden, *Tecumseh: A Life* (New York: Henry Holt, 1997); R. David Edmunds, "'A Watchful Safeguard to Our Habitations': Black Hoof and the Loyal Shawnees" in *Native Americans and the Early Republic,* ed. Frederick E. Hoxie, Ronald Hoffman, and Peter J. Albert (Charlottesville: University Press of Virginia, 1999).

6. R. David Edmunds, "Native Americans, New Voices: American Indian History, 1895–1995," *American Historical Review* 100 (February 1995): 718.

7. Historian Grant Foreman came closest to defining the political aspirations of the emigrant tribes. See Grant Foreman, *Indians and Pioneers: The Story of the American Southwest Before 1830* (Norman: University of Oklahoma Press, 1936). See also LaVere, *Contrary Neighbors.* Very little is known about Algonquian emigrants in the Southwest.

8. Other accounts of French and Spanish relations with the emigrant tribes include Carl J. Ekberg, *Colonial Ste. Genevieve: An Adventure on the Mississippi Frontier* (Gerald, Mo.: The Patrice Press, 1985); Gilbert C. Din and Abraham Nasatir, *The Imperial Osages* (Norman: University of Oklahoma Press, 1983); Abraham Nasatir, *Spanish War Vessels on the Mississippi, 1792–1796* (New Haven, Conn.: Yale University Press, 1968).

9. For more on this frontier zone and, in particular, relations between Indians and whites, see John Mack Faragher, "'More Motley than Mackinaw': From Ethnic Mixing to Ethnic Cleansing on the Frontier of the Lower Missouri, 1783–1833," in *Contact Points: American Frontiers from the Mohawk Valley to the Mississippi, 1750–1830,* ed. Andrew R. L. Cayton and Fredrika J. Teute (Chapel Hill: University of North Carolina Press, 1998), 304–26.

10. For more on Schoolcraft, see Mentor L. Williams, ed., *Schoolcraft's Narrative Journal of Travels* (East Lansing: Michigan State University Press, 1992), ix-xi. From one-quarter to two-thirds of Algonquian tribes and Cherokees voluntarily chose to immigrate west of the Mississippi prior to the passage of the Indian Removal Act in 1830. In January 1824, the secretary of war, John Calhoun, estimated the combined population of the Delawares, Kickapoos, Shawnees, Weas, Piankashaws and Peorias to be approximately 8,000. He added that their numbers were "constantly increasing by emigration from the remnants of their respective tribes which yet remain on this side of the Mississippi." See Clarence E. Carter, ed., *The Territorial Papers of the United States: Arkansas Territory* (27 vols.; Washington, D.C.: United States Government Printing Office), 19:591. For population figures on the emigrant Indians, see Henry Rowe Schoolcraft, *Information Respecting the History, Condition, and Prospects of the Indian Tribes of the United States,* Vol. 6, *1800–1825* (Philadelphia: Lippincott, Grambo, & Company, 1854), 583–86. Of the 17,000 Cherokees in 1820, some 6,000 lived west of the Mississippi River. See Russell Thornton, *The Cherokees: A Population History* (Lincoln: University of Nebraska Press, 1990), 48–49.

11. These figures are taken from the estimates of regional Indian agents. See Richard Graham to the secretary of war, 23 December 1823, in Carter, *Territorial Papers: Arkansas Territory,* 19:582. See also Thornton, *Cherokees,* 48–49.

12. For more on revitalization movements, see A. F. C. Wallace, "Revitalization Movements," *American Anthropologist* 58 (1956): 266. For more recent treatments, see Gregory Evans Dowd, *A Spirited Resistance: The North American Struggle for Indian Unity, 1745–1815* (Baltimore: Johns Hopkins University Press, 1992), and Joel W. Martin, *Sacred Revolt: The Muskogee's Struggle for a New World* (Boston: Beacon Press, 1991).

13. Vernon Kinietz and Erminie Wheeler-Voegelin, eds., *Shawnese Traditions: C. C. Trowbridge's Account,* Occasional Contributions from the Museum of Anthropology of the University of Michigan, no. 9 (Ann Arbor: University of Michigan Press, 1939), 8–9; James H. Howard, *Shawnee! The Ceremonialism of a Native American Tribe and Its Cultural Background* (Athens: Ohio University Press, 1981), 112–13.

14. Alford, *Civilization,* 201–6; John Archdale, "A New Description of That Fertile and Pleasant Province of Carolina, by John Archdale, 1707" in *Narratives of Early Carolina 1650–1700,* ed. Alexander S. Sally, Jr. (New York: Scribner's, 1911), 277–312; J. Leitch Wright, *The Only Land They Knew: American Indians in the Old South* (Lincoln: University of Nebraska Press, 1981), 107.

15. Most historians provide a range of years in the 1780s for the original Shawnee migra-

tion to Spanish Louisiana. For example, John Mack Faragher argues that the Shawnees migrated across the Mississippi during the 1780s and were invited there by the Spanish governor, Francisco Cruzat. See Faragher, "'More Motley than Mackinaw,'" 305–6. See also Nasatir, *Spanish War Vessels*, 71n27. For more on "Loramie's Town" in Ohio, see R. Douglas Hurt, *The Ohio Frontier: Crucible of the Old Northwest, 1720–1830* (Bloomington: Indiana University Press, 1996), 207–9; Abstract of Property in Cape Girardeau, Last Will of Louis Lorimier, 12 March 1808, Rodney Family Papers, Missouri Historical Society, St. Louis; Petition of Louis Lorimier on Behalf of the Shawnee & Delaware Indians, August 16, 1806, Box 1, Indian Papers, Missouri Historical Society, St. Louis. A short biographical sketch of Lorimier is included in John Frances McDermott, ed., "Audubon's 'Journey up the Mississippi,'" *Journal of the Illinois State Historical Society* 35 (June 1942): 167n25.

16. William Clark, Indians in Missouri Territory, 4 November 1816, Map Collection, Missouri Historical Society, St. Louis; several maps do exist with these town sites clearly identified. See H. P. Tanner, "The Travellers Pocket Map of Missouri with Its Roads and Distances," c. 1830, Missouri Historical Society, St. Louis; "Map of the States of Missouri and Illinois," (London: Hinton, Simpkin, and Marshall, 1832), Missouri Historical Society, St. Louis. This is the second location of Rogerstown following their removal to Missouri after the Treaty of Greenville. The original town site was located near the town of Bridgeton on the south side of the Missouri River near St. Louis. The original white captive's first name remains unclear. Jimmy Rogers's first name is variously given as William, Jimmy, and Henry. Given the prevalence of Jimmy, I refer to him throughout by this name. See Faragher, "'More Motley than Mackinaw,'" 309–31.

17. *American State Papers: Indian Affairs, Public Lands, Finance, Miscellaneous* (38 vols.; Washington, D.C.: Gales & Seaton, 1832–1861), 2:591; William Clark to William Henry Crawford, 20 September 1815, in *American State Papers*, 2:76; S. H. Long, "Account of an Expedition from Pittsburgh to the Rocky Mountains Performed in the Years 1819, 1820," in *Early Western Travels, 1748–1846*, ed. Reuben Gold Thwaites (32 vols.; Cleveland: Arthur H. Clark, 1905), 14:94–95.

18. James F. Keefe and Lynn Morrow, eds., *The White River Chronicles of S. C. Turnbo: Man and Wildlife on the Ozark Frontier* (Fayetteville: University of Arkansas Press, 1994), 5–7. For more on the Shawnee Bread Dance and gender, see Howard, *Shawnee!*, 223–28.

19. Pierre Menard to J. C. Calhoun, 19 September 1820, Shawnee File, Great Lakes-Ohio Valley Indian Archives, Glenn A. Black Laboratory of Archaeology, Indiana University, Bloomington (hereafter cited as GBLA).

20. William Clark to William Henry Crawford, 20 September 1815, in *American State Papers*, 2:76; McDermott, "Audubon's 'Journey Up the Mississippi,'" 154, 165. For more on the emigrant Indian economy, see Foreman, *Indians and Pioneers*, 228. See also S. G. Hopkins to Major R. Graham, 6 August 1825, Graham Papers, Missouri Historical Society, St. Louis.

21. Neal O. Hammon, *My Father, Daniel Boone: The Draper Interviews with Nathan Boone* (Lexington: University Press of Kentucky, 1999), 60, 119; J. J. Lutz, "The Methodist Missions among the Indian Tribes in Kansas," *Transactions of the Kansas State Historical Society* 9 (1905–1906): 170–71n21.

22. "The Journals of Jules de Mun," trans. Nettie Beauregard, in *Missouri Historical Society Collections* 5, 186; Rufus Babcock, ed., *Forty Years of Pioneer Life: Memoir of John*

Mason Peck, D.D. (Carbondale: Southern Illinois University Press, 1965), 111–14. For more on the Rogerstown Shawnees at Choctaw Academy, see Evelyn Crady Adams, "Kentucky's Choctaw Academy, 1819–1842: A Commercial Enterprise," *Filson Club Historical Quarterly* 26 (January, 1952): 29.

23. Babcock, *Forty Years of Pioneer Life,* 112–13; Jedidiah Morse, *A Report to the Secretary of War of the U.S. on Indian Affairs* (1822; New York: Augustus M. Kelley Publishers, 1970), 235–26.

24. Francois Lesieur & Son to Pierre Menard, 4 August 1825, Box 3, Graham Papers; S. G. Hopkins to Richard Graham, 6 August 1825, Box 3, Graham Papers; "Nuttall's Travels into the Arkansa Territory, 1819," in Thwaites, *Early Western Travels, 1748–1846,* 13:54. For more on the Indian economies of southeastern Missouri, see Foreman, *Indians and Pioneers,* 228n28. For the earthquake of 1811, see Neal Primm, *Lion of the Valley: St. Louis, Missouri, 1764–1980* (St. Louis: Missouri Historical Society Press, 1981), 102

25. Paithuckoosaw, Lailawsequa, and other Shawnee leaders to the President, 20 November 1831, National Archives, Records of the Bureau of Indian Affairs, Microfilm Publication RG 75, M234, Roll 300; Grant Foreman Collection, Thomas Gilcrease Museum of American History and Art, vol. 53, Box 28, 9 November 1827.

26. For a detailed description of Tecumseh's recruiting drives, and his relationship with Maisonville in Missouri, see Sugden, *Tecumseh,* 102, 210–11.

27. Louis Lorimier's will to his Shawnee wife and his métis children indicates that some Shawnees, particularly those from fur-trading families, owned considerable property, even slaves. See "Abstract of Property in Cape Girardeau, Last Will of Louis Lorimier"; Tanis C. Thorne, *The Many Hands of My Relations: French and Indians on the Lower Missouri* (Columbia: University of Missouri Press, 1996).

28. R. David Edmunds, *The Shawnee Prophet* (Lincoln: University of Nebraska Press, 1983), 11; Lewis Rogers & Missouri Shawnee Leaders to the Commissioner of Indian Affairs, n.d., RG 75, M234, Roll 300.

29. Nicolas de Finiels, *An Account of Upper Louisiana,* ed. Carl J. Ekberg and William E. Foley (Columbia: University of Missouri Press, 1989), 1, 35–36.

30. For Missouri population statistics, see Hattie M. Anderson, "Missouri—1804–1828: Peopling a Frontier State," *Missouri Historical Review* 31 (1937): 150–80.

31. William Clark, Ninian Edwards, and Auguste Chouteau to Wm. H. Crawford, 18 October 1815, *American State Papers,* 15:9–11; Godfrey Lesieur to Governor John Miller, 6 October 1831, Clark Papers, vol. 6, 610–12, GBLA; List of Horses, Cattle, Hogs and other Cattle Stolen from the Shawnees and Delawares, 1811–1814, RG 75, M856, Roll 2.

32. Morse, *Report to the Secretary of War,* 366, 362; William Clark, Ninian Edwards, and Auguste Chouteau to Wm. H. Crawford, 18 October 1815, *American State Papers,* 15:9–11; Godfrey Lesieur to Governor John Miller, 6 October 1831, Clark Papers, vol. 6, 620–12. The Apple Creek Shawnees understood the meaning behind the harassment; see List of Horses, Cattle, Hogs and other Cattle Stolen from the Shawnees and Delawares, 1811–1814. For a thorough description of the forced eviction of the Shawnee farmer named Petatwa from his farm, see Faragher, "'More Motley than Mackinaw,'" 321–23.

33. William Clark, Ninian Edwards, and Auguste Chouteau to Wm. H. Crawford, 18 October 1815, *American State Papers* 15:9–11; List of Horses, Cattle, Hogs and other Cattle Stolen from the Shawnees and Delawares, 1811–1814.

34. William Clark, Ninian Edwards, and Auguste Chouteau to Secretary of War, 18 October 1815, *American State Papers* 15:9–11;

35. William E. Foley and C. David Rice, *The First Chouteaus: River Barons of Early St. Louis* (Champaign: University of Illinois Press, 2000), 97. Governor Clark to the President, 22 January 1816, in Carter, *Territorial Papers: Territory of Louisiana,* 15:105; Resolutions of the Territorial Assembly to the Honourable the Senate and House of Representatives of the United States of America in Congress Assembled, 22 January 1816, in Carter, *Territorial Papers: Territory of Louisiana,* 15:105–7.

36. For a much more involved discussion of the conflict between McNair and Clark, see Primm, *Lion of the Valley,* 83, 105, 112, 117.

37. For Jefferson's own words on the dispossession of American Indians, see Thomas Jefferson to William Henry Harrison, 27 February 1803 in *Messages and Letters of William Henry Harrison,* ed. Logan Esaray (20 vols.; Indianapolis: Indiana Historical Commission, 1922), 7:69–73. For a recent treatment of Jefferson's Indian policies, see Anthony F. C. Wallace, *Jefferson and the Indians: The Tragic Fate of the First Americans* (Cambridge, Mass.: Harvard University Press, 1999), 17–19; Bernard Sheehan, *Seeds of Extinction: Jeffersonian Philanthropy and the Indian* (Chapel Hill: University of North Carolina Press, 1973). On the transition from Jeffersonian to Jacksonian Indian policy, see Reginald Horsman, *Race and Manifest Destiny: The Origins of American Racial Anglo-Saxonism* (Cambridge, Mass.: Harvard University Press, 1981), and Reginald Horsman, *Expansion and American Indian Policy, 1783–1812* (East Lansing: Michigan State University Press, 1967), 9.

38. For more on the transition from Jeffersonian to Jacksonian Indian policy, see Reginald Horsman, "The Indian Policy of an 'Empire for Liberty,'" in *Native Americans and the Early Republic,* ed. Frederick E. Hoxie, Ronald Hoffman, and Peter J. Albert (Charlottesville: University Press of Virginia, 1999), 37–61.

39. Col. Stephen Ross to William Clark, 30 April 1820, Clark Papers, Missouri Historical Society, St. Louis.

40. *Congressional Globe,* "Report of Mr. Benton, Committee on Indian Affairs," 14 May 1824, 18th Congress, 1st session, p. 79; Faragher, "'More Motley than Mackinaw,'" 321.

41. Matthew Adams, Statement, 16 May 1823, Shawnee File, GBLA. See also William Marshall and others, Statement on the Situation of the Indians, 16 April 1823, Shawnee File, GBLA. For more on Adams, see Keefe and Morrow, *White River Chronicles of S. C. Turnbo,* 265n7. For similar examples of de facto removal into marginal subsistence zones, see Karen I. Blu, *The Lumbee Problem: The Making of an American Indian People* (Cambridge, N.Y.: Cambridge University Press, 1980), and Daniel R. Mandell, *Behind the Frontier: Indians in Eighteenth-Century Eastern Massachusetts* (Lincoln: University of Nebraska Press, 1996).

42. Rufus Easton and B. Stephenson to James Monroe, 17 December 1814, Shawnee File, GBLA; Return J. Meigs to Secretary of War, 17 February 1816, quoted in Carter, *Territorial Papers: Territory of Louisiana,* 15:121–23; David G. Burnet to Bustamante, 6 October 1838, in Eugene C. Barker, ed., *The Austin Papers* (2 vols.; Washington, D.C.: Government Printing Office, 1924, 1928), 2:1669.

43. See Foreman, *Indians and Pioneers,* 218. See also William Clark to John C. Calhoun, 5 September 1823, Shawnee File, GBLA.

44. Dianna Everett, *The Texas Cherokees: A People between Two Fires, 1819–1840* (Norman: University of Oklahoma Press, 1990), 9, 50, 54, 61.

45. For more on the adoption of a legal code and the light horse company, see Rennard Strickland, *Fire and the Spirits: Cherokee Law from Clan to Court* (Norman: University of Oklahoma Press, 1975), 51, 67–68. For more on the Cherokees' transformation from an ethnic group to a nation-state, see John Phillip Reid, *A Better Kind of Hatchet: Law, Trade, and Diplomacy in the Cherokee Nation during the Early Years of European Contact* (University Park: Pennsylvania State University Press, 1976). See also William G. McLoughlin, *Cherokee Renascence in the New Republic* (Princeton, N.J.: Princeton University Press, 1986).

46. More recent titles follow Foreman's understanding of the emigrant Indian alliance as a contest for land and primacy with the Osages. LaVere, *Contrary Neighbors,* 22–27.

47. Thwaites, *Early Western Travels: Stephen Long's Expedition,* 19; William Clark to John Calhoun, May 8, 1821, Shawnee File, GBLA; Richard Graham to Secretary of War, June 1, 1821, Graham Papers, Box 2.

48. William Bradford to Secretary of War, Oct. 22, 1821, in Carter, *Territorial Papers: Territory of Arkansas,* 19:346–47.

49. Richard Graham to J. C. Calhoun, 4 June 1821, Graham Papers, Box 2; Richard Graham, Statement, n.d. (1822?), Box 2, Graham Papers; Richard Graham to J. C. Calhoun, 7 February 1822, Box 2, Graham Papers; Governor Miller to Secretary of War, May 1822, in Carter, *Territorial Papers: Territory of Arkansas,* 19:437–40.; William Clark to J. C. Calhoun, 24 July 1822, Shawnee File, GBLA.

50. Richard Graham to J. C. Calhoun, 20 September 1821, Graham Papers, Box 2; Richard Graham to J. C. Calhoun, 12 November 1821, Graham Papers, Box 2; Willard H. Rollings, *The Osage: An Ethnohistorical Study of Hegemony on the Prairie-Plains,* (Columbia: University of Missouri Press, 1992), 11–12.

51. John Campbell to Richard Graham, 25 July 1825, Graham Papers, Box 3.

52. Richard Graham to J. C. Calhoun, 12 November 1821, Graham Papers, Box 2; Pierre Menard to Major Graham, 3 January 1822, Graham Papers, Box 2.

53. *Ibid.*

54. "Treaty of Peace and Friendship between the Osage, and Delaware, Shawnee, Wea, Piankashaw, Peoria and Kickapoo," 21 September 1822, Shawnee File, GBLA.

55. Richard Graham to William Clark, 3 October 1822, National Archives, Shawnee File, GBLA; John C. Sullivan, "Boundaries of the Delaware & Shawnee Lands in Southwestern Missouri," 28 July 1824, Missouri Historical Society, St. Louis.

56. *Ibid.;* Keefe and Morrow, *White River Chronicles of S. C. Turnbo,* 264–66.

57. Richard Graham to Secretary of War, 23 December 1823, in Carter, *Territorial Papers: Territory of Arkansas,* 19:582.

58. Cherokees quoted in Foreman, *Indians and Pioneers,* 225n23.

59. Cherokee (West) Tolenliskee to William Clark, 21 February 1818, Foreman Collection, Gilcrease Museum, vol. 53, Box 28, pp. 91–93.

60. "1825 Cherokees West & Shawnees, Wm. Clark—Talks Relative to Delegation, etc," Foreman Collection, Gilcrease Museum, vol. 53, Box 28, pp. 319–20. See also Foreman, *Indians and Pioneers,* 193n21.

61. Col. Lewis, Civil John, and Wackanacky, "Memorial to the President," January 1816, Shawnee File, GBLA; Thomas L. McKenney and James Hall, eds., *The Indian Tribes of North America* (3 vols.; Philadelphia: E. C. Biddle, 1836–1844; reprint, Edinburgh: John Grant, 1933) 1:56.

62. McKenney and Hall, *Indian Tribes,* 3:181; *Ibid,* 1:249.

63. William Clark to John C. Calhoun, 5 September 1823, Shawnee File, GBLA.

64. *Daily National Journal,* 8 February 1825, p. 3; "1825 Cherokees West Delegation to John Calhoun," Foreman Collection, Gilcrease Museum, vol. 53, Box 28, p. 347.

65. Clark to Calhoun, 5 September 1823, Shawnee File, GBLA; Cherokees quoted in Foreman, *Indians and Pioneers,* 225n23.

66. Richard Graham to J. C. Calhoun, 20 September 1821, Graham Papers, Box 2, Missouri Historical Society, St. Louis; Richard Graham to J. C. Calhoun, 12 November 1821, Graham Papers, Box 2. For a much more detailed discussion of William Clark's increasing problems with frontier settlers in Missouri and the politicians who represented them, see Primm, *Lion of the Valley,* 83, 105, 112, 117.

67. Cornstalk, John Perry, Nolaseesay, and Shemanitoo to Commissioner of Indian Affairs, 10 April 1830, RG 75, M234, Roll 300.

68. Secretary of War to Maj. Bradford, Department of War, 12 May 1820, Foreman Collection, Gilcrease Museum, vol. 53, Box 28, p. 173; Col. Brearley to J. C. Calhoun, 24 April 1823, Adjutant General's Office, Old Records Division, War Department Files, Foreman Collection, Gilcrease Museum, vol. 53, Box 28, p. 271.

69. Governor Izard to Secretary of War, January 30, 1826, in Carter, *Territorial Papers: Territory of Arkansas,* 20:193.

70. For more on Isaac McCoy and his promotion of an Indian Canaan in the West, see George C. Schultz, *An Indian Canaan: Isaac McCoy and the Vision of an Indian State* (Norman: University of Oklahoma Press, 1972). For more on McCoy's role in promoting Indian removal on behalf of the Jackson administration, see William G. McLoughlin, *Cherokees and Missionaries, 1789–1839* (Norman: University of Oklahoma Press, 1995), 267–79.

71. Alford, *Civilization,* 200.

Chapter 4

1. "Lyman C. Draper's 1868 Shawnee and Delaware Field Notes," Folder 5, Box 31, Erminie Wheeler-Voegelin Papers, Newberry Library. For a population estimate of the Rogerstown village at the time of removal, see The United States Indian Department to James Williams, 25 May 1828, Box 4, Richard Graham Papers, Missouri Historical Society, St. Louis. For a description of the Rogerstown community and the challenges faced by the Missouri Shawnees prior to removal, see John Mack Faragher, "'More Motley than Mackinaw': From Ethnic Mixing to Ethnic Cleansing on the Frontier of the Lower Missouri, 1783–1833," in *Contact Points: American Frontiers from the Mohawk Valley to the Mississippi, 1750–1830,* ed. Andrew R. L. Cayton and Fredrika J. Teute (Chapel Hill: University of North Carolina Press, 1998).

2. "Shawnee in Old Mexico," Folder 3, Box 31, Voegelin Papers.

3. These villages were Wapakoneta and Hog Creek in Ohio, and St. Genevieve and Cape

Girardeau in Missouri. Each village maintained connections with smaller Shawnee bands and other multitribal villages in the vicinity of their respective territories.

4. Joseph B. Herring, *The Enduring Indians of Kansas: A Century and a Half of Acculturation* (Lawrence: University Press of Kansas, 1990), 1.

5. For an account of these changes among the Shawnees in Kansas, see Stephen A. Warren, "Shawnee Political Culture in the Reservation Era" (master's thesis, Arizona State University, 1994). For an excellent survey of the emigrant Indian communities of what is now Kansas, see Herring, *Enduring Indians of Kansas.* For a brief discussion of the Absentee Shawnees in Texas, see H. Allen Anderson, "The Delaware and Shawnee Indians and the Republic of Texas, 1820–1845" *Southwestern Historical Quarterly* 94 (October 1990): 231–60.

6. Mark Stephen Joy, "'Into the Wilderness': Protestant Missions among the Emigrant Indians of Kansas, 1830–1854," (Ph.D. diss., Kansas State University, 1982), 177. For Shawnee social organization, see Charles F. and Erminie Wheeler-Voegelin, "Shawnee Name Groups," *American Anthropologist* 37 (October-December, 1935): 617–35; James H. Howard, *Shawnee! The Ceremonialism of a Native American Tribe and Its Cultural Background* (Athens: Ohio University Press, 1981), 89–98.

7. Thomas D. Hamm, *The Transformation of American Quakerism: Orthodox Friends, 1800–1907* (Bloomington: Indiana University Press, 1988); Wilson Hobbs, "The Friends' Establishment in Kansas Territory," *Kansas Historical Collections* 8 (1903–1904): 250–71.

8. For more on the creation of reservations and the transformation of tribal leadership, see Loretta Fowler, *Arapahoe Politics, 1851–1878: Symbols in Crisis of Authority* (Lincoln: University of Nebraska Press, 1982), 68–70. See also Melissa Meyer, *The White Earth Tragedy: Ethnicity and Dispossession at a Minnesota Anishinaabe Reservation* (Lincoln: University of Nebraska Press, 1994), 46–47, and Rebecca Kugel, *To Be the Main Leaders of Our People: A History of Minnesota Ojibwe Politics, 1825–1898* (East Lansing: Michigan State University Press, 1998).

9. Belle Greene, "Life at Shawnee Mission," *Missouri Valley Historical Society: The Annals of Kansas City* 1 (1921–1924): 457; Nathan Scarritt, "Reminiscences of the Methodist Shawnee Mission: And Religious Work among That Tribe," *Missouri Valley Historical Society: The Annals of Kansas City* 1 (1921–1924): 437.

10. David D. Hall, ed., *Lived Religion in America: Toward a History of Practice* (Princeton, N.J.: Princeton University Press, 1997), 9.

11. John Sugden, *Blue Jacket: Warrior of the Shawnees* (Lincoln: University of Nebraska Press, 2000), 263.

12. J. J. Lutz, "The Methodist Missions among the Indian Tribes in Kansas," *Kansas State Historical Collections* 9 (1905–1906): 186, 186n40; Louise Barry, *The Beginning of the West: Annals of the Kansas Gateway to the American West, 1540–1854* (Topeka: Kansas State Historical Society, 1972), 350.

13. Martha B. Caldwell, *Annals of the Shawnee Methodist Mission* (Topeka: Kansas State Historical Society, 1977), 9. Two assessments of Shawnee–missionary relations in Indian Territory include Stephen A. Warren, "The Baptists, the Methodists, and the Shawnees: Conflicting Cultures in Indian Territory, 1833–1834," *Kansas History* 17 (Autumn 1994): 148–61, and Kevin Abing, "A Holy Battleground: Methodist, Baptist, and Quaker Missionaries among Shawnee Indians, 1830–1844," *Kansas History* 21 (Summer 1998): 118–37.

14. John Campbell to William Gordon, 20 May 1833, Fort Leavenworth Agency, Bureau of Indian Affairs, RG 75, M234, Roll 300; Kevin Abing, "A Fall from Grace: Thomas Johnson and the Shawnee Indian Manual Training School, 1839–1862," (Ph.D. diss., Marquette University, 1995); William Stewart Woodard, *Annals of Methodism in Missouri* (Columbia, Mo.: E. W. Stephens, 1893), 62–63. For the kin ties between the Shawnees and the Davis, Johnson, and McAllister families, see Patsy Moss, "Prelude to the Shawnee Methodist Mission: Family Connections of Sarah Johnson with the Shawnee Prophet," *Kawsmouth: A Journal of Regional History* 1 (Autumn 1999): 3–17.

15. Moss, "Prelude to the Shawnee Methodist Mission," 14; Don W. Holter, *Fire on the Prairie: Methodism in the History of Kansas* (Kansas City, Mo.: Editorial Board of the Kansas Methodist History, 1969), 29.

16. George C. Schultz, *An Indian Canaan: Isaac McCoy and the Vision of an Indian State* (Norman: University of Oklahoma Press, 1972), 5–7; William G. McLoughlin, *Cherokees and Missionaries, 1789–1839* (Norman: University of Oklahoma Press, 1994), 268; John Mack Faragher, *Sugar Creek: Life on the Illinois Prairie* (New Haven, Conn.: Yale University Press, 1986), 51.

17. Isaac McCoy, *History of Baptist Indian Missions* (Washington, D.C.: W. M. Morrison, 1840), 44, 36; McLoughlin, *Cherokees and Missionaries,* 267–68.

18. McCoy, *History of Baptist Indian Missions,* 404.

19. *Ibid.,* 405; Warren, "Baptists, the Methodists, and the Shawnees"; Abing, "Holy Battleground."

20. John Campbell to William Clark, 26 May 1833, RG 75, Roll 300, M234; William Gordon to William Clark, 12 August 1833, St. Louis Superintendency, Letters Received, Record Group 75, Roll 750, M234; Campbell to Clark, 20 May 1833, RG 75, Roll 300, M234.

21. Campbell to Clark, 26 May 1833, RG 75, Roll 300, M234.

22. Richard W. Cummins to Elbert Herring, 9 April 1833, RG 75, Roll 300, M234; William Clark to Elbert Herring, 29 April 1833, RG 75, Roll 776, M234; Stephen A. Warren, "Shawnee Political Culture in the Reservation Era," (master's thesis, Arizona State University, 1994), 71–73.

23. John Perry et al. to William Clark, 5 June 1833, RG 75, Roll 300, M234.

24. John Perry et al. to William Clark, 19 November 1833, RG 75, Roll 300, M234; Lewis Rogers & Shawnee Chiefs to the Commissioner of Indian Affairs, 6 March 1838, RG 75, Roll 301, M234.

25. Caldwell, *Annals,* 10–15; Abing, "Holy Battleground," 125; Lucius Bolles to Isaac McCoy, 3 January 1833, Isaac McCoy Papers, Roll 8, Manuscript Collection, Kansas State Historical Society, Topeka.

26. Richard Cummins to Elbert Herring, 30 June 1834, RG 75, Roll 300, M234; John Perry et al. to William Clark, 5 June 1833, RG 75, Roll 300, M234.

27. Warren, "Baptists, the Methodists, and the Shawnees"; Abing, "Holy Battleground."

28. Abing, "Holy Battleground," 125; Caldwell, *Annals,* 17–19; Douglas C. McMurtrie and Albert H. Allen, *Jotham Meeker, Pioneer Printer in Kansas* (Chicago: Eyncourt Press, 1930), 29.

29. Quoted in Abing, "Holy Battleground," 124.

30. *Ibid.*, 125.

31. Marston G. Clark to William Clark, 7 October 1834, McCoy Collection, Kansas State Historical Society manuscript collection (hereafter cited as KSHS). For more on McCoy's vision of an Indian state, see Schultz, *Indian Canaan.* The best statistics on Shawnee populations and the number interested in missions are from the U.S. Department of War, *Report of the Commissioner of Indian Affairs,* 25th Cong., 3rd Sess. S. Doc. 1 [338], 25 November 1838; U.S. Department of War, *Report of the Commissioner of Indian Affairs,* 26th Cong., 1st Sess. S. Doc. 1 [354], 25 November 1839. Based on these reports, 975 Shawnees resided on the reservation. Another 1,500 Shawnees lived in Texas.

32. Isaac McCoy to Elbert Herring, 9 January 1835, McCoy Collection, KSHS.

33. Mary W. Helms, *Ulysses' Sail: An Ethnographic Odyssey of Power, Knowledge, and Geographic Distance* (Princeton, N.J.: Princeton University Press), 4–5; McCoy, *History of Baptist Indian Missions,* 464.

34. Lutz, "Methodist Missions," 164–65n10.

35. George Catlin, *Letters and Notes on the Manners, Customs, and Conditions of the North American Indians* (2 vols.; New York: Dover Publications, 1973), 2:117.

36. For similar arguments, see Robert F. Berkhofer, Jr., *The White Man's Indian: Images of the American Indian from Columbus to the Present* (New York: Vintage Books, 1978), 119. Berkhofer writes that "not only did the image of the savage Indian rationalize European conquest but it also spurred missionaries to greater zeal and their patrons to larger contributions."

37. Edwin S. Gaustad, *A Documentary History of Religion in America: To the Civil War* (Grand Rapids, Mich.: Eerdmans, 1982), 386; Schultz, *Indian Canaan,* 198–203.

38. Journal of Jotham Meeker, MS 174, 32–44, esp. 44, Jotham Meeker Papers, KSHS.

39. *U.S. Congressional Document Series Set,* S. Doc. 413, [359], 23 May 1838.

40. *Ibid.*, 44, 86.

41. *American Baptist Magazine* 15, no. 6 (June 1835): 223–24; *American Baptist Magazine* 21, no. 6 (June 1841): 173; *American Baptist Magazine* 21, no. 9 (September 1841): 283.

42. "Lyman C. Draper's 1868 Shawnee and Delaware Field Notes," Box 31, Folder 5, Voegelin Papers; "Petition of Shawnee Now Serving in Florida," 12 March 1838, RG 75, M234, Roll 301. See also Virginia Bergman Peters, *The Florida Wars* (Hamden, Conn: Archon Books, 1979), 146. For detailed information on Tecumseh's background and his birthplace, see John Sugden, *Tecumseh: A Life* (New York: Henry Holt, 1998), 16, 25, 31; J. Leitch Wright, Jr. *Creeks and Seminoles: The Destruction and Regeneration of the Muscogulge People* (Lincoln: University of Nebraska Press, 1986), 249.

43. John Perry et al. to William Clark, 7 February 1835, RG 75, Roll 300, M234.

44. Isaac McCoy to C. A. Harris, 21 August 1838, RG 75, Roll 301, M234.

45. Lelahsekah to Joshua Pilcher, 1 August 1839, RG 75, Roll 301, M234; Anderson, "The Delawares and Shawnees of Texas," 243. See also two recent monographs: Kelly F. Himmel, *The Conquest of the Karankawas and Tonkawas, 1821–1859* (College Station: Texas A&M University Press, 1999), 37–69, and Gary Clayton Anderson, *The Indian Southwest, 1580–1830: Ethnogenesis and Reinvention* (Norman: University of Oklahoma Press, 1999), 251–65.

46. Journal of Jotham Meeker, 4 December 1841, 248, KSHS.

47. Dickson D. Bruce, Jr., *And They All Sang Hallelujah: Plain-Folk Camp-Meeting Religion, 1800–1845* (Knoxville: University of Tennessee Press, 1974), 76; Journal of Jotham Meeker, 25 March 1842, 259, KSHS.

48. Sydney E. Ahlstrom, *A Religious History of the American People* (New Haven, Conn.: Yale University Press, 1972), 322; Bruce, *And They All Sang Hallelujah,* 122.

49. "Church Records of Shawnee Baptist Mission Church," Francis Barker Collection, KSHS; "List of Members," Francis Barker Collection, KSHS. The author gratefully acknowledges historian Rebecca Kugel's assistance in exploring the connections between gender roles and conversion. For more on the intersection of religion and gender in Woodland tribes, see Kugel, *To Be the Main Leaders.* For more on American Indian women and cultural change, see Theda Perdue, *Cherokee Women: Gender and Culture Change, 1700–1835* (Lincoln: University of Nebraska Press, 1998).

50. Statement of John Perry et al., 4 July 1835, RG 75, Roll 750, M234; Statement of Huron River Shawnees, February 1838, RG 75, Roll 301, M234. This small group of Shawnee men, no more than twenty in number, began identifying themselves as the Huron River Shawnees, rather than the Hog Creek Shawnees, after their removal to Kansas. Joseph Parks owned a tract of land on the Huron River, Michigan Territory, prior to removal. Parks and others used this land claim to negotiate as a separate village for some of the proceeds from the Wapakoneta Treaty of 1831.

51. Lewis Rogers et al. to C. A. Harris, n.d., RG 75, Roll 301, M234.

52. Ellen Eslinger, *Citizens of Zion: The Social Origins of Camp Meeting Revivalism* (Knoxville: University of Tennessee Press, 1999), 227, 225.

53. Joab Spencer, "A Short History of the Shawnee Methodist Mission," *Missouri Valley Historical Society: The Annals of Kansas City* 1 (1921–1924): 449.

54. "Iron sharpens iron, and one person sharpens the wits of another," "Proverbs 27:17," in *The HarperCollins Study Bible* (New York: HarperCollins, 1993), 978; Scarritt, "Reminiscences of the Methodist Shawnee Mission," 438–41.

55. Joab Spencer, "The Shawnee Indians: Their Customs, Traditions, and Folk-Lore," *Transactions of the Kansas State Historical Society* 10 (1908): 401–2.

56. Barry, *Beginning of the West,* 260, 335; Lutz, "Methodist Missions," 211.

57. *Ibid.*

58. Richard Cummins to William Clark, 12 December 1836, RG 75, M234, Roll 300; C. A. Hitchcock, Monthly Abstract of Disbursements, 31 July 1838, RG 75, M234 Roll 751.

59. "Lyman C. Draper's 1868 Shawnee and Delaware Field Notes," Voegelin Papers; "Recording Steward's Books for Indian Mission District," Hist. Indians, Box 7, XXII, Q, KSHS; "Visit to Mrs. William Johnson," n.d., Box 1, I, E, 1, Missions: Methodist, KSHS.

60. Bruce, *And They All Sang Hallelujah,* 75; "Indian Camp Meeting," *Western Christian Advocate,* 11 November 1842, p. 118.

61. Richard Cummins to C. A. Harris, "Report on Tribes within Fort Leavenworth Agency," 25 September 1838, RG 75, M234, Roll 301; "Journal of a Visit to Indian Mission Missouri Conference," 1843, C. C. Wagner Collection, Missouri Historical Society, St. Louis; "Census of the Shawnee Tribe," 1842, RG 75, Roll 301, M234.

62. "Recording Steward's Books for Indian Mission District," Missions: Methodist, KSHS.

63. Herring, *Enduring Indians of Kansas,* 1; Francis Paul Prucha, *The Great Father: The*

United States Government and the American Indians (2 vols.; Lincoln: University of Nebraska Press, 1984), 1:270–71.

64. Cummins to Harris, "Report on Tribes within Fort Leavenworth Agency"; Richard Cummins to T. H. Crawford, 13 February 1839, RG 75, Roll 301, M234.

65. Journal of Jotham Meeker, 29 December 1863, 769, KSHS.

66. J. D. Blanchard to R. W. Cummins, 28 September 1844, Hist. Indians, Missions, Delaware, Baptist, KSHS; Francis Barker to Solomon Peck, 8 January 1848, Barker Collection, KSHS.

67. Jon Butler, *Awash in a Sea of Faith: Christianizing the American People* (Cambridge, Mass.: Harvard University Press, 1990), 292.

68. Abing, "Fall from Grace," 400.

69. Jotham Meeker to S. W. Lynd and J. H. Miller, 26 September 1842, MS Box 617, Meeker Papers, KSHS Manuscript Collection; Ahlstrom, *Religious History of the American People,* 164.

70. J. S. Bacon to J. Meeker, 28 November 1842, Meeker Papers, KSHS Manuscript Collection.

71. The United States' removal of the Shawnees from 1825 to 1833 involved three different treaties which were signed by separate Shawnee villages in Ohio and Missouri, predominantly. Unlike previous land cessions, these treaties eliminated all Shawnee territory in the Old Northwest and Missouri, and forced the Shawnees to remove to a shared reservation.

72. "Undated Correspondency Concerning a Controversy over the Shawnee Baptist Mission," Roll 12, Isaac McCoy Papers, KSHS Manuscript Collection; "Communication from Methodist Missionaries," 12 March 1842, Roll 1, Pratt Papers, KSHS Manuscript Collection.

73. "Shawanoe Mission," *Baptist Missionary Magazine,* 23 (June 1843): 139; "Shawanoes," *Baptist Missionary Magazine,* 23 (Jan. 1843): 20; J. S. Bacon to J. Meeker, 28 November 1842, MS Box 617, Meeker Papers, KSHS Manuscript Collection. For more on this dispute and Blackfeather's effort to drive Barker from the reservation, see Abing, "Fall from Grace," 239–41.

74. Abing, "Fall from Grace," 242.

75. J. G. Pratt to Brother Bacon, 14 January 1843, Pratt Papers, KSHS; Francis Barker Collection, Correspondence, 1841–1908, KSHS; Meeker to Simerwell, 12 March 1845, MS Box 617, Meeker Papers, KSHS.

76. J. G. Pratt to Brother Bacon, 14 January 1843, KSHS; Francis Barker Collection, Correspondence, 1841–1908; Meeker to Simerwell, 12 March 1845, MS Box 617, Meeker Papers, KSHS; Johnston Lykins to Jotham Meeker, 15 December 1843, Meeker Papers, MS Box 617, KSHS.

Chapter 5

1. Francis Barker quoted in Louise Barry, *The Beginning of the West: Annals of the Kansas Gateway to the American West, 1540–1854* (Topeka: Kansas State Historical Society, 1972), 517; Jotham Meeker to A. J. Vaughan, 7 September 1846, Indian Missions—Schools, KSHS.

2. Paul Wallace Gates, *Fifty Million Acres: Conflicts over Kansas Land Policy, 1854–1890* (1954; reprint, Norman: University of Oklahoma Press, 1997), 3.

3. Indian Territory included what is now the states of Nebraska, Kansas, and Oklahoma until 1854. After the Kansas-Nebraska Act in 1853, Oklahoma became the last remaining tract of "Indian Territory" in the West. For statistics on the Santa Fe and Overland Trails, see Walter Nugent, *Into the West: The Story of Its People* (New York: Vintage, 1999), 45–46.

4. For more on Paschal Fish, see A. T. Andreas, *History of the State of Kansas* (Chicago: A. T. Andreas, 1883), 308; J. J. Lutz, "The Methodist Missions among the Indian Tribes in Kansas," *Transactions of the Kansas State Historical Society* 9 (1905–1906): 193; Evelyn Crady Adams, "Kentucky's Choctaw Academy, 1819–1842: A Commercial Enterprise," *Filson Club Historical Quarterly* 26 (January 1952): 29.

5. John D. Lang and Samuel Taylor, Jr., *Report of a Visit to Some of the Tribes of Indians, Located West of the Mississippi River* (New York: M. Day, 1843), 22.

6. Francis Barker to R. W. Cummins, 18 August 1847, Indian Missions—Schools, KSHS; Richard White, *"It's Your Misfortune and None of My Own": A History of the American West* (Norman: University of Oklahoma Press, 1991), 189.

7. Joab Spencer, "Captain Joseph Parks, Shawnee Indian Chief," *Transactions of the Kansas State Historical Society* 10 (1907–1908): 399–401; Adrienne Christopher, "Captain Joseph Parks: Chief of the Shawnee Indians," *Westport Historical Quarterly* 1 (June 1969): 13–17; Lutz, "Methodist Missions," 186n40.

8. Some confusion exists regarding the precise date of Joseph Parks's death. For example, Craig Miner and William E. Unrau list him as a candidate in the tribal election of 1862, three years after his death. In contrast, J. J. Lutz, a Methodist missionary who knew Parks, lists his death as April 4, 1859. Similarly, Martha B. Caldwell lists his death as April 3, 1859. See Craig Miner and William E. Unrau, *The End of an Indian Kansas: A Study of Cultural Revolution, 1854–1871* (Lawrence: University Press of Kansas, 1970), 94–95; Lutz, "Methodist Missions," 186; Martha B. Caldwell, *Annals of the Shawnee Methodist Mission* (Topeka: Kansas State Historical Society, 1939), 105.

9. Spencer, "Captain Joseph Parks," 399; Christopher, "Captain Joseph Parks," 14.

10. Charles Findlay to John Bell, n.d., Fort Leavenworth Agency, Bureau of Indian Affairs, RG 75, M234, Roll 303; "A Bill for the Relief of P. Chouteau, junior, and Company, 11 April 1848, RG 75, M234, Roll 303. John Bell was a member of the Committee on Indian Affairs and submitted this bill on Parks's and Findlay's behalf. Bell probably assisted the Shawnee delegation in their meetings with Orlando Brown, the commissioner of Indian affairs. While Brown seemed to favor the Shawnee delegation's request, the superintendent of Indian affairs, T. H. Harvey, resisted the settlement, believing that the Shawnee chiefs should be cut off entirely from government support and their claims dismissed. See T. H. Harvey to William Medill, 25 January 1849, RG 75M234, Roll 303. For a brief description of Bell, see Alban W. Hoopes, *Indian Affairs and Their Administration: With Special Reference to the Far West* (1932; reprint, Philadelphia, 1972), 218.

11. *Ibid.* Joseph Parks, Chauwe, and Joseph Barnett to Orlando Brown, 17 January 1850, RG 75, M234, Roll 303; Statement of Orlando Brown, 24 January 1850, Hist. Indians, Box 6, XXII, M, KSHS. Brown clearly respected Parks and the other members of the Shawnee

delegation. Nevertheless, Brown did not comply with their request for the $9,600 claim or the 100,000-acre settlement.

12. Findlay to Bell, n.d., RG 75, M234, Roll 303; Parks, Chauwe, and Barnett to Brown, 17 January 1850, RG 75, M234, Roll 303.

13. Henry Harvey, *History of the Shawnee Indians, from the Year 1681 to 1854, Inclusive* (Cincinnati: E. Morgan and Sons, 1855), 282; Mayahwathkucka, Mathapahkah, Lewis Rogers, and William Rogers to T. H. Crawford, 30 March 1844, RG 75, M234, Roll 302; John Perry, P. A. Lahcumme, and Joseph Parks to T. H. Crawford, 30 March 1844, RG 75, M234, Roll 302.

14. Francis Parkman, *The Oregon Trail* (1846; New York: Penguin Books, 1978), 23. On the ownership of slaves, see Caldwell, *Annals,* 60–61. By the 1840s, Thomas Johnson and Joseph Parks were the only reported slave owners on the reservation. However, in 1906, Mrs. Julia Stinson, granddaughter of Henry Rogers, recalled that her grandparents owned more than twenty slaves. Rogers's contemporaries on the reservation did not confirm or deny Mrs. Stinson's report. See Lutz, "Methodist Missions," 170–71n21.

15. Asbury C. Farnham to Allen F. Farnham, 29 December 1845, Indian Papers, Box 2, Missouri Historical Society, St. Louis.

16. Between 1834 and 1847, U.S. policies dictated that treaty annuities were to be paid to chiefs. For more on this practice, see Francis Paul Prucha, *The Great Father: The United States Government and the American Indian* (2 vols.; Lincoln: University of Nebraska Press, 1986), 1:309–10.

17. Joab Spencer, "The Shawnee Indians: Their Customs, Traditions, and Folk-Lore," *Transactions of the Kansas State Historical Society* 10 (1908): 389; Charles Fish, James Captain, John Fish, William Rogers et al. to Orlando Brown, 22 April 1850, RG 75, M234, Roll 303.

18. William H. Goode quoted in Lutz, "Methodist Missions," 180.

19. To cite just one example, the Shawnee manual labor school averaged between 110 and 115 students in 1844, as compared to forty students at the Quaker school. The Baptist school rarely surpassed thirty students. See Caldwell, *Annals,* 53; T. H. Harvey to T. Hartley Crawford, 8 October 1844, St. Louis Superintendency, Letters Received, Record Group 75, M234, Roll 753.

20. William Patton quoted in Caldwell, *Annals,* 59. For a detailed explanation of the central manual labor school's creation, see Kevin J. Abing, "A Fall from Grace: Thomas Johnson and the Shawnee Indian Manual Training School, 1839–1862" (Ph.D. diss., Marquette University, 1995), 72–80.

21. For more on the removal of the Black Bob band to Indian Territory, see Caldwell, *Annals,* 7. For more on the cultural history of the Black Bob band, see Noel W. Schutz, Jr., "The Study of Shawnee Myth in an Ethnographic and Ethnohistorical Perspective" (Ph. D. diss., Indiana University, 1975), esp. 372; Grant Foreman, *The Last Trek of the Indians* (Chicago: University of Chicago Press, 1946), 35. On the connection between Black Fish and the Black Bob band, see Neal O. Hammon, *My Father, Daniel Boone: The Draper Interviews with Nathan Boone* (Lexington: University Press of Kentucky, 1999), 60–61, 119. On the Bread Dance, see Draper Manuscripts, 23 S, p. 168, State Historical Society of Wisconsin, Madison.

22. Mayahwathkucka, Mathapahkah, Lewis Rogers, and William Rogers to T. H. Crawford, 30 March 1844, RG 75, M234, Roll 302.

23. John Perry, P. A. Lahcumme, and Joseph Parks to T. H. Crawford, 30 March 1844, RG 75, M234, Roll 302.

24. U.S. Cong. Senate. *Report.* 29th Cong., 1st Sess. S. Rpt. 319, 19 April 1844; John Perry, et. al. to T. H. Crawford, 30 March 1844, RG 75, M234, Roll 302; Joseph Parks to T. H. Crawford, 26 April 1844, RG 75, M234, Roll 302.

25. Richard Cummins to Thomas H. Harvey, 13 January 1849, RG 75, M234, Roll 303; Cummins to Harvey, 16 January 1849, RG 75, M234, Roll 303; Thomas H. Harvey to William Medill, 25 January 1849, RG 75, M234, Roll 303.

26. Recording Steward's Book for Indian Mission District, 28 August 1848, Missions: Methodist, KSHS; Luke Lea to D. D. Mitchell, 23 November 1849, RG 75, M234, Roll 303.

27. Chas. Findlay to John Bell, n.d., RG 75, M234, Roll 303. For more on Stephen, Joseph Parks's runaway slave, see Sworn Statement of Joseph Barnett, 24 January 1850, Hist. Indians, Box 6, XXII, M, KSHS; Joseph Parks, Statement to the Senate and House of Representatives, January 1850, *ibid.*

28. Thomas Johnson and Joseph Parks shared similar views on the needs of the tribe. The citizenship and severalty proposal provides just one example of the agreement between the two men. Johnson quoted in Caldwell, *Annals,* 66; Statement of Orlando Brown, 24 January 1850, Hist. Indians, Box 6, XXII, M, KSHS.

29. R. W. Thompson to A. A. Singhery, n.d., RG 75, M234, Roll 303.

30. Abelard Guthrie, "The Shawnee Indians of Kansas," 1868, n.p., Gilcrease Museum, Tulsa, Oklahoma; Miner and Unrau, *End of an Indian Kansas,* 7–9.

31. T. H. Harvey to William Medill, 25 January, 1849, RG 75, M234, Roll 303.

32. John Johnston to Charles Cist, 14 May 1846, Papers of John Johnston, Mss. no. 42, Roll 3A, Ohio Historical Society, Columbus; John Wolf to John Johnston, 20 July 1846, *ibid.;* Francis Barker to Solomon Peck, 3 April 1848, Francis Barker Collection, KSHS.

33. Caldwell, *Annals,* 59; Asbury C. Farnham to Allen F. Farnham, 29 December 1845, Box 2, Indian Papers, Missouri Historical Society, St. Louis; Indian Associated Executive Committee of Friends on Indian Affairs, "Visitors from Oklahoma," Ohio Historical Society, Columbus.

34. Parks's main contact in Washington was an attorney named R. W. Thompson, who assisted Parks in winning the $9,600 claim against the tribe for services in the Second Seminole War. Parks also had ties with the famous Indian trader from the Midwest, George W. Ewing. Both men helped Parks establish contacts with prominent members of the Committee on Indian Affairs and other politicians, including John Bell.

35. Charles Fish et al. to Orlando Brown, 22 April 1850, RG 75, M234, Roll 303.

36. Joseph Parks, Chauwe, and Joseph Barnett to Orlando Brown, 17 January 1850, RG 75, M234, Roll 303; Luke Lea to Rev. Markham, 20 March 1850, RG 75, M234, Roll 303.

37. Charles Fish et al. to Orlando Brown, 22 April 1850, RG 75, M234, Roll 303.

38. Caldwell, *Annals,* 60–61; *The Liberator,* 23 June 1854, vol. 24, no. 25.

39. Joseph Parks, Chauwe, and Joseph Barnett to Orlando Brown, 17 January 1850, RG 75, M234, Roll 303.

40. Richard Cummins to T. H. Harvey, 16 January 1849, RG 75, M234, Roll 303.

41. Francis Barker to Solomon Peck, 2 February 1847, Francis Barker Collection, KSHS.

42. *Baptist Missionary Magazine,* July 1847, p. 259.

43. R. W. Thompson to Geo. W. Manypenny, 4 April 1852, RG 75, M234, Roll 364.

44. For a thorough explanation of the 1847 law and government efforts to deal with problems related to annuities and alcohol, see Prucha, *Great Father,* 1:309–10.

45. Joseph Parks, Big Bone, and others to the Commissioner of Indian Affairs, 22 July 1853, RG 75, M234, Roll 364; R. W. Thompson to George W. Manypenny, 4 April 1852, RG 75, M234, Roll 364.

46. Millard Fillmore to Luke Lea, 17 April 1852, RG 75, M234, Roll 364; Thomas Moseley to D. D. Mitchell, 4 March 1852, RG 75, M234, Roll 364.

47. Thomas Moseley to Luke Lea, 20 July 1852, RG 75, M234, Roll 364.

48. Joseph Parks, Big Bone, and others to the Commissioner of Indian Affairs, 22 July 1853, RG 75, M234, Roll 364.

49. Thomas Moseley to D. D. Mitchell, 18 November 1852, RG 75, M234, Roll 364; Statement of Thomas Moseley, 10 December 1852, RG 75, M234, Roll 364.

50. R. W. Thompson to George W. Manypenny, 4 April 1852, RG 75, Roll 364, M234; Samuel Johnson Huffacker to the Shawnee Nation, 7 July 1853, RG 75, M234, Roll 364.

51. A. Cumming to George Manypenny, 11 July 1853, RG 75, M234, Roll 364; Prucha, *Great Father,* 1:332.

52. B. F. Robinson to A. Cumming, 31 March 1855, RG 75, M234, Roll 364.

53. Cumming to Manypenny, 11 July 1853, RG 75, M234, Roll 364.

54. Joseph Parks, Big Bone, Black Hoof, George McDougal et al. to the Commissioner of Indian Affairs, 22 July 1853, RG 75, M234, Roll 364.

55. R. W. Thompson to George Manypenny, 29 July 1853, RG 75, M234, Roll 364.

56. For an extensive description of the discussions leading to the creation of the first Shawnee constitution, see Harvey, *History of the Shawnee Indians,* 283–96, esp. 283.

57. Blue Jacket v. Commissioners, 3 Kans. 294 (1865).

58. Guthrie, "Shawnee Indians of Kansas," 2. The Missouri Shawnees who negotiated the 1854 treaty were Black Bob and Graham Rogers. The Ohio Shawnees were Joseph Parks, Black Hoof, George McDougal, Longtail, George Blue Jacket, and Henry Blue Jacket. See "Treaty with the Shawnee, 1854," in Charles J. Kappler, *Indian Affairs: Laws and Treaties* (2 vols.; Washington, D.C.: Government Printing Office, 1904), 1:619.

59. Harvey, *History of the Shawnee Indians,* 282–83, 287–88; Richard Cummins to T. H. Harvey, 13 January 1849, RG 75, M234, Roll 303.

60. Cummins to Harvey, 13 January 1849, RG 75, M234, Roll 303.

61. U.S. Cong. Senate. *Report.* 32nd Cong., 1st Sess. S. Rpt. 658, 1 September 1852; U.S. Cong. Senate. *Report.* 34th Cong., 1st Sess. S. Rpt. 810, 26 November 1855; Francis Barker, "Annual Report of the Shawnee Baptist Mission," 24 January 1853, Francis Barker Collection, KSHS.

62. Francis Barker to Solomon Peck, 3 April 1848, Francis Barker Collection, KSHS.

63. U.S. Cong. Senate. *Report.* 33rd Cong., 1st Sess., S. Rpt. 690, 26 November 1853.

64. For statistics on the Manypenny treaties of 1854–1855, see Gates, *Fifty Million Acres,* 1, 16–19, 22.

65. For the 1854 treaty with the Shawnee, see Kappler, *Indian Affairs,* 1:619. For further evidence of various subagents' ability to intervene in Shawnee affairs, see B. F. Robinson to A. Cumming, 10 June 1854, RG 75, M234, Roll 364; Shawnee Council to Commissioner of Indian Affairs, 6 February 1860, Shawnee Agency, RG 75, M234, Roll 811.

66. For a detailed description of the acreage of lands reserved for the Shawnees and missionaries, see Kappler, *Indian Affairs,* 1:619; see also Gates, *Fifty Million Acres,* 36–37. Shawnee subagent Arnold provided detailed population figures for the Black Bob band and those Shawnees who accepted 200-acre allotments. See A. Arnold to G. Manypenny, 23 March 1858, Shawnee Agency, RG 75, M234, Roll 809.

67. Robinson to Cumming, 10 June 1854, RG 75, M234, Roll 364; George Manypenny, Explanatory Statement, *Senate Executive Documents and Reports,* 33rd Cong., 1st Sess., 14 July 1854.

68. Jotham Meeker to Solomon Peck, 1 September 1854, MS Box 618, Jotham Meeker Papers, KSHS.

69. R. Miller to A. Cumming, 21 May 1855, RG 75, M234, Roll 809. For more on the independence of Shawnee Baptists from missionary supervision, see H. L. Taylor to N. B. Taylor, 1 August 1867, Indian Missions—Schools, KSHS.

70. Manypenny disliked Johnson's tendency to use his religious influence to advance his own political interests. He was particularly angry with Johnson over allowing the first territorial governor, Andrew Reeder, to use the Methodist mission as his political headquarters. See Thomas Johnson to George Manypenny, 2 November 1855, RG 75, M234, Roll 809.

71. B. F. Robinson to G. W. Manypenny, 12 December 1854, RG 75, M234, Roll 364.

72. For more on the Fort Leavenworth Indian ring, see Miner and Unrau, *End of an Indian Kansas,* 2, esp. 108–114.

73. A. Cumming to George Manypenny, 25 June 1856, RG 75, M234, Roll 809. For more on the Shawnees' plight immediately prior to Gay's death, see William McCoy to A. Cumming, 15 February 1856, RG 75, M234, Roll 809.

74. For the larger context of Gay's murder, see Miner and Unrau, *End of an Indian Kansas,* 16, esp. 18–19; see also Gates, *Fifty Million Acres,* 40, 58.

75. Samuel Cornatzer to J. Thompson, 8 July 1858, RG 75, M234, Roll 810. Craig Miner and William Unrau discuss Cornatzer's letter in terms of the inadequacy of the Shawnee agents and their failure to act as responsive intermediaries between the tribes and the U.S. government. See Miner and Unrau, *End of an Indian Kansas,* 50–51.

76. Ben Newsom to A. M. Robinson, 2 September 1858, RG 75, M234, Roll 810.

77. Robinson to Cumming, 31 March 1855, RG 75, M234, Roll 364.

Chapter 6

1. Annie Heloise Abel, *The American Indian as Slaverholder and Secessionist: An Omitted Chapter in the Diplomatic History of the Southern Confederacy* (Cleveland: Arthur H. Clark, 1915), 22n10; Kevin J. Abing, "A Fall from Grace: Thomas Johnson and the Shawnee Indian Manual Labor School, 1839–1862," (Ph.D. diss., Marquette University, 1995), 330; Jay Monaghan, *Civil War on the Western Border, 1854–1865* (Lincoln: University of Nebraska Press, 1995), 56–62.

2. Monaghan, *Civil War on the Western Border,* 60–62; A. T. Andreas, *History of the State of Kansas* (Chicago: A. T. Andreas, 1883), 308.

3. For the best description of allotment and its legal ramifications for the Shawnees, see John W. Ragsdale, "The Dispossession of the Kansas Shawnee," *University of Missouri-Kansas City Law Review* 58 (Winter 1990): 209–56.

4. The dispute between Parks and his business associate Charles Findlay over the payment of debts incurred during the Second Seminole War reveals much about their plans for citizenship and a lump-sum payment to the Shawnees for debts and treaty obligations over the years. Charles Findlay to John Bell, n.d., Fort Leavenworth Agency, Bureau of Indian Affairs, RG 75, M234, Roll 303.

5. Ragsdale, "Dispossession of the Kansas Shawnee," 242–43.

6. U.S. Cong. House. *Report.* 38th Cong., 2nd Sess., H. Exec. Doc. 1, Rpt. 1220, 15 November 1864.

7. David M. Emmons, *Garden in the Grasslands: Boomer Literature of the Central Plains* (Lincoln: University of Nebraska Press, 1971); Vine Deloria, Jr., and Raymond J. DeMallie, eds., *Documents of American Indian Diplomacy: Treaties, Agreements, and Conventions, 1775–1979* (2 vols.; Norman: University of Oklahoma Press, 1999), 2:1344; James B. Abbott to H. B. Branch, 8 July 1861, RG 75, M234, Roll 812.

8. The three Marshall decisions are *Johnson v. McIntosh* (1823), *Cherokee Nation v. Georgia* (1831), and *Worcester v. Georgia* (1832). Taken together, these cases make clear that the federal government, rather than the states, has the ultimate authority in relations with the tribes. For more on the Marshall Trilogy, see Charles F. Wilkinson, *American Indians, Time, and the Law* (New Haven, Conn.: Yale University Press, 1987).

9. Paul Wallace Gates, *Fifty Million Acres: Conflicts over Kansas Land Policy, 1854–1860* (Norman: University of Oklahoma Press, 1997), 46–47.

10. U.S. Cong. House. *Report.* 37th Cong., 3rd Sess., H. Exec. Doc. 1, Rpt. 1157, 26 November 1862.

11. Ragsdale, "Dispossession of the Kansas Shawnee," 241–44; *Blue Jacket v. Commissioners of Johnson County,* 3 Kans. 294 (1865), *rev'd.* 72 U.S. 737 (1866).

12. Charles Fish et al. to James Buchanan, 6 February 1861, RG 75, M234, Roll 812; J. J. Lutz, "The Methodist Missions among the Indian Tribes in Kansas," *Transactions of the Kansas State Historical Society* 9 (1905–1906): 186, 167, 207.

13. J. P. Usher to William P. Dole, 27 December 1862, RG 75, M234, Roll 812; Abelard Guthrie to William P. Dole, 6 November 1862, RG 75, M234, Roll 813; Loyalty Oath, 3 January 1863, RG 75, M234, Roll 813.

14. For more on Thomas Johnson and his connections with the confederacy, see Abing, "Fall from Grace."

15. Black Bob to the Commissioner of Indian Affairs, 21 April 1862, RG 75, M234, Roll 812.

16. B. J. Newsom to A. M. Robinson, 17 March 1860, RG 75, M234, Roll 811.

17. Morris W. Foster, *Being Comanche: A Social History of an American Indian Community* (Tucson: University of Arizona Press, 1991).

18. For more on George Ironsides and his family history, see Helen Tanner, "The Glaize in 1792: A Composite Indian Community," *Ethnohistory* 25 (Winter 1978): 25. See also O. M. Spencer, *The Indian Captivity of O. M. Spencer,* ed. Milo Milton Quaife (New York:

The Citadel Press, 1968); Shawnee Council to the Commissioner, 6 February 1860, RG 75, M234, Roll 811; J. Thompson to C. E. Mix, 17 July 1860, RG 75, M234, Roll 811.

19. Matthew Brown to William P. Dole, 27 March 1863, RG 75, M234, Roll 813.

20. See B. J. Newson to A. M. Robinson, 17 March 1860, RG 75, M234, Roll 811.

21. Thomas Johnson was murdered by a group of unknown assailants on 2 January 1865. For more on Shawnee attitudes toward the mission during the war, see Martha B. Caldwell, *Annals of the Shawnee Methodist Mission* (Topeka: Kansas State Historical Society, 1939), 106–7, 114. On the closing of the mission, see Abing, "Fall from Grace," 398. For the impact on Shawnee education and religious practice after the closing of the Methodist mission, see James B. Abbott to William P. Dole, 10 April 1862, RG 75, M234, Roll 812; Report of the Commissioner of Indian Affairs, Voegelin Papers, Folder 4, Box 34, Newberry Library, Chicago; Sallie Gore to Joab Spencer, 17 June 1907, Papers of Mrs. S. B. Gore, KSHS.

22. James B. Abbott kept detailed records of Shawnee migrations onto the reservation. The greatest influx of Absentee Shawnees arrived in 1863 and 1864. For the initial report, see James B. Abbott to H. B. Branch, 5 June 1863, RG 75, M234, Roll 813.

23. For more on the move and reunification with the Black Bob band, see Thomas Wildcat Alford, *Civilization and the Story of the Absentee Shawnees* (Norman: University of Oklahoma Press, 1936; reprint, University of Oklahoma Press, 1979), 11–12. For population figures on the Absentee/Black Bob Shawnees, see Shawnee Council to Commissioner of Indian Affairs, 2 August 1866, RG 75, M234, Roll 814. For the Ohio/Cherokee Shawnees, see Cherokee-Shawnee Census, 1869, MS 1097, KSHS; Statement of Henry Edmund, Clerk of the Election, 28 January 1863, RG 75, M234, Roll 813.

24. See Statement and Protest of the Black Bob Settlement, n.d., RG 75, M234, Roll 814.

25. James B. Abbott to William P. Dole, April 6, 1863, M234, Roll 813.

26. *Ibid.* As historian Rebecca Kugel has pointed out in a related study, "the Ojibwe understood that Americans categorized Native people as either 'good' or 'bad' Indians, and they learned to play themselves off against these images." See Rebecca Kugel, *To Be the Main Leaders of Our People: A History of Minnesota Ojibwe Politics, 1824–1898* (East Lansing: Michigan State University Press, 1998), 207.

27. James B. Abbott to H. B. Branch, 25 September 1862, RG 75, M234, Roll 812.

28. *Ibid.* By 1866 they claim to have 768 Shawnees allied with them. Prior to the Quantrill raid, those Shawnees who held their lands in common were better off than those who had accepted allotments through the 1854 treaty. Like the Black Bob Shawnees, historian Joseph Herring has found that the Prairie Potawatomis were more prosperous than their kinsmen on allotments in Kansas. The reason, according to Herring, is that "they had refused allotment and had peacefully retained their lands in common." See also Joseph B. Herring, *The Enduring Indians of Kansas: A Century and a Half of Acculturation* (Lawrence: University Press of Kansas, 1990), 134.

29. Abel, *American Indian as Slaveholder and Secessionist,* 54–57; Christine Schultz and Benton R. White, *Now the Wolf Has Come: The Creek Nation in the Civil War* (College Station: Texas A&M University Press, 1996), 70, 73.

30. Abel, *American Indian as Slaveholder and Secessionist,* 329.

31. William W. Newcomb, Jr., *The Indians of Texas: From Prehistoric to Modern Times*

(Austin: University of Texas Press, 1961); Omer C. Stewart, *Peyote Religion: A History* (Norman: University of Oklahoma Press, 1987), 119; David LaVere, ed., *Life among the Texas Indians: The WPA Narratives* (College Station: Texas A&M University Press, 1998), 40–41, 63–65.

32. Abel, *American Indian as Slaveholder and Secessionist,* 329.

33. Laurence M. Hauptman, *The Iroquois in the Civil War: From Battlefield to Reservation* (Syracuse: Syracuse University Press, 1993), 16–17; LeRoy H. Fischer, ed., *The Civil War in Indian Territory* (Los Angeles: Lorrin L. Morrison, 1974), 20–21; Perry Fuller to Charles E. Mix, 14 September 1863, RG 75, M234, Roll 813.

34. William A. Ochiltron to J. B. Abbott, 12 October 1864, MS 1259, Roll 2, James Burnett Abbott Collection KSHS; S. R. Curtis to J. B. Abbott, 13 October 1864, *ibid.*

35. Monaghan, *Civil War on the Western Border,* 320–36.

36. James B. Abbott to William P. Dole, 7 January 1865, RG 75, M234, Roll 814; Graham Rogers and Charles Tucker, Statement of Competency, 18 May 1869, RG 75, M234, Roll 814.

37. James B. Abbott to William P. Dole, 27 August 1864, RG 75, M234, Roll 813; Paschal Fish et al. to William P. Dole, 15 September 1864, RG 75, M234, Roll 813; Abelard Guthrie to William P. Dole, 29 September 1864, RG 75, M234, Roll 813.

38. The following citation was written by the Absentee/Black Bob tribal council, which emerged in 1863 and operated independently from the Ohio Shawnee/Maykujay tribal council. Shawnee Council to the Commissioner of Indian Affairs, 2 August 1866, RG 75, M234, Roll 814.

39. This citation reflects the Ohio Shawnee/Maykujay response. Shawnee Council to Commissioner of Indian Affairs, 2 August 1866, RG 75, Roll 814, M234.

40. Delaware and Shawnee Tribal Registers, Rolls, and Publications, August 11, 1869, MS 1097, KSHS; "Agreement with the Shawnee Tribe of Indians, 1867," *Indian Affairs, Laws and Treaties,* ed. Charles J. Kappler (2 vols.; Washington, D.C.: Government Printing Office, 1904), 2:708–13.

41. Cherokee-Shawnee Census, 1869, MS 1097, KSHS. For more on the Cherokee-Shawnee agreement and landholdings after allotment, see Kent Carter, *The Dawes Commission and the Allotment of the Five Civilized Tribes, 1893–1914* (Orem: Ancestry.com, 1999), 105, 108; Vine Deloria, Jr., and Raymond J. DeMallie, eds., *Documents of American Indian Diplomacy: Treaties, Agreements, and Conventions, 1775–1979* (2 vols.; Norman: University of Oklahoma Press, 1999), 1:717–18. See also Janet A. McDonnell, *The Dispossession of the American Indian, 1887–1934* (Bloomington: Indiana University Press, 1991).

42. "Shawnee Tribe Receives Federal Recognition," *The Shawnee Journal* 1, no. 1 (Winter 2002): 1–2; Author interviews with Greg Pitcher (Shawnee), Lamont Laird (Eastern Shawnee/Black Bob), and Rebecca Hawkins, Miami, Oklahoma, 21 June 2002; with Linda Cox (Shawnee), Miami, Oklahoma, 4 February 2003; and with Greg Pitcher (Shawnee), Miami, Oklahoma, 4 February 2003.

43. Author interview with Pitcher, Laird, and Hawkins, 21 June 2002.

44. James B. Abbott notified the commissioner of Indian affairs, William P. Dole, that the Shawnees would send a delegation to "select and make some arrangements for a new home" later that September. Given Abbott's consistent support for the Ohio Shawnee national council, it is more than likely that Abbott helped this branch of the Shawnee

tribe negotiate an agreement with the Cherokees during this visit to the Indian Territory. See James B. Abbott to William P. Dole, 23 August 1864, RG 75, M234, Roll 813.

45. Author interview with Jennifer Makaseah (Absentee Shawnee), Shawnee, Oklahoma, 6 February 2003.

46. For the best firsthand account of their removal and its aftermath, see Alford, *Civilization,* 14n2.

47. Herring, *Enduring Indians of Kansas,* 133–34; Peter R. Hacker, "Confusion and Conflict: A Study of Atypical Responses to Nineteenth Century Federal Indian Policies by the Citizen Band Potawatomis," *American Indian Culture and Research Journal* 13, no. 1 (1989): 79–95; *Citizen Band Potawatomi Indian Tribe of Oklahoma v. Collier,* 23 ILR 3259 (W.D. Oklahoma, 1996).

Index

STEPHEN WARREN is an assistant professor of history at Augustana College in Rock Island, Illinois.

The University of Illinois Press
is a founding member of the
Association of American University Presses.

University of Illinois Press
1325 South Oak Street
Champaign, IL 61820-6903
www.press.uillinois.edu